C0-DKN-412

EIGHTEENTH-CENTURY ENGLISH DRAMA

a comprehensive collection of over two hundred representative plays, reproduced with critical introductions by leading scholars

General Editor
PAULA R. BACKSCHEIDER

A GARLAND SERIES

The Plays of
DAVID MALLET

Edited with an introduction by
FELICITY A. NUSSBAUM

GARLAND PUBLISHING, INC.
New York & London
1980

For a complete list of the titles in this series
see the final pages of this volume.

These facsimiles have been made from copies in the Yale University Library except for the 1755 *Britannia*, which has come from the Library of Congress, and the Garrick plate, which has come from the Clark Memorial Library of the University of California at Los Angeles.

Library of Congress Cataloging in Publication Data

Mallet, David, 1705?– 1765.
The plays of David Mallet.

(Eighteenth-century English drama)
Includes bibliographical references.
CONTENTS: Eurydice.—Mustapha.—Alfred.—Alfred (rev. 1751).—Prologue to the Mask of Britannia. [etc.]
I. Nussbaum, Felicity. II. Title. III. Series.
PR3545.M4A6 1980 822'.5 78-66605
ISBN 0-8240-3602-6

The volumes in this series are printed on acid-free, 250-year-life paper.

Printed in the United States of America

To my parents

CONTENTS

INTRODUCTION

When Samuel Johnson was engaged in writing the *Lives of the Poets*, James Boswell asked him if he would write the life of any poet the booksellers pleased: "I asked him if he would do this to any dunce's work, if they should ask him. JOHNSON. 'Yes, Sir; and *say* he was a dunce.'"[1] Among the *Lives of the Poets* is Johnson's "Life of Mallet" which, though only about two thousand words in length, captures the popular eighteenth-century view of the Scotsman David Mallet as untalented, untrustworthy, and unscrupulous. The "Life of Mallet" is riddled with inaccuracies, and Johnson even seems to suggest that the details are not worth seeking. "Of David Mallet, having no written memorial," Johnson begins, "I am able to give no other account than such as is supplied by the unauthorised loquacity of common fame and a very slight personal knowledge."[2] These dual themes—that Mallet is unknown to the world and that his only fame was infamy—recur in every paragraph of the short biography.

Johnson's contempt for Mallet is apparent in his immediate association of Mallet with the Macgregor clan, a clan so notorious that the author's father changed his name to Malloch. Johnson's antipathy extends to David Malloch's changing his name to Mallet: he "took upon him to change his name from Scotch Malloch to English Mallet, without any imaginable reason of preference which the eye or ear can discover."[3] Mallet's biography does not interest Johnson; in fact, Johnson appears to boast of his lack of knowledge when he writes, "Of his works, I know not whether I can trace the series," or, of *Eurydice*, "I know not the reception nor the merit, but have heard it mentioned as a mean performance," or, "What other proofs he gave of disrespect to his native country I know not. . . ." Johnson frequently structures the paragraph to offer Mallet limited praise, and then he turns to undermine it. Of *William and Margaret*, for example, Johnson writes, "he has been envied the reputation, and plagiarism has been boldly charged but never proved," and later, "he has Thomson's beauties and his faults." Mallet's poem in defense of Pope, *Of Verbal Criticism*, discussed "a subject which he either did not understand or willingly misrepresented." Mallet's not producing his long-promised *Life of the Duke of Marlborough* becomes an object lesson in "how little confidence can be placed in posthumous renown." Though Johnson must acknowledge that *Amyntor and Theodora* evidences "elegance of language, vigour of sentiment, and imagery," he adds that "it is lost in forgetfulness." Johnson compliments the ease and elegance of his conversation, but he denies him any parting tribute: "The rest of his character may, without injury to his memory, sink into silence."

Mallet, Johnson suggests, was a trifler who styled himself a man of significance. His pretensions extended beyond avoiding Scots pronunciation to relying heavily throughout his life on the influence of others. Mallet "had not virtue, or had not spirit, to refuse the office" of harming Pope's memory, though Pope had been his friend and advisor. Johnson asserts that Mallet intentionally sought to disguise himself, and this "prettiest drest puppet about town"[4] based his self-conceit on ignorance. Johnson uses the genre ironically in order to undermine the ostensible purpose of preserving a memorable life. Though Johnson once argued that no man had led a life unworthy of being recorded, he implies that Mallet scarcely deserves the dignity of our attention. The

"Life of Mallet" is the biography of a man who should justly be forgotten: "His Dramas had their day, a short day, and are forgotten. . . ." His writings, "conveying little information and giving no great pleasure, must soon give way, as the succession of things produces new topicks of conversation and other modes of amusement." Johnson's *Lives of the Poets* are structured to reveal those who are weak in character, and Mallet is stripped bare.

The details Johnson eschewed are, nevertheless, of interest to the reader of his plays. The most authoritative biography remains Frederick Dinsdale's memoir in his edition of Mallet's *Ballads and Songs* (1857). Tradition held that Mallet came from lower class origins (a fact Johnson thought Mallet sought to hide), though more recent evidence shows instead that Mallet was the son of James and Beatrix Malloch, tenants on Lord Drummond's farm near Perth. Dinsdale notes that Mallet probably shunned his Scots heritage because, as a Roman Catholic and a Jacobite, he would not have been welcome in Hanoverian England. This may help to explain his obsequiousness to Frederick, Prince of Wales, and his constant seeking of support from influential gentlemen of London. On the other hand, we must take into account that patriotism — or perhaps nostalgia — led him to request of Dr. Burney, in 1751, that he set *Alfred* to Scots tunes, and that Mallet himself expressed affection for Scots ballads and poems.

On entering Oxford in 1733, Mallet gave his age as 28, probably an inaccurate number he offered in order to guarantee his admission. Dinsdale argues he was born in 1702. Mallet's earlier education took place in the parish school at Crieff. Johnson indicated he had been a janitor at the high school in Edinburgh, and Boswell and his friends had taunted him with the charge in *Critical Strictures on the New Tragedy of Elvira* (1763); but it has since been established that the janitor held a position of considerable responsibility, and it was not solely menial custodial work. That Mallet was in fact a janitor was much disputed but now well accepted.[5]

In order to support himself while he pursued studies at the University of Edinburgh, Mallet boarded as a tutor to the children of Mr. Home of Dreghorne where he remained until 1723. He left the university and Scotland, without a degree, to become tutor to the sons of the Duke of Montrose, later traveling with them to London and then Shawford. It was at the university that he met James Thomson, as well as Allan Ramsay, who probably encouraged him in his early literary endeavors. His poems during this period included a "Pastoral" published in the *Edinburgh Miscellany* (1721), an imitation of Milton called *The Transfiguration*, and a long ballad, *William and Margaret*.[6]

At a ceremony in 1725 honoring James Fraser, a wealthy philanthropist, with the degree of Doctor of Civil and Canon Law (J.U.D.), John Ker, former classical master at Mallet's high school and later professor at the University of Edinburgh, read *Donaides*, a Latin poem of his own composition.[7] Mallet's *Donaides*, for which he was awarded an honorary M.A. from the University of Aberdeen in January 1726, is an English imitation of this. After a brief sojourn in Europe with his pupils in 1727, he returned to England and published *The Excursion* (1728), a Gothic poem of the graveyard school, in two cantos. Still a tutor to the sons of the Duke of Montrose, he relied on his position to gain favor with a variety of eighteenth-century notables, including Young, Lyttleton, Pope, and, of course, Frederick, Prince of Wales. Mallet once supposedly indicated that he changed his name because no Englishman could pronounce "Malloch," and perhaps one of these literary friends urged him to make the pronunciation easier for the English tongue.

In the same year that Mallet's first play, *Eurydice*, was

produced (1731), Mallet left Montrose to become tutor to Lady Knight's son, John. Tutor and pupil traveled abroad, and some time after they attended St. Mary Hall, Oxford, until Mallet received the B.A. and M.A. in 1735 from the University of Oxford. He also sought and received his M.A. from the University of Edinburgh. The literary works which he subsequently published indicate a history of Mallet's friendships and political loyalties. His *Of Verbal Criticism* (1733) compliments Pope at the expense of Theobald. The play *Mustapha* (1739), dedicated to the Prince of Wales, presented a partial parallel to the political intrigues of Walpole, Queen Caroline, and King George II in support of the Opposition. Similarly *Alfred*, first produced in 1740 with James Thomson and with music by Thomas Arne, celebrated the birthday of Frederick's daughter Princess Augusta and the anniversary of George I's accession. Mallet and Thomson had been given a small pension by the Prince of Wales, but they lost these pensions in 1748 when their supporter Lord Lyttleton fell out of favor with the prince. Mallet published his own works in 1743 and those of Lord Bolingbroke in 1754. Mallet's *Life of Bacon* earned some small praise, though Samuel Johnson reports Warburton's remark that "he had forgotten Bacon was a philosopher."[8]

The masque of *Britannia* appeared in 1755, and it, along with the prologue spoken by David Garrick in the character of a drunken sailor, was among the works included in a 1759 collection of Mallet's prose and poetry in three volumes. His poetry, including the ballad *Edwin and Emma* (1760), was collected in *Poems on Several Occasions* (1762). *Elvira* (1763), dedicated to Lord Bute, won Mallet an assignment as Keeper of the Book of Entries in London, but he soon left England to join his wife in France. He returned alone, and after a period of illness, died April 21, 1765, "aged sixty-three years."[9] In January 1741/42 his first wife, Susanna, had died, and in

October of that same year he married Lucy Elstob, a woman noted for both her vanity and learning. In addition to his wife, Lucy, he was survived by four children, two from each marriage. The only one who achieved fame was Dorothy Mallet Celesia, who wrote the play *Almida* (1771) and the poem "Indolence" (1772). *Almida*, acted at Drury Lane, January 1771, set in ancient Greece, is significant for its Gothic elements.[10]

What most hurt Mallet's reputation were incidents that occurred in his later career when he acted as Bolingbroke's agent in attacking Pope posthumously in *The Patriot King*, as well as his lifelong pretension that he was industriously writing the "Life of Marlborough," though he never completed a line of it. Samuel Johnson says, "He groped for materials, and thought of it, till he exhausted his mind."[11] Johnson, who triumphed painfully but repeatedly over his own indolence, had little patience for a man who found himself unable to do the same. Johnson's opinion of Mallet should be balanced with Alexander Pope's kindness and friendship, Professor John Ker's strong affection, testimonials from the parents of his pupils, Aaron Hill's regard, and James Thomson's complimentary words in his preface to *Winter*, but Johnson's view was the popular view.

It is the plays of Mallet which concern us here. Though David Mallet earned his literary reputation for his poetry and prose, he wrote three plays and two masques. Like many mid-century plays, Mallet's masques and plays rely heavily on their sources, but an occasional original construction deserves our attention. His first play, *Eurydice. A Tragedy*, was acted at Drury Lane for the first time on February 22, 1731. Rather well received, it ran for six days in February, seven in March, and one in April.[12] Mrs. Porter played the title role with Mr. Marshall as Procles and Mr. Mills as Periander. Mallet apparently sent Pope portions of early versions of

Eurydice for his comments and support as much as a year earlier than the production.[13] William Aikman wrote to Sir John Clerk on January 13, 1729 / 30, "You desir'd to know what Thomson & Malloch are about, they have both finish'd the Tragedies they were about this Summer and both are presented to the Old Playhouse . . . Mr. Malloch's Periander is much approv'd of by Mr. Pope, Dr. Arbuthnot and most that have seen it, but am afraid it will be too late to act it this winter as there are two already accepted before it."[14] At the request of David Mallet, Aaron Hill wrote both the prologue and epilogue. Robert Wilkes, who spoke the prologue, wished to omit four lines at the conclusion of the speech, and Hill concurred in his decision. The lines appear in the 1731 edition printed here, but they are omitted in Mallet's 1759 edition. Wilkes was not an actor in the play, and after delivering the prologue, he took his place in the orchestra, the long narrow section reserved for a few musicians and particularly prestigious members of the audience.[15] Hill composed the epilogue and sent it to Mallet on February 18, 1731.When the play was produced, the epilogue was delivered by a lively Miss Robinson in a breeches role. Hill complained on February 23 of changes in the epilogue perpetrated by "C-b-r (I conclude it him from his known Shamelessness)" and that he "has taken to alter, dismember, and destroy the humour and propriety of my Epilogue."[16]

In writing *Eurydice*, Mallet chose a popular subject, for Lincoln's Inn Fields had produced John Tracy's *Periander* a few weeks earlier on January 13–16 and January 25, 1731. Both plays have as their common source the Chevalier Ramsay's *Travels of Cyrus*. Genest criticizes John Tracy for following Ramsay's versions of the story rather than Herodotus or Diogenes Laertius. He finds Herodotus superior because there Procles possesses a much more sinister motive in his passion for Melissa (Eurydice) since he is her father. Genest also notes that "Mallet has however made considerable changes in the story, particularly in the character of Polydore, and in the manner of Eurydice's death. . . ."[17] Periander kills his wife in the source, for he assumes she intends to poison him, and his sons were wooed by Procles as enemies of their father (though they later relent).

John Tracy's play *Periander* places considerably more emphasis on Periander's relationship to the citizens of Corinth. Both Tracy's play and Mallet's play lack the engrossing nature of the prose narratives in which Periander is a tyrant who has an incestuous relationship with his mother, kills his wife, burns his concubines, and banishes his son. While in *Eurydice*, political motivations are secondary to the conflict between Procles and Periander for Eurydice, *Periander* focuses on civil unrest. In *Periander* the violent Procles is more openly aggressive against the virtuous Eurydice. Hypsenor, the go-between in *Periander*, takes a more central role than his counterpart, Medon, and Tracy follows the source in having a belatedly remorseful Periander kill his wife. The horrors of tyranny, not of jealousy, are the central issue of the earlier play.

Though *Eurydice* was called a libel against George II and a defense of the Pretender, *Periander* has far more political overtones.[18] A pamphlet published in 1731, *Remarks on the Tragedy of Eurydice* (Dublin, 1731), claims that *Eurydice* is a libelous tragedy, but the author suggests someone other than Mallet may have made the scurrilous revisions without Mallet's knowledge.[19] The accusations are ludicrous. For example, Periander's fetters being cut off in Act III is parallel to the Pretender's first invasion of Scotland; the death of Eurydice signifies the grief of the Pretender when his wife withdrew from him; Ariston represents Colonel Hay, who tried to prevent a reconciliation between the Pretender and Princess Sobiesky. This extraordinary interpretation of the play concludes with a regret that Mallet chooses to end with a catastrophe. Instead, the author suggests, he should have used as a model the pleasant humor of Congreve's *Mourning Bride.*

When Aaron Hill read Mallet's manuscript version of *Eurydice*, he heaped extravagant praise on the play and on its author in his letters to Mallet in February 1731. In the initial letters, he casually mentioned, when pressed for suggestions for revision, that Mallet might change Lycophon (the son's name)—since he had "dignified *Melissa* into *Eurydice*."[20] But in a letter three days later he suggested that the moral of the tragedy might be made more pointed if Periander and Eurydice were held accountable for their sufferings. Hill wanted Mallet to unfold the moral of the play through Leonidas, the wise counselor, who could burst into complaint against the injustice of the gods. Periander's guilt would be the greater if he stressed his pain at having broken an oath to his father, and the audience would be made to fear the judgment of the gods. The greater Periander's guilt, the more just his sufferings.

Mallet responded by indicating that the moral of the play was jealousy, not the avoidance of rash resolutions, and he thus underscores his lack of political intention in the play. Hill urged revisions that would increase the religious terror and the political implications while lessening the domestic tragedy. He wrote, "It had been juster for both *Periander* and *Procles* to have been ruined, by the personal effects of jealousy, without involving the interests of a nation; whereas, in the other more public light, you raise the importance of your Story, attach the general, to the particular sufferings; augment the terror, refine the pity, vindicate the punishment, and exalt the moral of your subject."[21]

The characters in *Eurydice* repeatedly mention the woefulness of their fate. Eurydice herself rather tediously bemoans the circumstances which have separated husband and wife, parent and child, and she laments the depths to which she has fallen. Until Eurydice begins to evidence her willingness to die as a falsely accused wife in order to save Periander's life in the middle of the play, she appears to be a character without complexity who demonstrates little courage, conviction, or even feminine softness. Procles turns to subdue Eurydice, and in taking pleasure in denying Periander her favors, his evil character is made incredible in the extreme.

In fact, the love between Periander and Eurydice becomes secondary to the rivalry between Periander and Procles. Though we are urged to feel sympathy for Periander's plight (I, ii; III, iii), he hates being the object of Procles' scorn as much as he longs for Eurydice. The two rulers represent very simple contrasting philosophies. Procles seeks "bliss"; he promotes riot and sensuality. Periander stands for law and order; he wishes to fight a "fair war" with Procles rather than have his crown usurped. Set in opposition is the longing for the stability of Periander's father's rule, a stability Periander had vowed to restore. Yet Periander is hot-tempered, and he is quick to assume that Eurydice is unfaithful because he finds her in Procles' presence.

Periander, like Eurydice, maintains faith in the gods while bemoaning his fate. Periander seeks divine guidance through Leonidas, who acts as the voice of the gods but without the didacticism Aaron Hill desired. He returns to Mallet's theme: "O Jealousy! thou merciless destroyer, / More cruel than the grave!" (V, i). The play concludes with Periander cursing his broken vow to his father, but jealousy seems more important in Leonidas' final words: "O Jealousy! / This is thy dreadful work. May future times / Learn here thy power, and mark with heedful eyes, / From thy blind rage what mighty mischiefs rise." Having Eurydice kill herself instead of having Periander murder her is an improvement, for it allows us to feel the futility of her death more poignantly and it characterizes Periander as wise too late, more tragic than violent and tyrannical.

Aaron Hill was extravagant in his praise of the play before it was produced, noting its scope of invention, delicacy, and propriety,[22] but he levied considerable criticism at the production when he attended its opening performance. Pleased with Wilkes's presentation of the prologue, he urged that the licentious sections of his epilogue (apparently added by Cibber) be expurgated. He further argued that only the actors playing Leonidas and Polydore acted their roles satisfactorily. Though he criticized the "whining monotony" of Mrs. Porter as Eurydice, this is surely a fault of the play as much as of the acting. Hill also berated Mills for the incongruity between his voice and his facial expressions, for, "in the midst of all his startings, and convulsive agitations of body, he looks not, as if he were in earnest."[23]

The play was revived with slight alterations and limited success on March 3, 1759, with Garrick as Periander and Mrs. Cibber as Eurydice.[24] Of the revival, Arthur Murphy commented laconically that "It loitered on the stage nine nights, and sunk into oblivion."[25] The play continued on March 6, and 13 and 17, but never attracted much interest.

The play touches on themes of broken vows, religion, politics, and domestic turmoil, but none of these ever becomes significant enough to unify the play or to sustain the tragedy. Periander has worldly stature but seems gratuitously cruel and even stupid in his unwillingness to attend to Eurydice's protest of fidelity. Procles is a heartless tyrant, Eurydice too passive and simple, Leonidas a moral mouthpiece for Mallet's intentions, and Polydore an awkward remnant of the source.

Mallet's second play, *Mustapha*, was recognized as more

explicitly political when it was first produced at Drury Lane on February 13, 1739. A more successful play than *Eurydice* with a run of fourteen nights, *Mustapha* was twice presented upon the command of the Prince and Princess of Wales, and in the published version it was dedicated to the Prince of Wales. Pope remarked to Aaron Hill, on December 8, 1738, that Mallet would defer to him for the first presentation of Hill's *Caesar.*[26] Mallet wrote to Hill of the frustration in producing his play and in dealing with Fleetwood, manager of Drury Lane. He had spent "ten days' attendance in town upon the Patentee" on behalf of his own tragedy and for Hill's *Caesar*.[27] Apparently Mallet had solicited favorable opinions about the play from Lord Bolingbroke and Pope, for he commented in a letter to Hill that both had a high opinion of the tragedy. Mallet continued in a letter on February 3, 1738, "The manager (if that is a name for him) will not be at the expense of one shilling towards the dressing or decorating it. He even carries away the actors that are to play in it, from the rehearsals to boxing matches at Totenham Court, where he himself presides as umpire."[28] Finally it was the Prince of Wales who sponsored the play. Hill reported "that the *prince* has been so just as to insist on Mr. *Mallet's* Tragedy, as the first to be brought on, this season."[29]

In spite of poor acting, "W. Q." commented in the *Gentleman's Magazine* (February 1739) that the play was well-received, and he printed the dedication, prologue, epilogue, and a portion of the scene in which Zanger urges Mustapha to flee for his life. "Amasius" directed to Mr. Mallet a panegyric which focused on the tyranny and ambition of Solyman and praised Mallet's "tow'ring genius" and ability to arouse "the tend'rest passions." The poem concluded with the charge, "Be *Mustapha* the proof, where pleas'd we find, / Sense, conduct, beauty, wit and judgment join'd." The Earl of Egmont provided a few specific remarks: "In the evening I went to [*Mustapha*]. The language of it is lofty but not bombast, the sentiments fine and justly expressed, characters kept up to, and the principles of honour and virtue inculcated; in a word, to one of our best modern tragedies."[30] Pope too liked the play, though with considerably more reserve: "It succeeded (hitherto at least, for yesterday was the first day) as well as I could expect; but so vilely acted in the women's parts and the men's (except two) that I wonder it could succeed."[31] Later he commented, "I heartily rejoice in the success you so justly merit, and so fortunately have met with, considering what a stage, and what a people you have to do with. I hope you have secured a side box on the sixth night for Mrs. Blount, Lady Fanny, &c. . . ."[32]

As he had in *Eurydice*, Mallet again chose a familiar story with a political application. Allardyce Nicoll remarks on the similarity between *Eurydice* and *The Tragedy of Mustapha, the Son of Solyman the Magnificent* (1690) by Roger Boyle, Earl of Orrery, and especially draws a parallel concerning the portrayal of Zanger.[33] Herbert Starr provides much more detail in his specific tracing of sources in the Orrery play as well as in Richard Knolles's *Generall Historie of the Turkes* (1603) and Fulke Greville's *Mustapha* (1609, 1633).[34] Starr correctly notes that Mallet made little use of the Orrery play and less of the Fulke Greville version. His chief source was Knolles's *Generall Historie of the Turkes*, best known as the source for Johnson's *Irene*.

Mallet included two scenes between Solyman and Mustapha and concluded with Solyman convinced of his son's innocence. Certainly Mallet knew Orrery's play, and Pope alluded to it in a letter to Mallet, December 17, 1739, when he cleared Mallet of a libel insinuation by saying, "that you have no sort of reason to answer a fact that is false in itself, and appears plainly so to every man, that reads your Mustapha and my Lord Orrery's."[35] Starr determined that Mallet made several original contributions to the story. He added Mustapha's secret marriage to Emira, her plea to Solyman for Mustapha's life, Zanger and Achmet's attempt to rescue Mustapha, Rustan's death, and Mustapha's portrayal "as wholly aware of the plots against him from . . . his first appearance on the stage."[36] While I agree that Mallet was most influenced by Knolles, attributions of originality to Mallet are not all accurate. For example, in Knolles, after Mustapha is sent to govern Caramania at Roxolana's urging, and after she sends him "certain rich apparel" in Solyman's name, she tricks Solyman by an elaborate ruse into "manumising" her and then marrying her. The account reads, "he fearing the worst, would not touch it [a poison apple rather than 'rich apparel'] before he had caused it to be worne by one of his servants, by which wariness (as it was thought) he for that time prevented the treason of his wicked stepdame, and made her malicious practice manifest to the world."[37] This is a very explicit statement indicating Mustapha's knowledge of his mother's treachery. Also Solyman's lack of retaliation against Roxolana is explained in Knolles by supernatural intervention. Trongilla, a Jew, bewitched the emperor so that he did not perceive Roxolana's subterfuge. Starr also is in error in suggesting Mallet added Mustapha's secret marriage to Emira to the play. In Knolles's account, Rustan and Roxolana tell Solyman that Mustapha has secretly married Emira. Mallet, then, is even more heavily in Knolles's debt than has previously been assumed. Emira's special plea for Mustapha's life appears, however, to be original with Mallet.

James Quin (1693– 1766), the actor Smollett satirized in *Peregrine Pickle*, played Solyman with the famed artificial and formal style he had previously shown in numerous classical tragic roles, including Jaffeir in *Venice Preserv'd* and Coriolanus in Thomson's play. Like *Eurydice*, *Mustapha* was interpreted as being filled with political implications. The poet in *Gentleman's Magazine* alludes to the play as portraying the tragic effects of uncontained power when "dastard slaves the sov'reign's nod obey." The machinations of Queen Caroline and Sir Robert Walpole had been the subject of another recent play, Thomson's *Agamemnon*, in which Quin had acted the title role. Also, Mallet had written the prologue to *Agamemnon*, and Thomson returned the favor with the prologue to *Mustapha* as an injunction against the lawless monarchy which breeds cruelty and hate. *Agamemnon* focuses, of course, on Clytemnestra's treachery against Agamemnon rather than on the parent / child conflict, but the differences between father and son, George II and Frederick, Prince of Wales, function to create more exact political innuendoes between Mallet's Solyman and Mustapha. The parallel between Rustan and Walpole as the evil minister who exacerbates the tension between father and son was certainly intended, and though the death of Queen Caroline in November 1737 relieved the political application, it remains surprising that the Licenser allowed the play to be performed. Thomas Davies comments, "On the first night of its exhibition were assembled all the chiefs in opposition to the court; and many speeches were applied by the audience to the supposed grievances of times, and to persons and characters."[38] That *Gustavus Vasa* and *Edward and Eleonora* were soon after refused license may perhaps be attributed to the roaring success of Mallet's play.

The various subplots provide the potential for the subtlety that is missing from Mallet's earlier play, *Eurydice*. Knolles emphasized Mustapha's conflict of conscience in his account. Mustapha ponders whether to kill his father and rule the world, or whether to succumb as an innocent and injured victim, but one who has led a blessed life. The latter choice prevails to enforce the moral that virtue matters more than sovereignty. Mallet's play emphasizes to a greater degree than its source Solyman's love for both Roxolana and Mustapha, and it adds the significant subplot of the loving brothers, Zanger and Mustapha, a subplot which affords some of the best scenes in the play. Mustapha is a well-drawn character shown as loyal, true, and unjustly maligned by Roxolana. Solyman too is fully realized as a just ruler, but he ultimately is destroyed by his blind passion for Roxolana and his trust in Rustan, his close adviser. Mustapha's love for Emira is made parallel to Solyman's for Roxolana, though Mustapha maintains (Act III) that he values his mind more than his passions. But when Emira confesses to Solyman that she has married Mustapha, he is convinced that Mustapha is in collusion with the enemy. Genest accurately judges the last act to be the weakest because "Rustan's voluntary confession of guilt is unnatural, and Roxalana's conduct seems inconsistent."[39] Orrery had allowed Zanger to reveal the truth to his father, but in Mallet's play, Roxolana and Zanger become the center of the final act, and they are less interesting as characters than Solyman and Mustapha. Though the scenes between Mustapha and his father and brother allow for some fine rhetoric, the strength of the play is not its exploration of the ideas of love versus duty or family versus country. Rather, Mallet has made skillful use of his sources to create the interweaving of plot and subplot, and, in addition, the characters of Mustapha and Solyman occasionally surprise us with the intricacy of their motivations. Finally, the epilogue, spoken by Quin in the role of Solyman, is historically noteworthy because it urges the expulsion of "wanton jokes" from tragedies in order to maintain their tragic dignity.

Mallet next composed two dramatic pieces as masques, a form surprisingly popular in the eighteenth-century playhouse. Thomas Arne's revival of *Comus* (1738), for example, was produced repeatedly at mid-century, seven times in Drury Lane in 1740. The masque, originally intended, of course, as a private court entertainment, provided music, dancing, and spectacle for the eighteenth-century English stage. The masque, a production requiring singing and acting, became a successful rival genre to the notoriously unsophisticated Italian opera which dominated the English theatre in the first decade of the eighteenth century.[40] Mallet wrote two such masques, the first *Alfred* with James Thomson (1740), revised in 1751, and later *Britannia* (1755). Mallet's masques, as well as other eighteenth-century specimens of the genre, were not an integral part of another play which served as a framework, but independent works to be performed separately. Because eighteenth-century masques frequently included spoken dialogue, they resembled operettas or musical plays. Masques were often performed as afterpieces, and, though brief, the masques frequently required considerable expense in their production.

The history of *Alfred: A Masque* is very intricate, and some aspects of portions of the story have been fully traced.[41] The principal versions of *Alfred* were in 1740, 1745, 1751, 1753, 1759, and 1773. Thomson and Mallet wrote the 1740 *Alfred*. Mallet revised and rewrote the 1751 version, and Garrick revised Mallet's version in 1773. Mallet had little to do with the other productions and variations, and he died well before Garrick's farewell performance in the 1773 version. Only those productions in which Mallet had a significant hand will concern us here. None of these performances was extraordinarily successful, but the coalescing of military and patriotic fervor around Alfred, founder of the British navy, in a pastoral and musical setting repeatedly struck a universally popular theme throughout the mid-eighteenth century.

The original production in 1740 by Mallet and James

Thomson concluded with a rousing arrangement of the song "Rule, Britannia," and it is for that alone that the masque has continued to attract interest. Though the occasion was momentous, the birthday of the Princess of Brunswick and the commemoration of the accession of George I, the masque itself fails to provide a strong characterization of the British king or any memorable dramatic scenes. The *London Daily-Post* report, often recounted, described the varied entertainments of the evening:

> On Friday last [August 1740] was perform'd at Cliefden (by Comedians from both Theatres) before their Royal Highnesses the Prince and Princess of Wales, and a great Number of Nobility, and others, a Dramatick Masque call'd *Alfred*, written by Mr. Thomson; in which was introduc'd Variety of Dancing, very much to the Satisfaction of their Royal Highnesses, and the rest of the Spectators, especially the Performance of Signora Barbarini . . . and the humorous Pantomimical Scene of The Skeleton taken from the Entertainment of Merlin's Cave, by Mr. Rich and Mr. Lalauze. The whole was exhibited upon a Theatre in the Garden compos'd of Vegetables, and decorated with Festoons of Flowers, at the End of which was erected a Pavilion for their Royal Highnesses the Prince and Princess of Wales, Prince George, and Princess Augusta. The whole concluded with Fireworks made by Dr. Desaguliers, which were equal in their kind to the rest of the Performance. Their Royal Highnesses were so well pleas'd with the whole Entertainment, that they commanded the same to be perform'd on Saturday last, with the Addition of some favourite Pantomime Scenes from Mr. Rich's Entertainments,

> which was accordingly began, but the Rain falling very heavy, oblig'd them to break off before it was half over; upon which his Royal Highness commanded them to finish the Masque of *Alfred* in the House.[42]

Mallet and Thomson both received pensions from the Prince of Wales, and most analysts have credited Mallet with little responsibility for *Alfred*. The intention of the play was, of course, to flatter the Prince of Wales by comparing his situation to Alfred's courage in spite of his misery, and to urge his continuing support of the two poets. Thomas Arne, the prolific composer, provided the music for the masque. The score required a lavish collection of instruments in order to present an overture, a march, and eight songs.[43] Musicians universally praise "O Peace, thou fairest child in Heaven," and two other songs, "Sweet Valley" and "If those who live in Shepherd's Bower," have also had many admirers. The cast of characters listed in the printed play does not indicate that Mrs. Arne apparently sang the part of a spirit and Thomas Salway, who played Corin as well as the Bard, sang "Rule, Britannia" at its premier, an honor often mistakenly given to Thomas Lowe.[44] "Rule, Britannia" was published with full score with *The Judgment of Paris* in 1742. Some of the settings to the 1740 score were published with Arne's revivals of *Alfred* in 1745, but the 1753 score is the first to document fully the music. The first production of *Alfred* after 1740, joined with *The Judgment of Paris*, took place in Aungier Street Theatre, Dublin, March 10 and 17, 1744, but Hogarth, in commenting on *The Judgment*, gives no details of *Alfred*.[45] Arne added numerous songs to *Alfred* and presented it as "an opera" March 20 and April 3, 1745, at Drury Lane.

While Thomson and Mallet undoubtedly intended to flatter the Prince of Wales and his family with the role of

Alfred, the part is relatively static. The Earl of Devon, Eltruda, and the Hermit encourage the passive Alfred to attempt to regain his former power and glory. The songs are intended to arouse the king's patriotic feelings. In Act I the Hermit urges Alfred to turn his political affliction to advantageous action. When Act II finds him still pensive, awaiting word of Devon's attempt to oust the Danes from the one remaining English fortress, the Hermit appeals to Alfred's parental and husbandly feelings as well. Alfred's internal ponderings are personified in visions of Edward III, Philippa, and the Black Prince.

The play itself is usually assumed to have been principally written by Thomson, largely on the evidence of Mallet's own comments concerning his revisions in 1751. When Mallet rewrote the play after Thomson's death, he greatly increased the significance of Alfred's role. Mallet's friend Aaron Hill died the year before Mallet's 1751 revision of the play, but apparently Mallet acceded to Hill's strong criticisms of the play. His letter to Mallet is undated, but his remark that the masque is with the Licenser provides a date for the letter as after February 9, 1740 / 41. Hill assumed that Mallet had a major part in the writing of the original masque, and he urged him to make Alfred more active than the Hermit and the Earl of Devon: "You will, I know, permit your *readers* to expect, that a brave king, so active, and so famed, as *Alfred*, should do more in his own drama, . . . than condescend to hear himself advised, blamed, spurr'd, and comforted."[46] He further urged Mallet to place Eltruda and the children under the Hermit's tutelage and create an occasion for a dissertation on educating the young prince. The Danish prince Hubba (whose name, Hill notes, ought to be changed) should be captured, tamed, and converted to Christianity. The entire masque should end with the king's creating a fleet to protect the country from future invasions.

Hill's objections and suggestions were sound, and apparently Mallet remembered them well as he prepared the play for its 1751 production which opened at Drury Lane.

With Edward Moore's *Gil Blas*, *Alfred* was one of two new main pieces acted in the 1750/51 season. February 23, 1751, was the first of nine performances at Drury Lane. Of Garrick's acting, Murphy wrote, "He hoped, it seems, when the eye was gratified with splendid scenery, and the ear charmed with vocal and instrumental music, that the play would have been crowned with brilliant success. He was much disappointed, and Mallet did not add a sprig of laurel to his brow."[47] The prompter Cross remarked that the play received "great Applause, only some of the Dances, being too long were dislik'd, & some of the Songs had ye same reception."[48]

The 1751 text from the Beinecke Library reproduced here shows John Genest's clear markings of the additions and alterations to the 1740 text. Mallet himself remarks in the Advertisement that he made Alfred the major figure, rejected many of his earlier scenes, and retained only "three or four speeches" of Thomson and "part of one song." We cannot know how much of the 1740 text was Mallet's, but Genest charges that he was "an impudent liar" in regard to his additions to the 1751 text.[49] Mallet expands the cast, limits Devon's rehearsal of the defeat of the British, and inspires Alfred to take quick command by reporting his popular support. Mallet introduces the idea that "Complaint is for the vulgar: kings must act," and he also creates a religious subtheme in the Hermit's attitudes. Three Danes enter the play as Eltruda's attackers in a subplot contrasting their barbarity to Alfred's fear of God. Though the Hermit reveals unnamed spirits to Eltruda in the interval while Alfred goes to battle, the spirits of Edward, Philippa, and the Black Prince are omitted. Furies, a Pyrrhic Dance, and a triumph over the Danish King are also new to Mallet's version. The play concludes with Alfred's desire to insure protection from attack and with the Hermit's prophecy and discovery of the future. Mallet even adds stanzas to "Rule, Britannia," perhaps in an effort to make it seem to be his own. Finally, the singer Mrs. Clive provides an epilogue which affords an opportunity for discovery of more spectacle. Many of Mallet's changes thus followed Aaron Hill's much earlier suggestions, though the success of the play must be attributed to the enormous spectacle, including the discovery (III, vii) of triumphal arches adorned with garlands and a procession of shepherdesses, as well as the concluding extravaganza.

The musical additions to the play are so extensive that Thomas Arne denied association with the 1751 production. He stated in *The General Advertiser* that only "O Peace, thou fairest child" and "Rule, Britannia" were his compositions. Apparently Charles Burney wrote the music for the revival. Madame d'Arblay remarked in her memoirs of her father that "the mask of Alfred was by no means his sole juvenile composition," and that various productions from his pen were put forth as "offspring of a *society of the sons of Apollo.*"[50] Burne, serving as an apprentice for Arne during the 1745 revival of *Alfred*, had made a fair copy of it, occasionally teaching parts to the singers and attending the rehearsals. In a burst of Scottish chauvinism, Mallet oddly wanted the songs to be set to old Scotch airs, but in fragments of his *Memoirs* we see that Burney appropriately refused his request, "as Alfred was not a Scotsman, I thought it w^{d} be ridiculous to confine all the songs to Scotish melody. I therefore new set all the rest except 'Rule Britania,' wch had been so happily set by my Master Arne. . . ."[51]

There were other revisions and productions of *Alfred* in 1753, 1754, 1759 (with a Benefit for the Use of the Marine

Society), and 1762, before Mallet's death in 1765. Those of 1753 and 1759 were principally Arne's work. In 1773 Garrick revived Mallet's version with new music by T. Smith. The promptbook of the 1751 edition survives with alterations in Garrick's hand, an important document for tracing staging practices.[52] Again the revival celebrates the spectacle of the play with a procession of Alfred and a procession of the Danish king added. Records of the musicians paid indicate the wide variety of instruments (in the tradition of the 1740 *Alfred*) with trumpets, clarinets, horns, and bassoon used. It was acted eight times, opening October 9, 1773, with Reddish as Alfred.[53]

Of course, "Rule, Britannia" was retained and sung with gusto. One observer remarked, "This Masque is very well got up with New Scenes & Decorations particularly a Representation of the Grand Naval Review design'd by Mons De Loutherberg & vastly well Executed had great Applause the piece is very dull."[54] As Carola Oman notes, "A play about the founder of Britain's Navy seemed appropriate in the year of the Grand Naval Review at Portsmouth."[55] The play was an enthusiastic patriotic call filled with extravagant display—never more than that—and it appealed to an important element of the eighteenth-century audience throughout the century.

The subject of the glory of England became extraordinarily popular in the early and mid-eighteenth century, and at the beginning of the French and Indian War (1755), the call to patriotism was heard in the rousing masque *Britannia*. *Britannia* is a trifle which seems to have inspired little notice. The masque, with a prologue by Garrick, was introduced on May 9, 1755, along with *Zara* as the main piece. It played throughout the month with various plays, including *The Mistake*, *Fair Penitent*, *The Chances*, *The Mourning Bride*, and *Barbarossa*, all at Drury Lane. It was revived February 10, 1756, with *Zara*, and May 11, 1757, for the Marine Society with *The Suspicious Husband*, and on both occasions the masque and the prologue were performed. The prompter Cross reported that books of the masque were sold at the theatre on several occasions, beginning May 14, 1755.[56] Garrick's prologue to the play was apparently extraordinarily popular, though Arthur Murphy's account that the audiences demanded the prologue alone on numerous occasions is probably erroneous. Murphy wrote, "A French war had broke out at this time; and to rouze the British spirit, Mr. Mallet prepared a *Masque*, intitled *Britannia*. The music was composed by Dr. Arne, and was a great support of the piece." It was revived in 1756, 1757, and 1758, apparently a popular afterpiece. Murphy continued, "The Prologue was written by Garrick, and, as it was understood at the time, had some lines from the pen of Mr. Mallet. It was spoken by the manager, in the character of a *Drunken Sailor*. It was delivered with the greatest humour, and from the nature of the subject was so popular, that it was called for many nights after the *Masque* itself was laid aside, and Garrick was obliged, though he did not act in the play, to be in readiness to answer the public demand."[57] The same week *Britannia* was produced at Drury Lane, "Rule, Britannia" was performed at Covent Garden after *The Old Batchelor*. Probably the most interesting production of *Britannia* took place May 11, 1757, when the play was presented to benefit "Friendless Boys and Men for the Sea," the Marine Society.[58] In addition to allowing the spectators to view the clothing they had purchased for the sailors, at the conclusion of the performance they saw the gentlemen sent off to the fleet at Portsmouth.

The masque itself, with music by Thomas Arne, is a spectacular call to a holy war intended to inspire soldiers, patriots, parents, and even mistresses to support Britain. The libretto is undistinguished. The soldiers' girlfriends, Nancey and Sukey, are convinced to forego their beguiling attempt to keep their lovers home, and they too become patriots in the cause. The prologue, however, unquestionably provides the only humor in the play. In slapstick fashion, it produces a comic counterpoint to the oppressive chauvinism of the masque with its appeal to the pit and its opportunity for Garrick to shine as a mildly ribald and drunken sailor. After damning the masque for its "trite thoughts and hackneyed metre," Thomas Davies noted that Mrs. Jefferson as Britannia was the one saving aspect of the play. She presented "the most complete figure in beauty of countenance and symmetry of form I ever beheld."[59]

Mallet is probably best known for his *Elvira*, not because of the excellence of the play but because of James Boswell's *Critical Strictures on Elvira*, written with his friends Erskine and Dempster. *Elvira* opened Wednesday, January 19, 1763, at Drury Lane, to an audience that apparently included both Boswell, prepared to damn the play, and Gibbon, ready to applaud it. The cast was headed by David Garrick as Don Alonzo, Mrs. Cibber as Elvira, and Mrs. Pritchard as the Queen of Portugal. An extraordinarily gifted actress, Mrs. Pritchard simultaneously rehearsed for the tragic *Elvira* and the comic *Way of the World*, as Edward Gibbon recounts:

> I went with Mallet to breakfast with Garrick; and from thence to Drury-Lane house, where I assisted at a very private rehearsal, in the Green-room, of *Elvira*. As I have seen it acted, I shall defer my opinion of it till then; but I can't help mentioning here the surprising versatility of Mrs. Pritchard's talents, who rehearsed, almost at the same time, the part of a furious Queen in the Green-room, and that

> of a Coquette on the stage; and passed several times from one to the other with the utmost ease and happiness.[60]

Mrs. Pritchard apparently quibbled at taking the character of the immoral queen. Mallet supposedly responded, "Why, Madam, you have always played *Lady Macbeth*; just such another part as this I designed for you, and yet you never complained of the former."

Elvira may have been unpopular because it was regarded "as a ministerial play."[61] Several sources indicate *Elvira* ran only thirteen nights as a result of the falsely labeled political aspects of the play. In any case, audiences assumed that Mallet was praising Lord Bute, who had recently concluded the unpopular peace with France. The play was produced during the half-price riots, the call to maintain the practice of allowing half-price admission after the third act. The mob sometimes damaged property and had even forced cancellation of *Two Gentlemen of Verona* on January 25 in that same year.[62]

The first night of *Elvira* marked the eve of Gibbon's long-anticipated journey to Lausanne and Italy. With the Seven Years War ended and his military and filial responsibilities fulfilled, Gibbon could at last return to his beloved Switzerland.[63] The relationship of Gibbon and Mallet had begun when Gibbon's father mistakenly entrusted his son to David Mallet's tutoring at the recommendation of the Rev. Mr. Philip Francis, though the deist Mallet was marked as being synonymous with the devil Moloch in a much-repeated popular joke.[64] Mallet urged Gibbon to read Swift and Addison, helped him publish *Essai sur l'étude de la littérature à Londres*, and provided him a letter of recommendation to friends in France. Thus it is that Gibbon wrote that his "last act in town was to applaud Mallet's new tragedy of Elvira."[65] Gibbon gave a specific account of the performance:

> My father and I went to the Rose, in the passage of the Play-house, where we found Mallet, with about thirty friends. We dined together, and went from thence into the Pitt, where we took our places in a body, ready to silence all opposition. However, we had no occasion to exert ourselves. Notwithstanding the malice of a party, Mallet's nation, connections and indeed imprudence, we heard nothing but applause. I think it was deserved. The plan was borrowed from *de la Motte*, but the details and language have great merit. A fine Vein of dramatick poetry runs thro' the piece.[66]

Boswell's visit to the first night's performance of *Elvira* was also a memorable day, for it was the day he began to suspect his having contracted "Signor Gonorrhoea" from the actress "Louisa." George Dempster, Andrew Erskine, and Boswell determined to gratify a whim, "which was that on the first day of the new tragedy called *Elvira's* being acted, we three should walk from the one end of London to the other, dine at Dolly's and be in the theatre at night; and as the play would probably be bad, and as Mr. David Malloch, the author, who has changed his name to David Mallet, Esq., was an arrant puppy, we determined to exert ourselves in damning it."[67] They walked through London, breakfasted at Somerset Coffee-house, went on top London Bridge and round to a public house, taking their inspiration from the *Spectator*'s remarks on the variety of London. At four they seated themselves in the pit "with oaken cudgels in our hands and shrill-sounding catcalls in our pockets, sat ready prepared, with a generous resentment in our breasts against dullness and impudence, to be the swift ministers of vengeance."[68] Their goal, to prevent the play from running past the first night, was defeated, almost from the first, for they were unable to muster enough support to call for a popular song, a defeat Boswell compares to a party losing its moderator. The three revived their spirits at Lady Betty Macfarlane's and planned to draft a six-penny pamphlet mocking the play.

Garrick told Boswell he found "half a dozen as clever things in the *Strictures on Elvira* as he ever had read," but most reviewers thought little of the pamphlet.[69] Mallet was a popular subject for ridicule because of his arrogance, his supposed desire to rid himself of his Scots affiliation, his posthumous attacks on Pope, and his fallacious claim that he was writing the life of Marlborough. A fragment of Boswell's early poem *The Turnspittiad* with Mallet as butt of the joke is an indication of Boswell's early and longstanding dislike of his fellow Scotsman.[70] Popular tradition, in an effort to explain how Mallet could have duped Garrick into producing *Elvira*, maintains that he appealed to Garrick's vanity. Mallet claimed he was industriously at work on the life of Marlborough and had introduced Garrick's name into the history. In a magnanimous moment, Garrick encouraged his writing something for the stage (in spite of the limited success of *Eurydice* and *Mustapha*): "'Why, faith,' said Mallet, 'to tell you the truth, I have, whenever I could rob the Duke of an hour or so, employed myself in adapting La Motte's Inès de Castro to the English stage, and here it is.' The manager embraced Elvira with rapture, and brought it forward with all expedition."[71]

The printed play begins with a dedication to the Earl of Bute, who is celebrated as the father of his country, and the prologue extolls the pleasures of peace:

War is no more: those thunders cease to rowl,
That lately shook the globe from pole to pole.

The play had previously been seen in London and Paris, the prologue claims, but of course the reference is to the source, a much criticized but popular play produced April 6, 1723, at Théâtre Francais, Lamotte-Houdar's *Inès de Castro*, and to the Portuguese poet Camoëns in the epic *Lusiad*, a debt Mallet readily acknowledges in a postscript to the printed version. There Mallet also records the elaborate detail of Don Pedro's adulation of Elvira's corpse. Mallet does allow for political implications of the play, for England had sided with Portugal against Spain. The villainess is a Spaniard, and Mallet calls for a war against Spain at the end.[72]

Gibbon and Boswell were at odds in their opinions of the play. Boswell criticized the play but complimented the actors; Gibbon deplored "entrusting fine Speeches to indifferent Actors."[73] More significantly, both of the men had experienced early and repeated conflicts with their fathers, a significant theme in *Elvira*. Though Boswell was much moved by scenes of paternal tenderness and filial obedience in other plays, he stood apart to mock the lack of pathos in *Elvira*: "Our great Author possesses, in its utmost Perfection, the happy Art of uniting rival Ladies, and of setting at Variance a virtuous Father and Son. How intimate his Acquaintance with Human Nature! How deep his Knowledge of the Passions!"[74] Gibbon, accompanied by his father to the performance, noted that the father-son scenes "awaken[ed] almost every sensation of the human breast. . . ."[75] Gibbon expands on the point. Don Alonzo's motivation in condemning his son to death for marrying Elvira seems excessive, and even incredible, for Don Pedro's offense is more a private than a public matter. The consequences of Don Pedro's marriage to Elvira are not great, and Don Alonzo thus exerts "an unequal and superior severity." The scene, and Gibbon's response to it, recalls his own desire to marry Suzanne Curchod against his father's wishes. Gibbon, unlike Don Alonzo, sighed as a lover and obeyed as a son.

Various critics of the play understandably found the catastrophe unmoving. Murphy accurately stated that Elvira's destiny is clear from the first act and it can surprise no one.[76] The conflict cannot sustain the spectator's attentions for Don Alonzo is unjust, the Queen too cruel, and Elvira's death too long anticipated. Davies bemoans Mallet's lack of the sense of the dramatic. The play "is laboured and affected, void of nature and simplicity."[77] Boswell's *Critical Strictures* are silly and juvenile, but Mallet is an easy target. Mallet is particularly vulnerable for his amateurish use of conventions and his awkward maneuvering of his characters. *Critical Strictures* aptly holds him accountable for lengthy plot summary at the beginning of scenes, for violating credibility by letting prisoners out of prison for a chat, and, especially, for introducing Elvira's children quite suddenly in the last act.

The gratuitous cruelty of the Queen, the utter virtuousness of Alonzo and Elvira, and the undramatic nature of the catastrophe condemn the play to mediocrity. Garrick encourages the appropriate response in the epilogue, spoken by the deceased Elvira, who encourages the spectators to indulge their desire to laugh at the excesses of the play:

> Love, marriage, treason, prison, poison, death,
> Were scarce sufficient to compleat my fate;
> Two children were thrown in to make up weight.
> With all these suff'rings, is it not provoking,
> To be deny'd at last a little joking?

Johnson's judgment on Mallet's works, that they convey little information and give no great pleasure, is certainly applicable to his plays. Mallet's goal is never literary excellence, though it is literary fame he seeks, and that can be had by winning the support of a prince and relying on the kindness of friends such as Thomson, Pope, and Garrick. Mallet, like most eighteenth-century dramatists, sought to provide amusement rather than art in the theatre. What pleasure that derives from his plays must have come from watching a fine actor like Quin play Solyman or David Garrick deliver a prologue in a drunken stupor. Mallet's plays *are*, as Johnson predicted they would be, largely forgotten, though *Alfred* and *Elvira* occasionally gain literary historical attention because of their connections to Mallet's literary acquaintances. Mallet's arrogance and his tenacity in the pursuit of fame command our interest in his plays, even though those characteristics cannot always command our admiration.

Felicity A. Nussbaum
Syracuse University

Notes

1. *Boswell's Life of Johnson*, ed. George Birkbeck Hill, rev. L. F. Powell (Oxford: Clarendon Press, 1934–50), III, 137.

2. Samuel Johnson, *Lives of the English Poets*, ed. George Birkbeck Hill (Oxford: Clarendon Press, 1905), III, 400. All subsequent references to the "Life of Mallet" are to this edition. Other authoritative biographical accounts of Mallet include Robert Anderson, *Complete Edition of the Poets of Great Britain* (London, 1795), IX, 675–78; and Frederick Dinsdale's preface to David Mallet, *Ballads and Songs* (London, 1857), pp. 3–82.

3. In his *Abridged Dictionary*, Johnson uses the incident to define *alias* as "a Latin word, signifying otherwise; as Mallet *alias* Malloch; that is *otherwise* Malloch." Dinsdale notes that changing names was common in Scotland "not merely for the purpose of evading justice by the help of an *alias*, but from Highland pride and etiquette," *Ballads and Songs*, p. 13.

4. James Boswell, *Journal of a Tour to the Hebrides with Samuel Johnson, LL.D.*, ed. Frederick A. Pottle and Charles H. Bennett (New York: Literary Guild, 1936), p. 226.

5. See Herbert W. Starr, "Notes on Mallet," *N&Q*, 178 (1940), 277–78. Boswell comments on the epilogue to *Elvira*: "There was a Simile of a Bundle of Twigs formed into a Rod, which seemed to convey a delicate Allusion to Mr. *Malloch's* original Profession . . ." in James Boswell, Andrew Erskine, and George Dempster, *Critical Strictures on the New Tragedy of Elvira* (1763), intro. by F. A. Pottle, No. 35 (Los Angeles: Augustan Reprint Society, 1952), p. 22.

6. See G. F. Sleigh, "The Authorship of William and Margaret," *Library*, 8 (1953), 121–23, and A. E. H. Swaen, "Fair Margaret and Sweet William," *Archiv*, 136 (1917), 40–71. Mallet's claim to have created an original work has been much contested.

7. Irma Lustig provides a finely detailed description of the circumstances surrounding the composition of this poem in "'Donaus,' *Donaides*, and David Malloch: A Reply to Dr. Johnson," *MP*, 76 (1978), 149–62.

8. "Life of Mallet" in *Lives of the English Poets*, III, 404.

9. See *Scots Magazine* (1765), p. 224.

10. See Bertrand Evans, *Gothic Drama from Walpole to Shelley*, Univ. of California Publications in English, No. 18 (Berkeley: Univ. of California Press, 1947), pp. 40–41.

11. *Boswell's Life of Johnson*, III, 386.

12. John Genest, *Some Account of the English Stage from the Restoration in 1660 to 1830* (Bath: H. E. Carrington, 1832), III, 288–89.

13. See Pope's letter to Mallet, Nov. 1 [1729?], *The Works of Alexander Pope*, ed. Whitwell Elwin and William John Courthope (London: John Murray, 1886), X (Vol. V of *Correspondence*), 80.

14. Clerk of Penicuik Papers, Register House, Edinburgh, cited in

Douglas Grant, *James Thomson: Poet of 'The Seasons'* (London: Cresset Press, 1951), p. 85.

15. *The London Stage, 1729–1747*, ed. with critical intro. by Arthur H. Scouten, pt. III, v.1 (Carbondale: Southern Illinois Univ. Press, 1961), p. lxiv.

16. Aaron Hill, *The Works of the Late Aaron Hill, Esq., in 4 volumes consisting of Letters on Various Subjects* (London, 1753), I, 47.

17. Genest, III, 289 and 309.

18. John Loftis discounts the possibility of *Eurydice* as a political piece in *Politics of Drama in Augustan England* (Oxford, 1963), p. 108.

19. I cite with permission from the Henry H. Huntington Library copy of *Remarks on the Tragedy of Eurydice* (Dublin, 1731).

20. Hill, *Works* (Feb. 6, 1731), I, 31.

21. Hill, *Works* (Feb. 12, 1731), I, 41.

22. Hill, *Works* (Feb. 6, 1731), I, 30.

23. Hill, *Works* (Feb. 23, 1731), I, 45–57.

24. Genest, IV, 547. Mallet blamed the dullness of the revival on the actors' lack of pathos, a quality the author valued highly. See David Erskine Baker, Isaac Reed, and Stephen Jones, *Biographia Dramatica, or, A Companion to the Playhouse* (London, 1812), II, 207.

25. Murphy, *The Life of David Garrick* (Dublin: Brett Smith, 1801), p. 213.

26. Elwin–Courthope, X, 72.

27. Mallet to Aaron Hill, London, Jan. 6 [1738–39]. MS, cited in Elwin–Courthope, X, 73n.3.

28. See Elwin–Courthope, X, 72n.4.

29. Hill, *Works* (Jan. 15, 1738 / 39), I, 328.

30. *The Diary of the Earl of Egmont* (London: 1920–23), III, 23.

31. Elwin–Courthope (Feb. 12, 1738 / 39), X, 75. Herbert Starr, "Sources of David Mallet's *Mustapha*, a Tragedy," *N&Q*, 181 (Nov. 22, 1941), 285–87, notes that the play opened on Feb. 13, though the letter is dated Feb. 12; and he concludes the letter is misdated since there is overwhelming evidence that the play opened Feb. 13.

32. Elwin–Courthope (Feb. 1738 / 39), X, 93.

33. Nicoll, *A History of English Drama 1660–1900* (Cambridge: Cambridge Univ. Press, 1952), II, 83.

34. Starr, "Sources of *Mustapha*," pp. 285–87.
35. Elwin–Courthope, X, 94.
36. Starr, "Sources of *Mustapha*," p. 287.
37. Richard Knolles, *Generall Historie of the Turkes* (London, 1638), p. 760.
38. *Memoirs of the Life of David Garrick* (1808; rpt. New York: Benjamin Blom, 1969), II, 34.
39. Genest, III, 576.
40. See especially Enid Welsford, *The Court Masque* (1927; rpt. New York: Russell & Russell, 1962).
41. For the first version of *Alfred*, see Alan D. McKillop, "The Early History of *Alfred*," *PQ*, 41 (1962), 311–24. Roger Fiske concentrates on the musical interpretations of the masque in *English Theatre Music in the Eighteenth Century* (London: Oxford Univ. Press, 1973).
42. Thomas Davies, *Memoirs of Garrick*, records complaints of ill-treatment by the cast: "the players were not treated as persons ought to be who are employed by a prince" (II, 36).
43. Fiske, pp. 191 ff.
44. For accounts concerning the uncertainty over who first sang "Rule, Britannia," see McKillop, p. 312n.2, and Fiske, p. 190.
45. T. J. Walsh, *Opera in Dublin 1705–1797* (London: Allen Figgis, 1973), and Fiske, pp. 191, 224, and 226.
46. Hill, *Works*, II, 163–65.
47. Murphy, *Life of David Garrick*, p. 132.
48. Cited in *The London Stage, 1747–1776*, ed. with critical intro. by George Winchester Stone, pt. IV, v. 1 (Carbondale: Southern Illinois Univ. Press, 1962), p. 238.
49. Mallet left himself open to the ridicule of Genest and others with a reference to the clock, an anachronism because it was not invented until 1368. Genest is one who holds him accountable, IV, 323–24.
50. Madame d'Arblay, *Memoirs of Dr. Burney*, ed. Edward Moxon (London, 1832), I, 20.
51. *Frag. Mem.* (B. M. Add. MS. 48345, f. 15) cited in Roger Lonsdale, *Dr. Charles Burney* (Oxford: Clarendon Press, 1965), p. 34.

52. See Kalman Burnim, *David Garrick, Director* (Pittsburgh: Univ. of Pittsburgh Press, 1961), p. 89.

53. See *The London Stage, 1747–1776*, pt. IV, v. 3, p. 1756.

54. William Hopkins, MS. Diary, 1769–76, Folger Shakespeare Library, cited in *The London Stage, 1747–1776*, pt. IV, v. 3, 1750.

55. *David Garrick* (London: Hodder and Stoughton, 1958), p. 327.

56. *The London Stage, 1747–1776*, pt. IV, v. 1, 487.

57. Murphy, *Memoirs of Garrick*, p. 174.

58. *The London Stage, 1747–1776*, pt. IV, v. 2, 598.

59. Thomas Davies, *Memoirs of Garrick*, II, 53.

60. Nov. 26, 1762, in *Gibbon's Journal to January 28th, 1763*, ed. D. M. Low (London: Chatto & Windus, 1929), p. 185.

61. *Biographia Dramatica*, II, 191–92.

62. *The London Stage, 1747–1776*, pt. IV, v. 2, 973–74.

63. Edward Gibbon, *Memoirs of My Life*, ed. Georges A. Bonnard (New York: Funk & Wagnalls, 1966), p. 35.

64. See Joseph Knight, *David Garrick* (London: K. Paul, Trench, Trubner & Co., 1894), p. 185.

65. Gibbon, *Memoirs*, p. 124.

66. Gibbon's *Journal to Jan. 28th, 1763*, pp. 202–03.

67. *Boswell's London Journal, 1762–1763*, ed. Frederick A. Pottle (New York: McGraw-Hill Book Company, 1950), p. 152.

68. *London Journal*, p. 154.

69. *London Journal*, p. 226.

70. Frederick Pottle, *Critical Strictures on the New Tragedy of Elvira*, p. iii. "The Turnspittiad" appears in Jack Werner's volume, *Boswell's Book of Bad Verse* (London: White Lion Publishers Limited, 1974), p. 77.

71. The story is recounted in Davies, *Memoirs of Garrick*, II, 55–57, and Murphy, *Memoirs of Garrick*, pp. 246–48.

72. See *Critical Strictures on the New Tragedy of Elvira*, p. iv.

73. Gibbon's *Journal to Jan. 28th, 1763*, p. 204.

74. *Critical Strictures*, p. 14.

75. Gibbon's *Journal to Jan. 28th, 1763*, p. 203.

76. Murphy, *Memoirs of Garrick*, p. 249.

77. Davies, *Memoirs of Garrick*, II, 57.

EURYDICE

EURYDICE.

A
TRAGEDY.

Acted at the

THEATRE-ROYAL

IN

DRURY-LANE,

By HIS MAJESTY'S Servants.

LONDON:

Printed for A. MILLAR, at *Buchanan's Head*, over-against St. *Clement's* Church, in the *Strand*. M.DCC.XXXI.

(Price 1 *s.* 6 *d.*)

To His Grace

The Duke of *Montroſe*.

My Lord,

I Beg leave to ſhelter the following tragedy under your Grace's patronage: a ſmall, but ſincere, return of Gratitude for the many obligations I have to your Grace; and in particular, for the generous concern with which you eſpouſed and ſupported the intereſt of this performance:

and to which I am greatly indebted for its reputation and ſucceſs.

Permit me to add, in juſtice to your Grace, (and I do it with equal pride and pleaſure) that I received this indulgence, without being obliged to pay for it that adulation and baſeneſs of heart, which is, ſometimes, exacted by the vulgar Great; but is, more frequently, the voluntary, ill-judged offering of mean and venal writers. I am, with the trueſt zeal and attachment,

MY LORD,

Your Grace's moſt obliged,

and moſt faithful ſervant.

PROLOGUE.

Written by AARON HILL, Esq;

Spoken by Mr. WILKS.

IN youth, when modesty and merit meet,
How rare the union! and the force how sweet!
Tho' at small praise our humble author aims,
His friend may give him, what his blush disclaims.
Ladies!—to you he makes his chief address;
Form'd, to be pray'd to, and even born to bless!
He feels your power, himself, and makes it felt;
His scenes will teach each stubborn heart to melt:
And each fair eye, that now shines softly here,
Anon shall shine, still softer, thro' a tear.
Let not constraint your gen'rous sighs repress,
Nor veil compassion, nor repel distress.
Your sex's strength is in such weakness found;
And sighs and tears but help your charms to wound.
Of all the wonders taught us by the fair,
'Tis strangest, Tragedy *shou'd lose their care!*
Where Love, soft tyrant! in full glory reigns;
And sovereign Beauty holds the world in chains.
Less polish'd, and more bold, the Comic *Muse*
Unkings your Cupid, *or obstructs his views;*
Upholds presuming wit's familiar claim,
And blots out awe *from Love's diminish'd flame.*
Finds, or makes faults, and sets 'em strong in sight,
And dares draw WOMAN *false, or vain, or light.*
While Tragedy—*your servant, try'd, and true,*
Still to your fame devoted, and to YOU!
Enslav'd to Love, subdu'd ambition brings,
Firms Beauty's power, and crowns it king of kings.
Let wish'd attention grace our scene to-night,
And mourn'd afflictions move refin'd delight.
Each tender light of life we recommend;
Wife, husband, subject, parent, son, and friend!

All!

PROLOGUE.

All ! your impaſſion'd Int'reſts ſhall engage,
And hopes and fears, and pity, fire the ſtage.
Then, when ſoft ſorrow ſwells the fair one's breaſt,
And ſad impreſſions mix with nightly reſt,
Pleaſing remembrance ſhall our ſcene ſupply,
And the ſweet ſaddening influence never die.

EPI-

EPILOGUE.

Written by AARON HILL Esq;

Spoken by Miss ROBINSON, in boys clothes; tripping in hastily.

OH! *Gentlemen!—I'm come—but was not sent ye:*
A voluntier—*Pray does my* size *content ye?*
MAN, *I am yours—Sex!*—bless'd, *as heaven can make ye,*
And from this time, weak WOMAN! *I forsake ye.*
Who'd be a wife? when each new Play *can teach us,*
To what fine ends these Lords *of* ours *beseech us?*
At first, whate'er they do, they do—so charming!
But *mark what* follows; *frightful! and alarming!*
They feed too fast *on* Love; *then sick'ning tell us,*
They can't, forsooth, be kind—*because they're* jealous.
Who wou'd be woman, *then? to sigh—and suffer,*
And wish—and wait—for the slow-coming *proffer!*
Not I—farewel to petticoats, and stitching,
And welcome dear, dear, breeches! more bewitching.
Henceforth, new-moulded, I'll rove, love, and wander,
And fight, and storm—and charm—like PERIANDER.
Born for this dapper age; pert, short, and clever;
If e'er *I grow a* MAN—*'tis* now, *or never.*
Well! but what conduct *suits this transformation?*
I'll copy *some smart* soul *of conversation.*
Shou'd there be war, *I'd talk of fields and trenches;*
Shou'd there be peace—*I'd toast* ten *favourite wenches!*
Shou'd I be lov'd—*Gadso! how then?—no matter,*
I'll bow, as you do—*and* look foolish *at her.*
And so, who knows, that never means to prove ye,
But I'm as good a Man, *as any of ye!*
Well! 'tis a charming frolick—and I'll do't:
Sirs!—have I your consent?—What say ye to't?
Yet hold—Perhaps they'll dread a rival beau:
I may *be what I* seem, *for aught* they *know.*
Ladies! farewel—*I shou'd be loth to* leave ye,
Cou'd an increase *of* pretty fellows *grieve ye:*
Each, like myself, *devoted, ne'er to* harm *ye,*
And full as fit, *no doubt, to* serve *and* charm *ye.*

The Persons represented.

EURYDICE, Queen of *Corinth.*	*Mrs.* PORTER.
MELISSA, her Confidente.	*Mrs.* BUTLER.
LEONIDAS, a Nobleman, secretly in the Queen's interest.	*Mr.* BRIDGWATER.
PROCLES, Tyrant of *Epidaurus,* in possession of the Crown of *Corinth.*	*Mr.* MARSHALL.
MEDON, his Favourite.	*Mr.* W. MILLS.
PERIANDER, King of *Corinth.*	*Mr.* MILLS.
POLYDORE, his Son.	*Mr.* HALLAM.
ARISTON.	*Mr.* COREY.

Officers, Guards, Attendants.

The SCENE, Corinth.

EURYDICE.

A TRAGEDY.

ACT I. SCENE I.

EURYDICE, MELISSA.

EURYDICE.

YE heavenly Powers!
What means this dreadful war of ſea and sky!

MELISSA.

Dreadful indeed. It roſe not by degrees,
But all at once, a tempeſt wild and loud.

EURYDICE.

Hear! from the wintry north how keen it howls
Thro' theſe lone towers that rock with every blaſt,
Each moment threatning ruine on our heads.
But ſee—ſtand here, and caſt thy eyes below

O'er the broad ocean to the diſtant sky,
See what confuſion fills the raving deep!
What mountain-waves ariſe!—'Tis terrible,
And ſuiting to the horrors of my fate,
The deep deſpair that deſolates my ſoul.

MELISSA.

Ha! look, behold, due weſt where yonder rocks
O'erhang the beating tides——O ſight of woe!
Four goodly ſhips, abandon'd to the ſtorm,
Drive blindly with the billows; their drench'd ſails
Stript off, and whirl'd before the rending wind.

EURYDICE.

Aſſiſt them, all good Powers! The ſtorm is high,
And the flood perilous.
Look! now they climb a fearful ſteep, and hang
On the big ſurge that mixes with the clouds.
Save me! it burſts, and headlong down they reel
Into the yawning gulph——They cannot ſcape.
A ſea rowls o'er the foremoſt.

MELISSA.

Ah! ſhe ſtrikes
On yonder wave-worn cliff. The fatal ſhock
Has doubtleſs ſhiver'd her ſtrong ſide. She ſinks
So ſwiftly down, that ſcarce the ſtraining eye
Can trace her talleſt maſt.——Where is ſhe now!
Hid in the wild abyſs, with all her crew,
All loſt for ever!

EURYDICE.

Turn we from the ſight,
Too diſmal for a woman's eye to bear.
Ill-fated men! whom, knowing not, I mourn;
Whence, or what may they be? Even now, perhaps,
In ſome far-diſtant land, a faithful wife,

Or

Or tender parent, offers vows to heaven
For their return; and fondly numbers up
The lingring months of abſence. Fruitleſs love!
They never more ſhall meet!——By my own ills
Severely taught, I pity them; yet think
Their fate, all full of horror as it ſeems,
Is rather to be envy'd. They are now
Beyond the hand of Fate, at reſt for ever!
While I, MELISSA—

MELISSA.

Ah, EURYDICE,
My royal Miſtreſs, rather think the Gods
Would teach you, by this ſight of mournful ruine,
Patience and gentler thought. When others too
Are miſerable, not to know the worſt
Is ſome degree of bliſs.

EURYDICE.

MELISSA, no.
I tell thee, no ill fate, no face of death
Can be ſo dreadful as a life like mine.
Call to thy thoughts what I have been; how great,
How happy in a husband, and a ſon
The riſing boaſt of *Greece*. Behold me now
Caſt down to loweſt infamy; the ſlave,
The ſport of a foul Tyrant, who betray'd me,
And would deſtroy my honour.—Gracious heaven!
And ſhall this bold offender, who has broke
All bonds of holy faith, yet bids his ſoul
Rejoyce and take her eaſe; ſhall he long triumph
Here in the throne of *Corinth*, while its lord,
The injur'd PERIANDER, roams a fugitive,
Far, far from bliſs and me!

MELISSA.

These tears, my Queen,
These faithful tears, which sympathy of sorrow
Draws from my eyes, speak the sad share I take
In all your mighty ills.

EURYDICE.

Say now, MELISSA,
Is there among the daughters of Affliction
One so forlorn as poor EURYDICE?
A prisoner here, subjected to the power
Of impious PROCLES, daily doom'd to hear,
O deadly insult! his detested love.
What ill can equal this? Why did I trust
The brutal Tyrant?

MELISSA.

See, his Minion's here.

SCENE II.

EURYDICE, MELISSA, MEDON.

MEDON.

Hail, beauteous Queen! By me, the royal PROCLES
With lowly service bends him to your charms:
Bids smiling health, and gentle peace of mind
Light up your morn, and make your evening fair.
This, with the tenderest vows—

EURYDICE.

Canst thou inform me
Of those unhappy men, whom I but now
Saw perish on this coast?

MEDON.

MEDON.

Not who they are;
But what their fate, theſe eyes with dread beheld.
The King too, from the morning's chaſe return'd,
At this ſad ſight ſpur'd on with all his train
To ſave, if poſſible, whom the wild ſea
Caſts forth upon the land. But firſt his love,
That counts each moment's abſence from your eyes
An age of lingring torment, bade me fly
With health and greeting to the matchleſs fair,
That holds his ſoul enſlav'd.

EURYDICE.

Then bear him back,
From her whom he has wrong'd, betray'd and ruin'd,
Horror and loathing, unrelenting ſcorn,
And all a woman's hate, in juſt return
For his deteſted love. The tyrant coward!
To cruſh the fallen and helpleſs! to embitter
The pangs, the miſeries, himſelf has caus'd
With gall of mockery!

MEDON.

Your pardon, Madam,
If I, the humbleſt of your ſlaves, preſume
To place before your eyes in faithful proſpect
That mournful period, full of dread and danger,
Which late you ſaw. Behold then your falſe ſubjects,
Wantonly mad and ſpurning every tye
Of ſworn obedience, mix'd in one bold treaſon,
Threatning and univerſal: your loſt husband
Abſent, involv'd in unſucceſsful war:
His troops averſe and mutinous. From them
Bold faction with contagious ſwiftneſs ſpread
To *Corinth* too; where the wild herd arrous'd
Inſulted you, and drove you to this Fortreſs.

Say

Say where was then your hope, when meagre Famine
Join'd his devouring ravage; and your eyes
Saw daily, hourly perifh thofe poor few
Whofe faith had kept them yours?

EURYDICE.

O would to heaven
I then had perifh'd too!

MEDON.

Such was your ftate,
Loft even to hope, when generous PROCLES flew
Impatient to your aid, difpers'd and quell'd
The general treafon. May I dare to urge
Thefe fervices? But what are thefe? His throne,
His heart is yours: he lays them at your feet:
He bids you reign in both.

EURYDICE.

Thou bafe of heart!
To flaves like thee, who flatter and inflame
Their prince's crimes, are owing half the plagues
That curfe mankind. Has not thy cruel Mafter,
Whofe guilt this fhameful praife of thine brings home
On thy own foul, fay, has not he ufurp'd,
With perfidy avow'd, the very crown
He fwore to fave? And I too—thy bold infult
Shews I indeed am wretched. But away.
'Tis bafe to parle with thee, the fycophant
Who leads him on from guilt to guilt, and fwears
He grows a God by finning.

SCENE

SCENE III.

EURYDICE, MELISSA.

MELISSA.

Ah, my Queen,
My heart forebodes ſome fatal conſequence
Will grow of this.

EURYDICE.

Why let it come, MELISSA.
I merit all that fortune can inflict,
For truſting this betrayer, this curſt PROCLES.

MELISSA.

Alas, what could you do?

EURYDICE.

I ſhould have dy'd.
He was the known and mortal foe of *Corinth*.

MELISSA.

Yet his fair-ſeeming might have won belief
From doubting Age, or wary Policy.
By frequent, urgent meſſage he conjur'd you
To ſave yourſelf. With open honour own'd
His antient enmity; but, by each Power
Celeſtial and infernal, ſwore 'twas paſt.
Nay more, that as a king and as a man,
Juſt indignation at your impious ſubjects,
And pity of your fate, had touch'd his heart.

EURYDICE.

But Fame had ſpoke him faithleſs, bold, ambitious.
No; 'twas the coward woman in my ſoul,
Th' inglorious fear of dying, that betray'd

My vertue into the Deceiver's power.
For this my heart, each conſcious hour upbraids me,
As faithleſs to my truſt, weak, and unworthy
Even of the baſe precarious life I hold.
For this, O crown of miſery! I'm doom'd
Daily to hear the Tyrant's impious paſſion,
His horrid vows and oaths.

MELISSA.

That way indeed
I dread to turn my thoughts. A ſoul ſo brutal,
And flown with nightly inſolence and wine,
What may he not attempt?

EURYDICE.

O curſe! to know
That I am in his power, and yet compell'd
To ſuffer hated life!—for can I die
Unheard, unjuſtify'd; while yet perhaps
Th' unhappy PERIANDER thinks too hardly
Of my late error?—King of gods and men!
Whoſe univerſal eye beholds each thought
Moſt ſecret in the ſoul, give me to clear
My faith to him; I ask of heaven no more
For my paſt miſeries.

MELISSA.

What ſhouts are theſe?
[*looking out.*
Ah me! th' inhuman triumph of the croud,
The hard-ſoul'd many, who have watch'd the ſtorm
For driving wrecks, the ſpoils of periſh'd wretches.

EURYDICE.

Unfeeling beaſts of prey!—Methinks the ſtorm
Is almoſt overblown. The waves ſubſide,
And fall their fiercer roarings. But alas!
Of all the four, not one remaining ſail
Is to be ſeen around.

 MELISSA.

MELISSA.

Either my eyes
Deceive me, or the good LEONIDAS
Moves towards us.

EURYDICE.

'Tis he: and on his brow
Sits ſome afflicting thought. Ha! whence is this?
What mean theſe ſecret ſhiverings, this dark horror
Of ſome approaching ill?

SCENE IV.

EURYDICE, MELISSA, LEONIDAS.

LEONIDAS.

Forgive me, Madam,
That I appear before you to impart
A mournful meſſage: but by PROCLES' order—

EURYDICE.

Whate'er proceeds from him, LEONIDAS,
Muſt needs be fatal to me. But ſay on.
No form of ruine is ſo dreadful now,
As being in his power.

LEONIDAS.

Unhappy Queen!
Your fate might melt the hardeſt breaſt, and teach
Even Cruelty's remorſeleſs eye to weep.
How ſhall I ſpeak the reſt?

EURYDICE.

LEONIDAS!
What is this fatal tale too ſad for utterance?
I cannot bear ſuſpenſe, that worſt of tortures—
Is PERIANDER ſafe?

LEONIDAS.

This ruinous ſtorm,
Whoſe ſudden outrage—

EURYDICE.

Ha! what ſhips were theſe,
Say, ſpeak, that ſunk but now before our eyes
In ſight of ſhore?

LEONIDAS.

The very fleet deſign'd
To reſcue you; to free repenting *Corinth*
From this betrayer, this deteſted PROCLES.
The King was there embark'd.

EURYDICE.

Then all is loſt!

MELISSA.

Ah heaven! ſhe faints.

LEONIDAS.

Behold, ye Gods! this ſight.
Remember the curſt Author of this ruine.
My eyes, my ſoul's in tears to ſee her thus.

EURYDICE.

O PERIANDER! my much-injur'd Lord!
Would I had dy'd for thee—Ah! gentle maid,
Was it then he, my husband, whom theſe eyes
Saw periſh in the ſtorm! whoſe fate I wept,
Nor knew that all the cruel wreck was mine!

MELISSA.

Unhappy day!

EURYDICE.

Undone EURYDICE!
But I will die—I ſhould have dy'd before
When my mean cowardice, my dread of death,

Betray'd

Betray'd me to falſe PROCLES. I had then
Dy'd innocent: I had not then deſerv'd
A ruin'd husband's curſe.—O thought of horror!
Perhaps his lateſt breath, even in the hour
Of dreadful fate, charg'd me with all his wrongs,
His life and honour loſt! perhaps expir'd
In imprecations on me!

MELISSA.

Oh, for pity,
Forbear theſe fatal thoughts. They but inflame
The rage of real ills, and wound you deeper.

LEONIDAS.

Would tears, my gracious Miſtreſs, aught avail us,
Methinks theſe aged eyes could number drops
With falling clouds, or the perpetual ſtream.
But while we mourn, our enemy rejoyces,
And ſounds his cruel triumph loud to heaven:
Heart-ſtabbing thought! Then ceaſe we tears and ſighs,
That aid for trivial ills. Call we inſtead
Heaven's ſlumbering juſtice down, and loud invoke
The Powers of vengeance to our aid. Who knows
But ſome more happy hour remains—

EURYDICE.

O no.
There is no happy hour in ſtore for me.
All, all are paſt and gone. Even Hope himſelf,
The wretche's lateſt friend, is fled for ever.
Death and the grave are now my only refuge:
There even my woes may reſt.

LEONIDAS.

And who will then
Befriend your orphan-ſon? What eye will pity;
What aiding hand rear his fair-ſpringing youth,

And ſhelter him from want, from woe? Oh none.
Think then you hear this darling of your ſoul,
Your POLYDORE, call loud on you to live,
To live for him, and by your guardian care
Supply a father's loſs.

EURYDICE.

Unhappy boy!
Too ſoon alas! acquainted with ill fortune.
And does he live?

LEONIDAS.

Thoſe few that ſcap'd the ſtorm
Gave me to hope he ſail'd not with the fleet.
But for this PROCLES, Madam, this betrayer;
If I have bow'd me to his impious will,
Tho' with that ſtrong abhorrence Nature feels
At what ſhe holds moſt mortal, 'twas to turn
Againſt the traitor his own treacherous arts,
And ruin him more ſurely. This may be.
Sad *Corinth* looks with horror on the hand
That ſcourges her each hour with whips of ſcorpions.
She waits but ſome fair chance, at once to riſe
And drive him from her throne.

MELISSA.

Theſe trumpets ſpeak
His near approach.

EURYDICE.

Father of human kind!
Eternal Juſtice! hear theſe guilty ſounds!
Behold this Tyrant's revel! while a King,
Thy great reſemblance, floats a cold pale corſe;
Or on the naked beach caſt vilely out,
Unknown, unhonour'd lies. LEONIDAS,

By

By all my griefs I beg thee, ſearch theſe ſhores,
Each cliff and cavern where the wild wave beats,
For my lov'd Lord, and to theſe widow'd arms
Give back his dear remains. But PROCLES comes.

SCENE V.

PROCLES, MEDON, LEONIDAS, *Attendants*.

PROCLES.

Hail glorious day! auſpicious fortune hail!
From this triumphant hour my future life
Runs fair and ſmiling on, no cloud of ill
To ſhade its brightneſs. MEDON, was it not
A wonderous chance?

MEDON.

Beyond our hope, my Lord.
Yet tho' the danger's o'er, with awe and trembling
I ſtill look back to the dread precipice
Where late you ſtood!

PROCLES.

'Tis true, he had well nigh
Surpriz'd me unprovided: but th' attempt
Is periſh'd with its author. From on high
Heaven arm'd his winds and ſeas to fight for me:
And victory is mine without my care,
Almoſt without my knowledge. Yes the Gods,
The Gods themſelves eſpouſe my happy cauſe!
For this, let flowery garlands wreathe their ſhrines;
Let hecatombs before their altars bleed,
And triumph reign thro' *Corinth*.

[*Attendants withdraw.*

Is the Queen
Inform'd of all, LEONIDAS?

LEONIDAS.

LEONIDAS.

She is.

PROCLES.

And ſhe receiv'd the news—

LEONIDAS.

With ſad ſurpriſe,
And many tears, my Lord.

PROCLES.

Juſt the fond ſex.
Such their vain grief; a moment's paſſing ſtorm,
Then all is calm. Be it thy farther care,
As the receding flood forſakes the ſhore,
To make ſtrict ſearch thro' all this coaſt around
For PERIANDER'S Corpſe. I would methinks
A while indulge my eyes; a while peruſe
The features of a rival once ſo fam'd,
So terrible in arms; whoſe partial fortune
Soar'd high above, and ever thwarted mine
In all the dearer aims that ſwell my thought,
Love and ambition.

LEONIDAS.

Mark this, righteous heaven!

SCENE VI.

PROCLES, MEDON.

MEDON.

At length, Sir, all the Gods declare for you,
And fortune is your own. Your native realm,
Fair *Epidaurus*, peaceful and reſign'd,
Acknowledges her Lord. Your rival's fate
Confirms his kingdom yours.

PROCLES.

PROCLES.

Yet I am ſtill
Unbleſt amidſt this flow of proſperous fortune.
Not all that charms Ambition's ſhoreleſs wiſh,
Empire and kneeling homage, can beſtow
The better joy I long for.

MEDON.

Ah, my Prince,
Forget, or ſcorn that proud ill-natur'd fair one.

PROCLES.

Impoſſible. By heaven my ſoul can form
No wiſh, no thought but her. I tell thee, MEDON,
With bluſhes tell thee, this proud charmer reigns
Unbounded o'er my reaſon. I have try'd
Each ſhape, each art of varied love to win her;
Alternate prayers and threats, the ſoothing skill
Of paſſionate ſincerity, the fire
Of rapturous vows: but all theſe arts were vain.
Her rooted hate is not to be remov'd.
And 'twas my ſoul's firſt aim, the towering point
Of all my wiſhes, to prevail in this;
To triumph o'er my rival too in love.
That had been great revenge! but baffled here,
I'm diſappointed ſtill.

MEDON.

Believe me, Sir,
When once the fit of wilfulneſs is o'er,
The burſt of tears diſcharg'd, ſhe'll quickly ſoften,
Stoop to your wiſhes, and forget a husband
Who is no more.

PROCLES.

Perdition on his name!
I dread his memory as my rival ſtill.
But if I have not won her to be mine,

At

At leaſt the hated husband reap'd no joy
From her fantaſtic honour. Stung to madneſs
For ill-requited love, I darkly ſpread
Surmizes of her truth. He thought her falſe:
And, as he doated on her, the dire tale
Was poiſon to his quiet. Jealouſy,
In all its horrors, muſt have ſeiz'd his ſoul.
I triumph'd there!

MEDON.

'Twas exquiſite revenge.
I too, my Lord, who live but for your pleaſure,
Your ever-faithful ſlave, I too combin'd
To aid your vengeance. You can ſtill remember
When in a dungeon's depth ARISTON lay,
ARISTON, PERIANDER's factious friend.
With looks of ſeeming pity I oft mourn'd
His hard impriſonment, complain'd of you,
Nay curs'd your cruelty; till I had brought
His unſuſpecting honeſty to credit
My fiction of the Queen. I told him then,
With well-diſſembled hatred of her crime,
Embittering every circumſtance, that ſhe,
Forgetful of her better fame, had heard
Your ſecret paſſion, and with equal ardor
Return'd its warmth. Nay that ſhe often urg'd you
To wreak your rage on him, the hated friend
Of PERIANDER. Having thus alarm'd him,
After long pauſe I let him ſcape at laſt
To find his maſter out.

PROCLES.

I thank thee, MEDON.
But this avails not much. My ſoul burns in me
With furious longings to ſubdue that woman;
To bend her pride of vertue to my paſſion.

I

I fancy, in her arms, tranſcendant joys,
A heaven of higher bliſs, not to be found
In unreſiſting Beauty, woo'd and won
At idle leiſure. Yet once more I mean
To try the fortune of my wiſhes with her:
And if I am repuls'd, away at once
All little arts of love.

MEDON.

Mean while, the banquet,
Which Pleaſure's curious hand hath furniſh'd out
With ſplendid choice, awaits you, and invites
To laughing thought and triumph. There the God,
Th' inſpiring God of wine, with roſe-buds crown'd,
Mirth in his look, and at his ſide the band
Of little playful Loves, fills high the bowl,
And bids it flow unbounded. Muſic too
Joins her enchanting voice, and wooes the ſoul
With all her powerful skill of moving ſtrains:
Till the gay hour is quite diſſolv'd in bliſs,
In ecſtacy of revel, all-unknown
To lean-look'd Temperance, and his peeviſh train.

PROCLES.

Come on then, MEDON. Life is vainly ſhort;
A very dream of being: and when death
Has quench'd this finer flame that moves the heart,
Beyond is all oblivion, and waſte night
That knows no following dawn, where we ſhall be
As we had never been. The Preſent then
Is only ours: and ſhall we let it paſs,
Untaſted, unenjoy'd? No; let us on.
Hail we the riſing ſhade: and now while night
Leads on the ſecret hour of free delight,
With wanton gayety, in naked ſtate,
Let Muſic, Mirth, and Love around us wait.

The End of the Firſt Act.

ACT II. SCENE I.

The ſcene a rocky coaſt, terminated by a view of the ocean.

PERIANDER *alone.*

BY the pale glimmering of the falling moon,
Amid the broken windings of theſe rocks
I wander on forlorn, and find no place
To truſt my head, or reſt my weary ſteps.
Horror purſues me cloſe. In each low blaſt,
And murmur of the main, methinks I hear
The murderous ſpies of PROCLES at my heels.
Thou mournful Queen of heaven! and ye dread Gods!
Who rule the fearful ſecreſy of night;
Behold me here, the ſport of human chance,
A nameleſs wretch, a ruine hardly ſav'd
From the devouring deep. There my laſt hopes,
My great revenge lies buried.—Is there more?
Away, away; a Traitor fills my throne,
Triumphant in his crimes: and I the while
Roam here a midnight fugitive. Yet this,
All this I could have borne. He was my foe,
The jealous rival of my power—But thou,
In whom my ſoul had treaſur'd up her heaven,

Friend.

Friendſhip, and faith, and love, EURYDICE!
Thou to betray me!
[*letting himſelf fall againſt the rock.*
Ha! by the moon's ſad beam, I can deſcry
The towers that hold this author of my ſhame—
Nay, PROCLES too, perhaps— and may not he,
Even now—confuſion! death! he may, he does
Invade my bed—O hell! ſhe ſmiles to hear
The ſtory of my fate—And now they give
A looſe to impious Joys.—All-ſeeing Powers!
And does your vengeance ſlumber? Are your bolts
Reſerv'd for me alone?—Ha!—yet 'tis juſt.
Conſcience, that in the day of fortune's favour,
Securely ſlept, now rouſes into ſtrong
And dread conviction of her crime. I broke
The ſacred oath ſworn to a dying father,
To free my country from her chains. My ſoul
Shakes, as I roll this thought. O Providence!
Awfully juſt, tho' Guilt may ſhut her eye,
Thine ever wakes to mark, to trace, to puniſh!

SCENE II.

PERIANDER, LEONIDAS.

LEONIDAS.

This way a diſtant ſound alarm'd my ear.
Broken it ſeem'd to be; the voice of mourning,
And deep diſtreſs. Methought it roſe juſt here,
From theſe deaf-ſounding cliffs. But all is ſtill!
Save the hoarſe deep yet working from the ſtorm.

 Some

Some Power direct my ſteps where I may find,
By this faint moon-light, my lov'd Maſter's corpſe,
To ſave his ſacred reliques from the rage
Of brutiſh tyranny.—Ha! what art thou?
A man, or fear-form'd Shadow of the night?

PERIANDER.

LEONIDAS!

LEONIDAS.

The ſame. But ſpeak again.

PERIANDER.

LEONIDAS!

LEONIDAS.

Ha! can it be, ye Powers!
My royal Lord?

PERIANDER *coming forward.*

A wretch that has no name.

LEONIDAS.

Oh all ye Gods! may I believe my ſenſes?
'Tis he! my Prince!—Juſt heaven to thee I kneel,
And thus adore thy gracious providence.
'Tis moſt amazing!

PERIANDER.

Riſe, LEONIDAS.
I am beneath thy care. Thou ſeeſt me here
The laſt of men, caſt off by all good Powers;
Sav'd from the deep to be more loſt on ſhore.

LEONIDAS.

My king and maſter, tho' my heart bleeds in me
With all your mighty ills, I muſt again
Bleſs that good heaven whoſe providence has ſav'd you.
'Tis great! 'tis wonderous all! But how, oh how

I Have

Have you efcap'd the Tyrant's jealous fearch?
His guards with ftrict furvey rang'd every cliff,
And hollow of thefe rocks.

PERIANDER.

I'll tell thee then.
We were in fight of *Corinth*, when at once
Broad darknefs hid the sky: at once the winds
Roar'd with mad blufter o'er us, and the feas
In rowling mountains rofe. A ftorm fo fierce,
So big with ruine, baffled our beft skill.
Defpair ftruck every heart. The fhip ran round
In giddy whirls, and bulg'd on fome hid rock.
O difmal moment! ftill methinks I hear
The general, dying fcream of multitudes
Juft drowning in th' abyfs. How poor a thing
Is a King then, LEONIDAS! I grafp'd
A floating wreck, the big fea roaring round me,
And burfting o'er my head; but, bury'd deep
Beneath the whelming tide, at once I loft
The light of heaven and life. A wave it feems
Lodg'd me within a cavern's fecret depth,
Near yon tall mountain.

LEONIDAS.

Miracle of fate!
Sure God's immediate hand conducted it,
Severely merciful.—How fhall I tell
What pangs, what agonies of foul I felt
At fight of your fad wreck?—But, Sir, the Prince,
What of his fate?

PERIANDER.

I know not what to think:
But to be mine, it feems, is to be wretched.

Half

Half of my fleet, yet riding in the port,
I left to his command, but with ſtrict charge
To ſail a few hours after. 'Twere in vain
To tell thee now the reaſon of my order.
This ſtorm, I fear, may have ſurpriz'd him too,
Unhappy boy!

LEONIDAS.

Your own eſcape, my Lord,
So full of wonder, and beyond all hope,
Inclines me to ſtrong faith that heaven is ſtill
Concern'd for your affairs.—But to behold you,
So late the firſt and happieſt of mankind,
Alone and wandering here at the dead hour;
No roof, but heaven's high cope to ſhelter you;
No couch, but this unhoſpitable earth
To reſt your brine-drench'd limbs—it kills my heart.
Curſe on the Tyrant!

PERIANDER.

Prithee think me not
So poorly ſoul'd to ſtoop beneath the preſſure
Of Fortune's hand. That were to merit it.
But there is ſtill behind—O death to honour!
One cruſhing blow that lays me low indeed!
That ſinks me in the duſt!

LEONIDAS.

What do I hear!
Your words amaze me.

PERIANDER.

How, LEONIDAS!
Surely thou art no ſtranger to my thought.
PROCLES—EURYDICE— Wilt thou not ſpeak
To ſave my ſhame. Say, tell me what thou know'ſt
Of that bad woman.

LEONIDAS

LEONIDAS.

With ſuch watchful care
The Tyrant's truſted ſpies obſerve her ſteps,
That till this fatal evening, when by order
Of PROCLES, I inform'd her of your death,
I have not ſeen her once.

PERIANDER.

Juſt what I fear'd.
That guilty ſecreſy was well contriv'd
To cover crimes too foul for honeſt eyes,
And heaven's fair light to ſee. None, none but PROCLES
Could gain admittance: and to him my gates,
My fortreſs, nay my bed it ſelf was open!

LEONIDAS.

O wrong her not, my Lord. Had you but ſeen
With what convulſive pangs of heart-felt anguiſh,
What bleeding agonies, ſhe heard the tale
Of your imagin'd death, your ſoul would melt
In pity of her woes. This PROCLES too
Call'd down each Power of heaven to witneſs for him,
He meant her fair. Hers was the common cauſe
Of kings, he ſaid; whoſe place and honour bound 'em
To ſcourge rebellion, in whatever ſhape,
Wherever found. And then what was her ſtate?
Death in his ghaſtlieſt form, devouring famine,
Hung inſtant o'er her head. O think of this,
And add not to her wrongs.

PERIANDER.

Ha! wrong her, ſay'ſt thou?
Anſwer me: has ſhe not entail'd diſgrace,
And vileneſs on my name? Has ſhe not made me
The laughter of my foe, the ſcoff of PROCLES?
O curſe! is there in all the wrath of heaven

A plague, a ruine, like that infamy!
Wrong her—I am too well inform'd of all;
Too certain of the blushful stain that cleaves
To me and mine for ever!

LEONIDAS.

Ah, my Lord,
By all good Powers, by your eternal quiet,
I beg you hear me—

PERIANDER.

I have heard too much,
Too much, just Gods! to hope for quiet more.
Those fates inexorable, that pursue
My life with utmost rigor, would not spare me
The knowledge of my shame. From my best friend
Blushing I learnt it——But hast thou e'er felt
That heart of anguish stab'd by murderous fears,
And shuddering with ten thousand mortal thoughts!
That tempest of the soul that knows no calm;
Tossing from love to hate, from doubt to rage,
To raving agony!

LEONIDAS.

Alas! my Lord,
Trust me, I weep to hear so sad a tale.

PERIANDER.

I'll tell thee all; for oh! my soul is full,
And must have vent. My aking memory,
Still fruitful to my torture, brings again
Those days, those months of horror I have known.
Abandon'd to distraction, I renounc'd
The commerce of mankind. I sought to vent
My ravings in the wildness of the woods;
To hide my shame in their profoundest night.
The morn still brought it back: the midnight-shade

Could

Could not conceal it. Her lone echoes groan'd
Unceaſing with my pangs: and her ſad ghoſts
Forbid to reſt even in the grave, in me
Beheld a ſoul more loſt, more curſt, than they.

LEONIDAS.

O Sir, no more—

PERIANDER.

When I call'd back paſt time,
Life's vernal ſeaſon, the ſoft hours of peace
And unſuſpecting love; our growing joys
In rearing one lov'd ſon; that heaven of bliſs
Which princes ſeldom find, and was all ours;
My ſoul dy'd in me. Solitary, wild,
I wept, I groan'd, in bitterneſs of heart.
But when curſt PROCLES flaſh'd on my remembrance,
My known, my deadly foe—that he of all,
That he had made her vile! 'twas then, 'tis now
Rage, fury, madneſs.—You at laſt arrous'd me
To thoughts of vengeance. With all ſpeed I ſail'd,
Feeding my frenzy with the gloomy joy
Of ſtabbing the betrayer in her arms;
Of plunging both to hell—but this curſt ſtorm!
Theſe treacherous waves!

LEONIDAS.

Ye Gods! what have I heard!
Alas! alas! all waves, all ſtorms are calms
To Jealouſy. O my lov'd Lord, beware
Of that deſtroyer, that ſelf-torturing fiend,
Who loves his pain, and feeds the cruel cares
That prey upon his life; whoſe frantic eye
Is ever open, ever prying round
For what he dreads to find. By all moſt dear
And inward to my ſoul, I think the Queen

As pure as Truth herſelf. This is, by heaven,
Some dark-laid treachery, the crime of PROCLES.

PERIANDER.

Of PROCLES, ſay'ſt thou?

LEONIDAS.

Oh you know him not.
Luſt and ambition are not all his guilt.
But now's no time, my Lord,
For farther talk. I tremble for your life.
This place is hoſtile ground: and Danger here
May find us out, tho' ſhrouded round with night.
Hence let us fly, where I may lodge you ſafe
In ſome obſcure retreat; till pitying heaven
Unravel this perplexity of ills,
And point us what to do.

PERIANDER.

Thou good old man!
By heaven, thy matchleſs honeſty and truth
Half reconcile me to diſgrace and ruine.
Yet bluſhing let me tell thee all my folly—
Might I but ſee EURYDICE.—Nay ſtart not:
I know 'tis baſe. I know ſhe is beneath
My cooleſt ſcorn. I hate and curſe this weakneſs.
Yet let me ſee her—If ſhe ſtill has kept
Her faith inviolate; fallen as I am,
My ruine will be light. If otherwiſe,
To know the worſt will be ſoft ſoothing eaſe
To this hot hell of doubt.

LEONIDAS.

I wiſh you, Sir,
To weigh the certain peril that attends
This raſh adventure. Should, which heaven avert,
Should PROCLES' guards diſcover you, oh think

What

What muſt enſue! Think, in your fate, the Queen
And Prince both ruin'd!

PERIANDER.

But my Genius prompts.
Fate calls; and I muſt on. No face of danger
Can be ſo dreadful as the vultur-thoughts
That gnaw my heart-ſtrings. But we both are ſafe.
The moon you ſee is down: and this mean babit
Hides me from all ſuſpicion. Who will dream
Of finding PERIANDER in this ruſſet?
This, when the ſtorm firſt roſe, I threw around me;
That if I periſh'd in it, and my corpſe
Were caſt aſhore, at leaſt my vulgar fate
Might ever reſt unknown—But hark what ſounds?

LEONIDAS.

Thus that curſt Tyrant revels out the night
In triumph o'er your ruine.—Let me think.
Yes; it may be. Now Riot rules the hour,
And all good order is relax'd: we may
Paſs on unqueſtion'd. Come, my gracious Lord,
This way our path lies. May ſome friendly God
Walk with us, and throw tenfold darkneſs round.

SCENE III.

EURYDICE *alone.*

O night of ruine, horror, and deſpair!
Walks there beneath thy univerſal ſhade
A wretch like me undone? All-ruling Gods!

Why have I liv'd to this? Why was my crime
Visited on the guiltless head? on him
For whom my soul would have met death with joy?
Where shall I turn my eyes? What hope remains
To misery like mine? Oh! I am lost
Beyond the hand of heaven to save me now.
LEONIDAS returns not—

SCENE IV.

EURYDICE, MELISSA.

MELISSA.

Gracious Gods
Defend my royal Mistress! As I watch'd
Without for good LEONIDAS, this moment
I saw the Tyrant cross the lower court,
Preceded by his Minion: as new risen
From the mad midnight's feast; his wanton robe
Loose-flowing from behind, and on his head
A festal wreath of roses—Ah! he's here.

SCENE V.

PROCLES, EURYDICE, MELISSA, MEDON.

PROCLES.

Hail young-ey'd God of wine! parent of joys!
Frolic, and full of thee (while the cold sons
Of Temperance, the fools of thought and care,

Lie

Lie ſtretch'd in ſober ſlumbers) we, the few
Of purer flame, exalt each living hour
With pleaſures ever new.—EURYDICE!
Thou queen of ſouls! thou rapture of my vows!
What means this penſive mood? O quench not thus
In fruitleſs tears thoſe eyes, that wont to ſmile
With all Love's ſweetneſs, all his dewy beams,
Diffuſing life around thee.

EURYDICE.

Hence, thou tyrant,
And leave me to my ſorrows. Ills like mine
Would draw remorſe and reverence from the ſavage,
Who howls with midnight wolves amid the deſart
In queſt of horrid prey. What then art thou?
Whoſe brutal rage adds bitterneſs to woe,
And anguiſh to the breaking heart!

PROCLES.

'Tis well.
Yet have a care: my temper but ill brooks
Upbraiding now. Be wiſe, and timely ſeize
The minute of good fortune, that by me
Invites thee to be bleſt.

EURYDICE.

Talk'ſt thou of bliſs?
Thou bane of all my happineſs! Caſt back,
Caſt back thy guilty eyes, and view the crimes
Thy ſoul ſtands charg'd with: view my bleeding wrongs,
Inſult, impriſonment, diſhonour, ruine!
All, all this guilt is thine— but heaven will find thee.
Thoſe Gods whom thou haſt proudly ſet at nought,
Will call thee to a dreadful reckoning.

PROCLES.

PROCLES.

No.
The Gods and I are friends: they crown my cauſe
With their beſt favour. Come, be thou too mine,
And imitate the great example ſet thee.

EURYDICE.

Thou vain and blind in ſoul! The righteous Gods,
Oft, in their anger, cloathe the worſt of men
With all the pride of fond proſperity,
To make his fall more terrible.

PROCLES.

Confuſion!
Still wayward and perverſe!—Off then this tameneſs,
Theſe ſupple, fawning arts. By all th' impatience
That goads my ſoul, I will not flatter more.
Know thou art in my power, and——

EURYDICE.

Tyrant, no.
I ſcorn thy baſe unmanly threats—Ah heaven!
Doſt thou look calmly on?—But be it ſo.
This friendly dagger ſets me free.
[*attempting to ſtab herſelf.*

PROCLES.

Ha! what,
What means thy frantic paſſion? This is wildneſs,
Th' extravagance of female wilfulneſs.
It muſt not be: you ſhall be gently forc'd
To live, and to be happy.

SCENE

SCENE VI.

EURYDICE, PROCLES, *an Officer*, &c.

OFFICER.

Sir, forgive
This rude intrusion. What I bring imports
Your present ear. As now I walk'd the round
Of this wide fort, where the steep-winding path
Ends at the northern gate, I spy'd a stranger,
Who sought to lie conceal'd. Forthwith I rous'd
The nearest watch; and, ere he was aware,
Surrounded him at once. His sullen silence,
And hands oft rais'd to heaven with earnest action,
Convince me he is of no common note.

EURYDICE *aside.*

My soul! what dost thou hear?

PROCLES.

'Tis well. I thank thee.
Haste, see him brought before us.

SCENE VII.

PERIANDER *guarded*, EURYDICE, PROCLES, *&c.*

EURYDICE *aside.*

Oh ye Powers!

PERIANDER *aside.*

Ha! poison to my eyes!

PROCLES.

PROCLES.

I know him not.
His dreſs is poor, and ſpeaks him of the vulgar.
He ſeems to labour with ſome ſtormy thought,
That deeply ſhakes his frame. What art thou? ſay
Why at this hour of ſilence lingring here?
Ha! ſpeak, reſolve me; or the rack ſhall tear
Confeſſion from thy pangs.

PERIANDER *aſide.*

Fate, thou haſt caught me!
But all is equal now.

[*to him.*

Then ſee before thee
The man on earth whom thou haſt injur'd moſt.
If guilt can know remorſe, what muſt thou feel
At ſight of PERIANDER?

PROCLES.

PERIANDER!

EURYDICE.

Now, now, we both are ruin'd.

PROCLES.

Heaven, I thank thee.
I form'd but one ſupreme, one crowning wiſh,
And thou haſt heard it! This is more than triumph!

EURYDICE.

O! my lov'd Lord—

PERIANDER.

Thou canſt no more betray me,
For thee, my ſoul ſtill unſubdu'd and free,
Diſdains to parle with thine.

PROCLES.

Yet thou art fallen
Beneath my wrath, the vaſſal of my nod,

To

To be chaſtis'd for mirth—Guards, drag him hence,
And plunge him in the dungeon's depth.

PERIANDER.

Away,
Unkingly boaſter. Can proſperity
Debaſe thee to the cowardice of inſult?
Thy brutal manners well revenge me on thee:
They ſhew thee as thou art—My nobler part,
Th' immortal mind, thy madneſs cannot reach:
Thy whips and racks can there impreſs no wound.
And for this weary carcaſs in thy power,
It is beneath my care. Lead to my dungeon.
Chains, ſcourges, torture, all that Nature feels,
Or fears abhorrent, cannot ſhock my thought
Like thy loath'd ſight, and that vile Woman's. On.

SCENE VIII.

EURYDICE, PROCLES, MELISSA, MEDON.

EURYDICE.

My lord, my husband, ſtay—Oh hear me! hear me—
Shame! rage! diſtraction!—Cruel tyrant, off.
I'll follow him to death.

PROCLES.

No. By the joys
That ſwell my ſoaring thought, you ſhall not ſcape me.
Revenge and love combine to crown this night
With matchleſs bliſs.

EURYDICE.

Inhuman! haſt thou eyes?
Haſt thou a heart? and cannot all this wreck
Of ruin'd majeſty, ruin'd by thee,
Move one relenting thought, and wake thy pity?

He feels not what I ſay: repeated crimes
Have ſavag'd his remorſeleſs ſoul.—Hear then,
Almighty JOVE! behold, and judge the cauſe
Of PERIANDER! number all his wrongs
In plagues, in horrors—

PROCLES.

Ha! by hell, this raving
But wings his fate. Since thy fond folly weds thee
To ruine with this rival, know he dies;
This very night he dies. Thro' him I mean
To wound thy heart indeed. Thou ſhalt behold him
When the rack ſtretches ſtrong his rending joints,
Burſts all his veins, and hunts the flying ſoul
Thro' every limb. Then, when convulſive agony
Grins hideous in his face, mangled and bleeding,
In the laſt throes of death, thou ſhalt behold him.

EURYDICE.

It is not to be borne! My life dies in me
At the deſtroying thought—Ah ſtay thee, PROCLES—
Aſſiſt me, pitying heaven!—See then, behold me
Thus proſtrate at thy feet. If thou haſt not
Renounc'd all manhood, feeling, and remorſe,
Spare me his life; ſave only that: all elſe,
His crown, his throne be thine.

PROCLES.

Off, let me go.
Thy words are loſt in air.

EURYDICE.

Nay hear me, PROCLES.
As is thy hope in heaven's forgiving goodneſs,
Shut not thy heart againſt the cry of miſery.
Baniſh us any whither; drive us out
To ſhame, want, beggary, to every woe

That

That moſt embitters life—I yet will bleſs thee,
Forget my crying wrongs, and own thee merciful.

PROCLES *aſide, and pauſing.*

This woman fools my rage—but to reſolve.
No—yes: it ſhall be ſo. Riſe then, and learn
Thy triumph o'er my ſoul. Yes he ſhall live,
This PERIANDER whom I deadly hate.
Nay more, he ſhall be free. LEONIDAS,
With ſuch ſafe conduct as thyſelf ſhalt name,
Attends him to our kingdom's fartheſt limit.
This, in the ſight of JOVE the ſupreme Lord,
I ſwear to do; ſo thou at laſt conſent
To meet my love—Ha! what! and doſt thou frown?
Weigh well what I propoſe; for on my ſoul,
His life, or death, awaits thy next reſolve.

SCENE IX.

EURYDICE, MELISSA.

EURYDICE.

Then kill me firſt—He's gone! and now, ye Gods,
Is there among the wretched one ſo loſt,
So curſt as I? O ſcene of matchleſs woes!
O PERIANDER! wert thou ſav'd for this?
Ye holy Powers in heaven! to whom belongs
The fate of vertue, and redreſs of wrongs,
Aſſiſt, inſpire me how to ſave his life;
Or to th' unhappy huſband join the wife.

The End of the Second Act.

ACT III. SCENE I.

EURYDICE, MELISSA.

MELISSA.

THIS chearless morning rises slow and sad.
The frowning heavens are black with stormy clouds;
And, o'er the deep, a hovering night of fogs
Lies dark and motionless.

EURYDICE.

That mournful face
Of nature is less gloomy than my soul:
All there is darkness and dismay. Ah me!
Was ever night, MELISSA, like the last?
A night of many terrors, many deaths!
How has my soul out-liv'd it? But, great Gods!
Can mortal strength, can human vertue bear
What PERIANDER feels? In one day's course
Wreck'd, made a captive, sunk into a dungeon,
To die or live as his curst foe decrees!
Distraction's in the thought. And what can I
To save his sacred life? [*After a pause.*
Ha! is it heaven
That darts this sudden light into my soul?
This glimpse of dawning hope?—It shall be try'd.
Yes, yes, ye Powers! my life and fame shall both
Be offer'd up to save his dearer life.

MELISSA.

Alas, what mean you, Madam?

EURYDICE.

Mean, MELISSA?
To do a noble justice on myself;

A deed for which, in nations yet unborn,
Chaſte wives and matrons ſhall renown my name.
I have wrong'd my husband greatly, and I mean
Ample atonement of my guilty weakneſs.
Go then, MELISSA——

MELISSA.

Whither muſt I go?
I tremble at your words.

EURYDICE.

Yet it ſticks here,
This fatal purpoſe. Can I leave behind me
A doubtful name, inſulted, wounded, torn
By cruel Calumny? I can; I dare
Throw off the woman, and be deaf to all
Thoſe nicer female fears that call ſo loud,
Importunate, and urging me to live
Till I may clear my truth from all ſurmize.
Go then, and in my name—'Tis worſe than death
To utter it—but go, inform the Tyrant,
So PERIANDER lives, and is ſet free,
I yield me to his wiſh.

MELISSA.

Forbid it heaven!

EURYDICE.

Thou faithful vertuous maid! Know then my laſt,
My fix'd reſolve. By this I mean to amuſe
His brutal hopes, and ſave me from his violence,
Till PERIANDER is beyond his reach.
Then, if he ſtill dare urge his impious purpoſe,
A dagger ſets me free. This arm at laſt
Shall do me right on him, myſelf, or both.

SCENE

SCENE II.

EURYDICE, LEONIDAS.

EURYDICE.

LEONIDAS!

LEONIDAS.

Ah Madam!

EURYDICE.

Dare I ask
Where PERIANDER is—ah where indeed?
Chain'd in a dungeon's airleſs depth, amid
Foul damps, and loneſome darkneſs! Oh that thought
Draws blood from my torn heart.

LEONIDAS.

Juſtice divine!
In thy great day of viſitation, mark
This man of blood. O let him feel the hand
He dares to disbelieve. To all his counſels
Send forth, in thy juſt wrath, that fatal Spirit
Of error and illuſion, that foreruns
The fall of guilty kings.
Ere morning-dawn,
Soft to the diſmal dungeon's mouth I ſtole,
Where, by the glimmerings of a dying lamp
I ſaw my great unhappy Maſter laid
On the cold earth along—

EURYDICE.

O hide the ſad
The fatal image from me. The dire thought
Will run me into madneſs.

LEONIDAS.

Yet even there,
Where pale Diſmay, the priſoner's drear aſſociate,

Sits

Sits ever ſad and ſleepleſs, he could reſt.
Superior to the cruel fate that cruſh'd him,
He ſlept as deep as Indolence on down.
Theſe eyes beheld it: and I would not break
His wiſh'd repoſe, but fix'd in ſilent wonder,
Stood weeping o'er the ſight.

EURYDICE.

Ah me! my life
Flows out at every word: What's to be done?

LEONIDAS.

Madam, I ſet my all at ſtake for him.
Old as I am, and broken with the load
Of threeſcore years, what is a life like mine,
But as it may be uſeful to my Maſter?
Already the ſad people know his fate:
And I, by faithful hands, will try to rouze
Their pity firſt, and next their rage. No hour,
No moment ſhall be loſt.

EURYDICE.

Thou good old man!
What words can ſpeak thy worth? Fair loyalty
And faith inviolate, which ſeem'd quite loſt
Among mankind, live in thy vertuous boſom.

LEONIDAS.

No more of this, my Queen. Might I but ſee
This haughty Tyrant, in ſome guilty hour
Of inſolence and riot, when his pride
Plumes all her vaineſt wiſhes, hurl'd at once
To ruine unforeſeen; my labours then,
My ſervices were greatly over-paid.

EURYDICE.

Heaven hear thy pious wiſh. I too the while,
To ſave my husband's life, have been contriving—

LEONIDAS.

LEONIDAS.

Madam, the Tyrant—I will find another
More favourable moment.

SCENE III.

PROCLES, MEDON, LEONIDAS.

PROCLES.

Hold thy ſelf
Prepar'd, LEONIDAS: I muſt employ thee
In an affair of weight.

[LEONIDAS *withdraws.*

Methinks I droop
With more than wonted heavineſs of heart.
But I will ſhake it off, and to the winds
Give every thought of care. 'Tis only fondneſs,
And fancy ſick with hope. EURYDICE
Bends to my wiſhes: and, in her, I hope
That heaven imagin'd, that ſole bliſs, which yet
My ſearch could never meet.

MEDON.

It moves my wonder
To ſee your love thus wedded to one boſom:
While all around bright crouds of rival beauties
Practiſe each art of charming, look, and talk,
And live for you alone.

PROCLES.

Alas, my friend,
Poor is the triumph over hearts like theſe:
This hour they pleaſes us, and the next they pall.
But to ſubdue the pride that ſcorns to yield;
To fill th' unwilling breaſt with ſighs and longings,
With all the ſoft diſtraction of fond love,

Even

Even while it ſtrives againſt th' invading victor,
And wonders at the change; that, that is conqueſt!
The plume of pleaſure! and from her alone
A glory to be won.

MEDON.

Well, may you find
In this proud fair one that enchants you thus,
Wha te'er Imagination's fondeſt eye
Beholds in rapturous viſion; or young Love
In all his wantonneſs of power can give.
But yet, forgive your ſervant's forward zeal,
Mean you to keep the promiſe you have made her?

PROCLES.

I do.

MEDON.

How Sir! what ſet her husband free?

PROCLES.

mean no leſs.

MEDON.

Your pardon, Sir: 'tis well.
But have you calmly weigh'd in reaſon's ſcale
The certain conſequence? Set free your rival!
A ſoul made furious with his mighty wrongs;
Boiling with hate, rage, jealouſy, revenge;
With the full-gather'd ſtorm of deadly paſſions!
The Gods forbid it, Sir—And all to dry
A froward woman's tears!

PROCLES.

No, no, my friend;
Nor liberty nor life ſhall long be his:
I never meant him either; but my faith
Is paſs'd to ſet him free. By that alone
The haughty Queen was overcome: and I
Will keep th' illuſive promiſe to her ear,
But break it to her hope.

MEDON.

As how, my Lord?

PROCLES.

Such inbred enmity my ſoul bears his
As Nature does to ruine; to the grave,
Where the whole man deſcends to riſe no more.
Hear then what I intend. Thou know'ſt the fortreſs,
That guards our frontier on the *Theban* ſide.
That way our foe muſt paſs; but thou ſhalt firſt
Poſt thither on the ſpur with wary ſpeed:
And with a choſen band, drawn from the fort,
Way-lay him on the farther hill, cloſe couch'd
In the deep covert of thoſe pendant woods,
That ſhade the path below.

MEDON.

Conclude it done.
Sleep ſhall not know my eyes, till his are clos'd
In everlaſting night. As to his priſon
I waited him, he call'd me minion, ſlave,
A traitor's paraſite, the baſe-ſoul'd miniſter
Of his looſe pleaſures: and I will repay him,
For each opprobrious name, a mortal ſtab.
Yes, he ſhall feel his fate. Inſult and taunt,
Embittering every blow, ſhall mock his pangs,
And give him ſevenfold death.

PROCLES.

So, now to try
This PERIANDER thoroughly. Go, MEDON,
Command him hither.

SCENE

SCENE IV.

PROCLES *alone.*

No. I cannot bear
His laſt night's haughty look and untam'd ſpirit.
It baffles my revenge, and I ſtill miſs
My nobleſt triumph; for I meant to bend him
To baſe dejection, and to feaſt my ſcorn
With his pale cheek and ſupplicating eye.
But I will hunt this pride thro' each receſs,
Each cloſer folding of the ſoul, till I
Have ſunk him to my wiſh.—Thou Jealouſy!
Almighty tyrant of the human mind,
Who canſt at will unſettle the calm brain,
O'erturn the ſeated heart, and ſhake the man
Thro' all his frame with tempeſt and diſtraction;
Riſe to my preſent aid: call up thy Powers,
Thy furious fears, thy blaſts of dreadful paſſion,
Thy whips, ſnakes, mortal ſtings, thy hoſt of horrors;
Rouſe thy whole war againſt him, and compleat
My purpos'd vengeance.—But he comes to prove it.

SCENE V.

PERIANDER, PROCLES, MEDON, *Guards.*

PROCLES *advancing.*

I have to talk with thee. Thy life, thou know'ſt,
Depends upon my will—

PERIANDER.

And therefore I
Am weary of the load. But let the Gods,

Who thus difpenfe our fates, account for them,
And vindicate their juftice.

PROCLES.

Be more calm.
The noble mind meets every chance of fortune,
Unruffled and ferene. I, tho' thy foe,
Perhaps may mean thee good.

PERIANDER.

Such good the Tyger,
Hungry for death and flaughter, means his prey.
But know my foul receives with equal fcorn
Thy hate and hollow love. I am not fallen
By thy fuperior fword, or nobler deed:
It was the guilt of fate!

PROCLES.

Call we it fo.
At leaft 'tis well thou muft of force acknowledge
Thy crown, thy liberty, thy life and death,
Hang on my nod. I can difpofe of all
As likes me beft.

PERIANDER.

Ha! doft thou boaft of that?
But thou wilt never know how poor a purchafe
Is power and empire gain'd for vertue loft.

PROCLES.

And yet, methinks, I read the difference plain
In thee and me. Thy vertue and thefe bonds
I weigh in equal fcale againft the crown
And fceptre of fair *Corinth*: and while thefe,
The glorious aim of each great heart that dares
Beyond the narrow fphere of earth-born fpirits;
While thefe are mine, I envy not thy tribe
A found, an empty name.

PERIANDER.

PERIANDER.

It joys my ſoul
To find the man, who bears me mortal hate,
At war too with the Gods. 'Tis great revenge!
Had not vain fortune made thee blind, the thought
Would change thy purple to the mourner's ſack-cloath
What are thy glorious acts?—Thou haſt undone
A woman, weak and worthleſs.—Yes, ye Powers!
This heroe, this fair warrior, well deſerv'd
To fill my vacant ſeat: he won it nobly!
Diſſembling, perjury, the coward's arms—
With theſe he fought his vertuous way to empire.
Thou ſeeſt I know thee.

PROCLES.

Doſt thou preach to me
The pedant-maxims of thoſe ſons of earth,
Whom the groſs vulgar fondly title wiſe?
Slaves, who to ſhades and ſolitude condemn'd,
Pine there with all-ſhun'd Penury and Scorn.
A monarch is above them, and takes counſel
Of his unbounded will, and high ambition,
That counts the world his own. I ever held thee
My foe, my deadly bane: and againſt ſuch,
Force, fraud, all arts, are lawful. I have won,
And mean to wear thy crown. Thou may'ſt the while
Seek ſome vile cell out, and grow poorly old
Amid the talking tribe of moraliſts.

PERIANDER.

Thro' this falſe face of arrogance, I read
Thy heart of real terror and diſmay.
Hence all theſe coward-boaſts. The truly brave,
Invincible to pride and fortune's flattery,
Know neither fear, nor inſult.—But I would not,
As thou ſurmizeſt, dream out uſeleſs life
In Sloth's unactive couch. Nay I could tell thee,
That tho' I ſhun thy ſhameful ways of conqueſt;

Still

Still heaven-born glory, won by vertuous deeds,
Has been my fair purſuit: ſtill would I ſeek her
In toils of war, and in the nobler field
Of juſtice, peace, and mercy.

PROCLES.

My ſoul longs
To prove thy higheſt daring, and to meet thee
Amid the din and peril of the battle.
Thy life is in thy hand: thou art no longer
Our priſoner. This moment ſets thee free.

PERIANDER.

How!—but thou dare'ſt not—Could I find thee there,
In open day, and honourable arms,
Oppoſing war to war, as monarchs ſhould;
I would forgive thee all, my crown uſurp'd,
Theſe ſlave-like bonds—But that fair hope is vain.
The fears that haunt thy ſoul—

PROCLES.

Strike off his fetters.
[*to* MEDON.
Haſte, find LEONIDAS. Bid him prepare
To guard the priſoner to our kingdom's frontier.
There he ſhall leave him free to chuſe what courſe
His fancy moſt affects.

PERIANDER.

What means all this?
Dares Guilt then be ſo brave? and doſt thou free
The man whom act of thine ſhall never win
To owe thee aught but deep and deadly hate?

PROCLES.

Go, ſee my orders inſtantly perform'd.
[MEDON *and Guards retire.*

PERIANDER *aſide.*

And is it ſo—I ſhudder with my fears.
Say, tell me firſt to what is PERIANDER
Indebted for this freedom?

PROCLES.

PROCLES.

Well it may
Surprize thy hope: 'twas what I never meant thee.
But that fond woman who enſlaves my ſoul
To all her wiſhes, and ſtill pitys thee,
With idle blandiſhments extorted from me
A ſolemn vow to ſet thee free.

PERIANDER.

Confuſion!

PROCLES.

Thus I, againſt my better mind, releaſe
My mortal enemy. But let it ſpeak
The greatneſs of my love: and what dull husband,
Thro' all recorded time, e'er gave ſuch proof
Of matchleſs fondneſs?

PERIANDER.

Plagues! perdition! hell!
Damn'd, damn'd adultreſs!—Villain, ſlave, 'tis falſe:
Thou ly'ſt—What thee! O curſe—

PROCLES.

At laſt 'tis done.

SCENE VI.

PERIANDER *alone.*

Have I then liv'd to this? to this confuſion?
My foe, the man on earth my ſoul moſt loaths,
Rejoices over me: and ſhe—even ſhe
Hath join'd his triumph!—Off, away, be gone
Love, manhood, reaſon—Come, ye ſiſter-Furies!
Daughters of hate and hell! ariſe, inflame
My murderous purpoſe; pour into my veins
Your gall, your ſcorpion-fellneſs, your keen horrors
That ſting to madneſs; till my burning vengeance

Hath

Hath her full draught of blood—

[*Walking with a diſturb'd motion.*

But how! where am I?

O this poor brain! ten thouſand ſhapes of fury
Are whirling there, and reaſon is no more.
Him! him! a caitif black with every vice!
Debaſe herſelf to him!—the thought is hell!
Well, well—and I, how have I doated on her
Whole years of fondneſs! cheriſh'd, pleas'd, adorn'd her
With all that love can give—Yet ſhe has done this!
Confuſion on my folly—Ha! ſhe comes.
Down, down tempeſtuous ſoul: let me be dumb,
And hide this ſhameful conflict that unmans me.

SCENE VII.

EURYDICE, PERIANDER.

EURYDICE *aſide.*

He muſt not know my ſecret fatal purpoſe,
That I am fix'd to die; leſt his great ſoul
Refuſe a life ſo dearly ſav'd—And now
All Powers that pity human kind aſſiſt me
In this important hour!

[*to him.*

O PERIANDER—

And is it thus we meet again!

PERIANDER *aſide.*

Ha! ſee,

She comes prepar'd. By hell, ſhe weeps a lye.
My rage will leap all bounds.

EURYDICE.

My Lord, my love,

I know you look on me as on the cauſe,
The fatal cauſe of all your ills; too true:
That guilt is mine—O would to heaven this head
Had been laid low in earth ere that ſad hour!

Why

Why did I ſhrink at ruine? why not bear
All pangs, all horrors of beſieging famine?
Alas! my love—But your falſe faithleſs ſubjects
To what have they reduc'd us?

PERIANDER.

No; not they:
Thou vile one, thou alone haſt made me wretched.
Thou! thou! whom I had treaſur'd in my boſom,
As my life's jewel—thou haſt heap'd upon me,
On this poor head, contempt and foul diſhonour.

EURYDICE.

Juſt Gods! what means my Lord?

PERIANDER.

Mean!—doſt thou ask?

EURYDICE.

Heaven! has the Traitor then—

PERIANDER.

Ha! does that gaul thee?
Perdition! ſhall I ſtab—But what? ſhall ſhe,
A woman, ſhake my ſoul's firm temper thus?
I will be dumb. Yet no—Yes he, thy minion,
The baſe one, has repaid thy broken faith
With equal perfidy: has loudly boaſted
To heaven, and earth, and me, how vile thou art.
Shame! death! diſtraction!—I too am become
A proverb of reproach, a tale, a word
For ribbald Scorn to mock at.

EURYDICE *aſide.*

O dire error!
Fatal miſtake! Now am I loſt indeed.
But be it ſo: what is my life and fame
To ſaving him?

PERIANDER *aſide.*

See! guilt has ſtruck her dumb.

EURYDICE.

My lord, my only love, by holy faith

I never was difloyal. Rags and penury,
Difeafe and death, fhock not my apprehenfion
Like that detefted crime—I dare no more.
O fly, my love; hafte from this fatal place,
And leave me to my fate. O fave your life,
While yet 'tis in your power.

PERIANDER.

My life! away.
And haft thou vilely barter'd for that life
Thy truth, and my fair fame? By yon bleft heaven,
I could have borne all woes that Wretchednefs
Groans under; age, affliction, pining anguifh:
And borne them like a man. I could have fmil'd
At fortune's keeneft rancor—But to know
My felf deceiv'd in thee! there, there I fink!
There manhood, reafon die!

EURYDICE.

O ye juft Powers!
Were ever woes like mine? What are the whips,
Rack, engines, all that murderous Cruelty
Hath yet contriv'd—what are they all to this?
This infamy that kills the foul itfelf?
Yet I will bear even this.
Then here, by weeping, bleeding love I beg you,
With ftreaming eyes, hafte from this fatal place.
The Tyrant may recall his word: and then—
I cannot utter more.

PERIANDER.

And thou can'ft weep?
Thou crocodile! Thefe falfe, thefe lying tears
Are daggers here. I go—But doft thou hope
Thy mean diffimulation hides thee from me?
Thou haft difhonour'd, ruin'd me; and now
My fight is hateful to thee.

[*returning.*

But fay, tell me
How have I merited thefe wrongs of thee?

What

What was my crime? Can all-beſtowing Love
Do more than mine for thee?—When I call back
The days that are no more! Thou wert my all
Of happineſs: my ſoul ne'er knew a joy
That was not thine: my doating fondneſs lull'd
Its hopes, its fears, its wiſhes, in thy boſom.
O heaven and earth!—and yet—EURYDICE—
Thou could'ſt forſake me! [*weeps.*

EURYDICE.

Oh this is too much!
Heaven knows I would have dy'd to ſave thy life:
But we will periſh both, both die together.
Thy tears diſtract me; I will tell thee all.

PERIANDER.

Curſe on this weakneſs. I could tear theſe eyes
From forth their orbs—Thou exquiſite deceiver!
Hence, leſt this arm ſhould do a deed of ſhame,
And ſtain me with thy blood.

EURYDICE.

O but one moment,
For mercy's ſake, allow me one ſhort moment.

PERIANDER.

No. In the ſight of all-beholding JOVE,
Here I renounce thee. What a ſlave to folly,
To thy curſt arts has PERIANDER liv'd!

EURYDICE.

O cruel! cruel! haſt thou caſt me out
For ever from thy heart? By all our loves;
By the dear pledge of our unſpotted flames,
Grant me one moment.

[*kneels.*

Here will I hang; grow to thy knees—Yes, ſpurn me;
Drag this bare bleeding boſom on the ground;
Yes, uſe me as the vileſt ſlave—but hear me.

PERIANDER.

Away, away.

EURYDICE.

Then ſtrike me dead at once.
Look here, my love; I ſhrink not from the blow.

PERIANDER.

That were poor vengeance. No; I meditate
A nobler ſacrifice—

[*alarm of trumpets.*

Ha! what is this?

[*alarm again.*

Th' alarm is urgent, big with war and dread.
I am the ſport of fortune.

SCENE VIII.

PERIANDER, EURYDICE, MELISSA.

MELISSA.

O! my Lord,
Some wonderous birth of fate is ſure diſcloſing.
PROCLES calls out to arms: his guards ſwarm round him,
Haſte in each ſtep, and fear in every eye.
This way too MEDON ſpeeds, and in his train
A gloomy band of ſoldiers.

PERIANDER.

Let him come.
Death has no terrors, when to live is ſhame.

SCENE

SCENE IX.

PERIANDER, EURYDICE, MELISSA,

MEDON *at the head of one party who hurry the Queen off the ſtage,* LEONIDAS *at the head of another who remove the King.*

MEDON.

Be quick, ſecure the Queen.

EURYDICE.

What mean'ſt thou, ruffian?
Muſt we then part?—Farewel, my Lord, for ever.

PERIANDER.

Thou too, LEONIDAS!—nay then—

SCENE X.

LEONIDAS *alone.*

O JOVE!
Eternal and ſupreme, whoſe nod controuls
The fate of empires; whoſe almighty hand
Suſtains the weak, and raiſes vertue fallen,
Now to this royal ſufferer deal thy mercy:
Aid his juſt arms, and teach mankind to know
That ſovereign juſtice ſways the world below.

The End of the Third Act.

ACT

ACT IV. SCENE I.

EURYDICE, MELISSA.

EURYDICE.

WHAT may this mean? The gloomy band of ruffians,
That bore me hence, vaniſh'd I know not how.
And hark! no ſound, no breath of human voice;
But all around the depth of ſolitude!
A dumb and death-like ſtillneſs! My ſoul trembles:
And Apprehenſion peoples the lone void
With fears of horrid form—But what can fate?
What can the wrath of all the Gods inflict
Beyond what I have known?

MELISSA.

My gracious Miſtreſs,
This awful moment is perhaps the criſis
Of all your future life. Your guards fled ſudden:
And late the neighbouring courts were loud with tumult,
Which dy'd away in ſlow and ſullen murmurs.
Some turn of fate is near. LEONIDAS
In haſte bore hence the king, doubtleſs to ſave him
From his dire foe: or at the people's head
Once more to place their ſovereign, and reſtore
You to your former ſtate.

EURYDICE.

All otherwiſe
My thoughts forebode. There is one deadly ill,
Which oh too ſure no time, no chance can heal!
And at the dawn of day, juſt as theſe lids
Reluctant clos'd to reſt, ARPASIA's Shade,

My

My much-lov'd mother, ſtood confeſs'd before me,
Pale as the ſhroud that wound her clay-cold limbs;
Her eyes fix'd on me, ſtill and motionleſs,
Streaming unreal tears. She groan'd, and thrice
In low, ſad murmurs bade me to her tomb,
To meet her there—and there, in death alone,
In the dark grave, can poor EURYDICE
Expect repoſe.

MELISSA.

O no; juſt heaven, I hope,
That ſees your innocence, has yet in ſtore
Much bliſs and many days of peace for you.

EURYDICE.

I know his heart is quite eſtrang'd, and ſhut,
For ever ſhut againſt the voice of love:
And can my heart ſurvive it? Shall I live
With public infamy? a theme of ſcorn
To all licentious tongues? Oh! in that thought,
Death's keeneſt dart has ſtab'd my ſoul already;
And what comes after is not worth my fear.

MELISSA.

Ha! Madam, this way caſt your eyes, and ſee
What ſwarms of men; theſe flying, thoſe purſuing.

EURYDICE.

Now, Lord of battles! join thy powerful arm;
Aſſert the cauſe of righteouſneſs—But hark!
The thunder of their ſhouts grows near and loud.
This way the combat turns. By all my hopes,
The Tyrant's party flies. Look, look, MELISSA,
Their broken numbers to the fortreſs bend.

MELISSA.

And now with eager ſpeed they climb th' aſcent
That leads to us.

EURYDICE.

But who is he, MELISSA,
That like the God of war, flames foremoſt yonder?

See

See his ſword lighten, and the foe fly ſcattering
From his tempeſtuous arm!—Ha—yes—O heaven!
'Tis he, 'tis he himſelf, 'tis PERIANDER!
O miracle! He looks again a monarch,
Dreadfully glorious. Throw, ye Powers! your ſhield
Of providence before him; think on all
His cauſeleſs wrongs, and do him juſtice now.

MELISSA.

Ah! PROCLES comes.

SCENE II.

PROCLES *followed by a party of his guards,* EURYDICE, MELISSA.

PROCLES.

Confuſion! all is loſt.
That Traitor has undone me: and thoſe ſlaves,
The falſe *Corinthians*, in a moment's flight,
Threw all their gates wide open to the foe.
Of hope abandon'd, and the Gods againſt me,
What now remains?—The Queen! by heaven 'tis well:
Their boaſted triumph is not yet compleat.
She's mine, ſhe's mine; and I am conqueror ſtill!
You, bear this woman thro' the poſtern-gate
[*to one party.*
Down to the ſouthern ſhore: I ſail this moment
For *Epidaurus*. You, the while make head
[*to another.*
Againſt the near purſuit, and bar its progreſs
Till ſhe's ſecur'd. This is my laſt great ſtake,
Of dearer price than victory. Away.

EURYDICE.

EURYDICE.

No, Tyrant: I will die firſt. Off, baſe ſlaves.
Dare ye, dare earth-born peaſants violate,
With your rude touch, the majeſty of kings?
Ah! heaven—

PROCLES.

Be quick, nor liſten to her raving.

SCENE III.

EURYDICE, PROCLES, MEDON, *&c.*

MEDON.

Undone! undone! The poſtern-gate is ſeiz'd.
That curſt LEONIDAS—

PROCLES.

Ha! ſay'ſt thou, MEDON?

MEDON.

By hell, our foes ſurround us on each hand.
We're taken in the toil.

PROCLES.

Unequal Powers!
And have you then deceiv'd me? rais'd me high
With traiterous kindneſs, but to plunge me deeper
In howling deſperation? Does the man,
Whom late my foot could ſpurn, behold my fall?
And fall I thus? my great ambition daſh'd?
My love unſatisfy'd? Shall he yet revel
In her fond arms, and hear her curſe my name?
No. Spite of heaven my ruine ſhall be glorious,
A pomp of horrors. I will make this day
For ever mournful to his aking heart.
Yes, he ſhall weep in blood amid the ſhouts
Of victory. One blow deſtroys his triumph,
And levels him at once to my deſtruction.

[*he draws a dagger.*

EURYDICE.

Strike, Tyrant, and compleat thy monſtrous crimes.
See, thou pale coward, ſee a woman braves
Thy guilty dagger.

PROCLES.

Ha! what's this I feel?
A ſhivering dew of horror ſweats all o'er me!
Some Power inviſible arreſts my arm!
It is heaven's ſecret hand—But ſhall I loſe
This only moment? No: be ſtrong my heart;
Be ſhut againſt all human thoughts, and ſcorn
Theſe warnings of thy hoſtile Gods—'Tis done.

SCENE IV.

POLYDORE *and ſoldiers*, PROCLES, EURYDICE, LEONIDAS, *&c.*

POLYDORE *puſhing back* PROCLES *with his lance.*

No, traitor, murderer, no. Heaven is more juſt
Than to permit a life ſo much its care
To fall by thy vile hand. Secure the Tyrant.
[*to his ſoldiers.*
My mother!

EURYDICE.

O my ſon!

POLYDORE.

Tranſporting joy!

EURYDICE.

O ecſtacy! and do I ſee thy face?
And do I hold thee in my trembling arms?
Thou darling of my love! thou early heroe!
O thou haſt ſav'd us all!

POLYDORE.

This, this is triumph!
And I can ask of bounteous heaven no more.
Was ever joy ſo full? This feeble arm,
O pride to think! has ſav'd the ſacred lives

From

From whom I drew my own.

EURYDICE.

And is this poſſible?
What ſhall I ſay?—But language all is poor
To ſpeak the tender yearnings of my ſoul.
O POLYDORE! did ever parents know
Such tranſports as do thine? Did ever ſon
Deſerve ſo well of parents?—Good LEONIDAS,
I ſaw thee not before; indeed I could not:
My eyes, my ſoul, were ſo cloſe fix'd on him.
But ſay, redouble this day's bliſs, and ſay,
Whence this amazing change?

LEONIDAS.

My royal Miſtreſs,
The Gods have done this. One half of the fleet,
As led by their peculiar hand, eſcap'd
Yeſterday's ruinous ſtorm, and with the dawn
Enter'd the port unſeen; their ſecret landing
Befriended by the morn's wide-hovering miſts.
Inſtant, inform'd of his great father's fate,
Your POLYDORE, this gallant royal youth,
Pour'd forth his eager troops; and at their head,
Swift as heaven's darted fire, flew towards *Corinth*,
Which open'd wide her arms to take him in.
His fortune ſpeaks the reſt.

EURYDICE.

O ſovereign Goodneſs!
Be thine the praiſe: this is thy wonderous work.
The King, how was he ſav'd?

LEONIDAS.

Struck with this danger,
The Tyrant had to preſent death devoted
His ſacred head. I counſel'd, and prevail'd
(PROCLES ſtill thought me his) in bonds to hold him
As our ſure pledge of ſafety, ſhould ſucceſs

Desert our arms. The following moment saw him
Free from his chains, and foremost in the fight—
And hark! these joyous strains proclaim his triumph.

EURYDICE.

Retire, my son; I would not meet him here.

SCENE V.

PERIANDER *attended*, LEONIDAS, ARISTON, PROCLES, MEDON.

PERIANDER *aside*.

She flies!--Thou coward, Guilt!—but hence that thought.
[*advancing towards* PROCLES.
At length the measure of thy crimes is full:
Thy high-plum'd pride lies humbled in the dust;
And awful Justice comes, array'd in terrors,
To make enquiry for the guilt that swells
Thy black account—But I will check my heart,
Nor learn of thee to triumph o'er the fallen.
Bear him to prison.

PROCLES.

Yet, I will be free,
And soon beyond thy power. Knowing the worst,
I laugh at all to come.

PERIANDER *to* MEDON.

For thee, thou vile one,
Thou pander to thy Master's lusts, thou sycophant,
(The most pernicious present angry heaven
Can make to princes whom it means to blind,
And ruin beyond mercy) thy just doom
Is instant. Spurn this slave into the streets.
The furious people, whom his earth-born pride
Has trampled on, and numerous rapines beggar'd,
Will find th' oppressor out, and as they tear
His guilty limbs, think all their wrongs o'er-paid.

SCENE

SCENE VI.

PERIANDER, LEONIDAS, ARISTON.

PERIANDER.

LEONIDAS, my father and preferver,
Rife to my arms. By heaven the joy that fmiles
Upon thy brow adds brightnefs to the morn.
This wonderous revolution of my fate,
This change that gives me back my crown and name,
Rejoices me yet lefs, than that I owe
The gift to thee.

LEONIDAS.

O facred Sir, forbear.
The tranfport to behold you thus again
Is great reward. Now your old man can fay
He has not liv'd in vain. Ye bounteous Powers!
Difmifs me now in peace; for I have feen
My Mafter bleft!

PERIANDER.

No recompence can equal
Such matchlefs goodnefs. But I will repay thee
A way more pleafing to a foul like thine,
By running ftill in debt to all thy vertues.
Thou know'ft th' unhappy, envy'd ftate of kings;
How perilous the height fo near to heaven,
Ten thoufand ways expos'd: here to the luft
Of lawlefs will; there to the darker ruine
Of venal flattery. Be near me ftill.
Thy life has roll'd thro' all the various round
Of human chance: and years of hoary thought,
Cool and unpaffionate, have taught thee wifdom.
Be ftill my guide, and fave me from the fnares
That thus befet me; fave me from myfelf.

LEONIDAS.

LEONIDAS.

My heart can only anſwer to this goodneſs
By ſilent gratitude and joy—But, Sir,
Forgive me if I ſay, another care
Demands your preſent thought.

PERIANDER *aſide.*

Fatal remembrance!
At once inflam'd my ſmother'd rage burns up
With fiercer blaze. He muſt not know the purpoſe
With which my boſom labours.

[*to him.*

Yes, my friend,
Of that we'll talk anon; but now I wiſh
An hour of privacy.—ARISTON, ſtay.

SCENE VII.

PERIANDER, ARISTON.

PERIANDER.

Thus far have I repreſs'd the ſtorm within me;
Held down its furious heavings: but they now
Shall have full flow. I am once more a king.
My foe is in my hand, and breathes this air
But till I doom him dead: yet is not he
So curſt, ſo ruin'd as his conqueror!

ARISTON.

What do I hear, my Lord?

PERIANDER.

Ah! good ARISTON,
The horrors of thy tale were true. She has,
She has betray'd me.

ARISTON.

Since the Queen is fallen,
There is no truſt in woman—

PERIANDER.

Nor no hope

For

For wretched PERIANDER. Not the grave
Can hide me now from ſcorn: not length of days
Will wear out this. O never-dying ſhame!
Worlds yet unfound will hear it: and where'er
The guilty tale is told, my fate will raiſe
Baſe mirth, or baſer pity.

ARISTON.

Could the Queen
Stoop to a thought of PROCLES? Falſe fond ſex!
Unfix'd by reaſon, ever wandering wild,
As Fancy whirls, from folly on to folly,
From vanity to vice. My gracious Lord,
She is beneath your anger. Caſt her out
From all your ſoul, and be yourſelf again.
Reſume that reaſon, Sir—

PERIANDER.

Away: can reaſon
Arreſt the whirlwind's wing? or quench the foreſt,
Struck by the hand of JOVE, when all its woods
In one broad conflagration blaze to heaven?
'Tis reaſon makes me wretched; for it tells me
How ſhameful this mad conflict of my paſſions:
But does that ſtill their uproar? Here, ARISTON,
Works the wild ſtorm that reaſon cannot calm.
I muſt, I will have eaſe.

ARISTON.

You may; but oh!
The remedy is dreadful, and will give you
Swoonings and mortal agonies. I tremble
To mention it; but ſuch your ſoul's deep malady,
No gentler cure can bring the health you want.
Her death, my Lord—

PERIANDER.

Ha! death—my ſoul ſhrinks back
From the dread image. How! for ever loſe her!
My queen! my wife! behold thoſe eyes no more

That were the light of mine! no longer hear
That voice whoſe every ſound was harmony!
Of power to ſooth tumultuous Rage, and heal
The wounded heart of Anguiſh—Can it be?
O miſery! why, why is this?

ARISTON.

Alas!
You love her ſtill, my Lord, and know it not.

PERIANDER.

Ye Gods, why am I thus? driven to and fro
By every blaſt that blows?—It is too true.
A traiterous ſoftneſs ſteals o'er my juſt rage,
And melts me to the dotage of low pity.
O thou mean heart! Is ſhe not falſe? And I,
Shall I ſit down with tame diſhonour? take
Pollution to my arms? grow vilely old,
A tale for drunkards in their wine? the mirth
Of midnight libertines, when they recount
Their triumphs o'er baſe women? No: ſhe dies.
I tear her from my breaſt, tho' the life-ſtream
Should iſſue with her. Hear me then, ARISTON,
Do thou prepare a ſecret draught of death,
Of power moſt ſwift and baneful; and be ready
Upon my fatal ſummons.

ARISTON.

Spare me, Sir;
I like not this employ.

PERIANDER.

It muſt be thine.
I have no friend in whom to truſt but thee:
And ſhe ſhall die—But think'ſt thou, good ARISTON,
I ſhould not hear her firſt?

ARISTON.

Hear her, my Lord?
Would you then have her live?

PERIANDER.

PERIANDER.

No; were my fate
Involv'd in hers, ſhe ſhould not live. But ſtill
Something within me crys that I ſhould hear her.
It is not, can't be love. 'Tis my revenge,
All direful now, that would enjoy her tears,
Her lying oaths of innocence, her new
And added perjuries: then ſink her down
To the dark world, with all her crimes upon her.

ARISTON.

You ſee not, Sir, the danger of that meeting.
Is your heart proof againſt the powerful charm
Of beauty ſoften'd into ſighs, and melting
With the mild languor of imploring eyes,
More winning now, and ſhedding gentler beams
Thro' ſhowers of ſorrow. Think you here behold her,
The kneeling charmer lovely in her tears,
Pleading for pity, ſinking at your feet,
And dying by your frown.

PERIANDER.

Art thou my friend?
O mercileſs! why doſt thou raiſe before me
This dangerous image? 'Tis not to be borne.
My brain turns round with madneſs. O ye Powers!
Why am I not at quiet? Why is life
Forc'd on the wretch who ſtrongly begs to die,
In bitterneſs of ſoul? who asks no more
But the grave's ſhade and ſilence, there at laſt
To ſleep for ever, nameleſs and forgotten?

ARISTON.

Alas for pity! I will talk no more
On this diſtreſsful theme.

PERIANDER.

ARISTON, ſtay.
Spite of theſe tears, ſpite of this fond diſtraction,
It ſhall be done. A king may live unhappy

But not with loſs of honour unreveng'd.
'Twas mad to think of this. I will not truſt
My eyes againſt the witchcraft of her charms.
Then ſummon all thy firmneſs, O my Soul!
And dare to be accurſt; ſince thy ſad choice
Is ſhame, or miſery. I am reſolv'd.
Ye Gods who watch o'er the chaſte marriage-bed!
Thou *Stygian* JOVE! and all ye Powers infernal!
Behold, I kneel as in your awful preſence.
By that inviſible, that dreaded Lake,
Th' irrevocable oath that binds even you,
Here I pronounce, and ſeal her doom of death.

SCENE VIII.

EURYDICE, PERIANDER, ARISTON.

EURYDICE *kneels to* PERIANDER, *who after looking on her ſome time with emotion, flings away without ſpeaking.*

EURYDICE *alone.*

Not hear me! not vouchſafe me one poor word!
'Tis hard indeed.—The Wretch of many crimes, [*riſing.*
Whom Mercy dares not ſave, is gentler us'd.
His rigid judge is leſs ſevere than mine.
Ye Powers! have I deſerv'd this? Did my heart
E'er harbour one looſe wiſh? Your ſelves can tell,
The morning's orient beam is not more pure,
More ſtainleſs than my truth. Was ever fate,
Were ever woes, like mine? Even in the hour
Of general joy to all, while pleaſing hope
Sprung faſt within my heart, I find my ſelf
Undone for ever! ſunk to riſe no more!

Not

Not hear me—then I know my doom is fix'd.
And ſhall I ſtay to hear the foul ſurmizes,
The ſcurril taunts, the falſe upbraiding pity,
The keen revilings, that muſt uſher in
My public ſentence? Can there be in death
Such pangs? ſuch piercing agonies? Impoſſible.
Death is repoſe and calm, is ſoft elizium
To thoughts like theſe. I will prevent their triumph,
And ſave myſelf this ſhame. 'Tis but to loſe
A few unhappy moments; 'tis to reſt
The ſooner from my cares; to feel no more
The bitterneſs of miſery and inſult
That bait my weary ſoul. Then it is fix'd.
Spite of the woman, no fond tear ſhall flow,
No ſigh ariſe, the coward-ſex to ſhew.
When life is ſhame, and glorious freedom nigh,
A *Grecian* and a Queen muſt dare to die.

The End of the Fourth Act.

ACT V. SCENE I.

PERIANDER *walking diſordered,* LEONIDAS *following.*

O MY lov'd Maſter! have I liv'd to ſee
This ſight of woe? Alas! is this to conquer?
Are theſe the fruits of victory?

PERIANDER.

Away,
Why nam'ſt thou victory to me, a ſlave
Subdu'd and tyranniz'd by his worſt foes,
His unrelenting paſſions? Talk of ruine,
And I will hear thee: talk of hopeleſs miſery;
No other ſtrain befits thy maſter's triumph.

LEONIDAS.

This is the language of ſupreme diſtreſs,
Impatient of itſelf. My gracious Lord,
Forgive an old man's talk, who would this moment,
Might his poor life bring back your peace of mind,
With joy reſign it.

PERIANDER.

That were to bring back
The darted ſun-beam, or recall the flight
Of unreturning time. O no: my ſoul
Has bid the laſt farewel to happineſs,
To hope itſelf. And yet I thank thy love,
Indeed I do: but leave me for a while.
I would be private.

LEONIDAS.

Sir, I dare not leave you—
Forgive theſe tears—I dare not leave you thus

At

At variance with your ſelf. I read too plain
The fatal thought that wakens in your boſom.

PERIANDER.

And would'ſt thou have me live this abject thing?
This ſlave of folly? For I tell thee bluſhing,
With ſhame and ſtrong abhorrence of my ſelf,
I cannot tear that Woman from my ſoul,
Falſe, faithleſs as ſhe is—Then I will die.
That juſt revenge is ſtill within my power.

LEONIDAS.

O Jealouſy! thou mercileſs deſtroyer,
More cruel than the grave! what ravages
Does thy wild war make in the nobleſt boſoms!
Too long, my Lord, you liſten to the whiſpers
Of that domeſtic foe, that boſom traitor.
For mercy's ſake, throw not away ſo raſhly
The jewel of your ſoul. Some unſeen error
Miſ-leads you from the truth, and ruins her.
Grant her a moment's audience.

PERIANDER.

I have ſworn,
That ſhe ſhall die.

LEONIDAS.

Is then her ſacred life
Of ſo ſmall price, to caſt her thus away
With blind precipitance? Your Queen, my Lord!
The faireſt form, the moſt exalted mind!
Once ſo ador'd and lov'd! to whom your ſoul
Still cleaves with fondneſs! Can you give her up,
The mother of your darling POLYDORE,
Unheard, untry'd, to death and infamy?
Can you do this?

PERIANDER.

O Thou! whoſe eye beholds
And pitys the frail heart of erring man,
Ruler of heaven and earth! or ſtill theſe paſſions,
That rage in tempeſt here: or ſtrike in mercy,

And

And free me from my pain.—What can I do?
My ſolemn vow is gone up to high heaven:
And would'ſt thou have me break it?

LEONIDAS.

That raſh oath
Nor does, nor ought to bind. The Gods refuſe it.
Should you, too late, diſcover ſhe is wrong'd—
Think on it well—O what a life of horrors
Remains for you! I tremble but to name 'em.
The ſad and ſilent meltings of vain ſorrow;
The thorn of keen remorſe; the ſting of love,
Inflam'd by fond reflection, hourly ſighing
For what he never, never hopes to find:
With theſe, late-coming, but no more to leave you,
Deſpair accurſt. Dreadful ſociety!
Yet ſuch will ſhare your day and night, and haunt
Your court, your throne, your ſolitude, your couch.
Alas, my Lord!

PERIANDER.

O by my ſoul's ſtrong anguiſh,
I would moſt gladly blot out from my thoughts
All memory of paſt time: I yet would queſtion
The waking evidence of every ſenſe,
To give her back that vertue, thoſe fair beams
That ſhone on our firſt loves. Then was I bleſt
Beyond the race of men, belov'd and loving,
Honour'd and happy; and my name as odor
Pour'd forth, and breathing freſhneſs all around.
O days of dear delight! that I could fix
For ever there, and think no farther on.
I will if poſſible.

LEONIDAS.

O happy change!
Confirm this gentle purpoſe, favouring heaven!
I fly to bring her hither.

PERIANDER.

PERIANDER.

Stay thee yet.
I would reſolve, but cannot. Love and rage
By turns aſſail me: melt me now to mercy;
Now rouſe me to diſtraction—O my heart!

LEONIDAS.

Then puniſh the ſole cauſe of all your pangs.
On the great criminal, on PROCLES' head
Diſcharge the fulneſs of a righteous vengeance,
And juſtify the Gods. Let the rack tear
The traitor's limbs; and as he howls with anguiſh,
Extort confeſſion from him of the lyes,
The dark aſperſions, that have well nigh ruin'd
Your injur'd, vertuous Queen, and tortur'd you.

PERIANDER.

What haſt thou done? O that deteſted name!
Thou know'ſt not half my madneſs—that curſt name
Has ſet my brain on blaze, and call'd up there
Ten thouſand furies. Hell! haſt thou not heard
What ſhame and ſcorn, what vileneſs and confuſion,
He heap'd upon my head—and ſhe the cauſe!

LEONIDAS.

Oh heaven, and is this retribution thine?
Muſt Vertue know, what Vice alone ſhould feel?

PERIANDER.

Forbear, fond man. That heaven thou dar'ſt accuſe,
Juſt, tho' myſterious, leads us on unerring,
Thro' ways unmark'd, from Guilt to Puniſhment.
I vow'd, alas! and with ſtrong adjurations
Bound that juſt vow, to ſet my country free.
This, to my Father on his bed of death,
Solemn I ſwore—But, O blind luſt of greatneſs!
Thro' wantonneſs of will I lightly weigh'd it,
Nor fear'd the hour of terrible account!
That hour is come: and what avails it now
That I, with equal hand and gentle rule,

Have

Have ſway'd my people? I am puniſh'd moſt,
Where I had bid my ſoul be moſt ſecure
Of happineſs for years—Ha! POLYDORE.

SCENE II.

POLYDORE, PERIANDER, LEONIDAS.

PERIANDER.

I ſaid I would be private.

POLYDORE.

O my father,
Here let me kneel for ever, weep theſe eyes
To blindneſs, and ne'er know a thought of comfort.

PERIANDER.

What would my POLYDORE?

POLYDORE.

Alas! what means
This common face of woe that meets my ſight
Where'er I turn? Even now while happy *Corinth*
Blazes with triumph; while the neighbouring ſhores
Reſound to heaven her voice of general joy,
The palace is in tears. Her ſilent courts
Are dark with mourning, as if Death and Ruine,
Not Victory, had fix'd their manſion here.

PERIANDER.

There is a cauſe, my ſon, a dreadful one.
But leave me to myſelf.

POLYDORE.

Am I then grown
A horror to your eyes? What is my crime,
That thus with alienated look you turn
As from ſome baleful object? Yet, my father,
Oft have you ſworn that in this face you ſaw,
And lov'd your darling Queen.

PERIANDER.

PERIANDER.

Away, thy looks,
Thy words diſtract me.

POLYDORE.

Whither ſhall I fly?
Where hide this hated head? My mother too,
As now I left her, preſſing full her eyes
With fix'd and earneſt mournfulneſs on mine,
Stream'd into tears: then claſp'd me to her boſom
With ſuch ſad paſſion, ſuch tranſported tremblings,
As parting lovers that muſt meet no more.
I beg'd to know the cauſe. Again ſhe preſs'd me
With fonder eagerneſs, and ſighing cry'd,
Say to the King, my heart has never err'd.

PERIANDER.

By heaven, my ſoul melts at the piteous tale.
O POLYDORE—

SCENE III.

PERIANDER, POLYDORE, LEONIDAS,

OFFICER.

My Lord, the priſoner MEDON
Attends, and prays admittance to your preſence.

PERIANDER.

Ha! MEDON! Doſt thou dream? MEDON alive?
Did I not charge thee ſtrict to caſt him forth
That moment to the fury of the people?
How haſt thou dar'd to diſobey?

OFFICER.

Dread Sir,
As to his fate I led him pale and trembling;
At ſight of the tumultuous croud around,
With utmoſt inſtance he requeſted of me
To ſave him yet a moment; for he had
Secrets of prime concernment that requir'd

The King's immediate ear. We hardly ſcap'd
Into the ſouthern tower: th' unnumber'd rabble
With cries and threats demanded forth their foe.
At hazard of my life I ventur'd down,
Sooth'd, flatter'd, promis'd 'em they ſhould have juſtice.
They are but now diſpers'd.

PERIANDER.

LEONIDAS,
My heart miſgives me at that miſcreant's name.
But let him enter.

SCENE IV.

PERIANDER, POLYDORE, LEONIDAS, MEDON.

MEDON.

O King! renown'd for gentleneſs and mercy,
The nobleſt praiſe; ſee proſtrate at your feet
A criminal, who comes to merit pardon
By fair diſcovery of ſome weighty truths,
That much import your ſoul's repoſe and health.

PERIANDER.

Say on: and if thy heart has form'd a hope
Of one hour's after-life, take heed thy tale
Be ſtrictly juſt to truth.

MEDON.

Thus groveling here,
With ſhame and ſharp remorſe I own my crime.
Miſled by that Uſurper, who with me
Now ſhares the due reward of guilt like ours,
To pleaſure him, unhappy that I was!
I told, I know not what of your good Queen.
Would I had periſh'd firſt! for all was falſe,
And ſhe moſt innocent.

PERIANDER.

Perdition on thee!
What do I hear?

MEDON.

MEDON.

I fill'd ARISTON's ears
With monftrous tales, which his plain honefty
Alas, too rafhly credited—

PERIANDER.

Ye Gods!
And could your thunder fleep? Pernicious flave,
Hadft thou as many lives as crimes, not one
Should fcape my juftice—Ah LEONIDAS,
Was ever fuch black treachery?—Forgive thee?
Thy doom fhall be of fignal dread and warning
To all fucceeding Minions. Drag him hence,
[*to the guards.*
And guard him at the peril of your heads.

SCENE V.

PERIANDER, POLYDORE, LEONIDAS.

LEONIDAS.

Amazing villainy!

PERIANDER.

O fly, my fon,
Find the poor mourner out, and in my name
Say all that weeping Penitence can plead,
Or Love returning promife. My full heart
Will more than make it good—and may the power
Of foft perfuafion wait upon thy lips.

SCENE VI.

PERIANDER, LEONIDAS.

PERIANDER.

As from enchantment freed, the mifts difperfe
By which my eyes were held.—That injur'd Fair!
How fhall I meet her foft forgiving look,
Whom I fo much have wrong'd!

LEONIDAS.

Thrice happy turn
Of unexpected fate!

PERIANDER.

But let me fly
Into her gentle arms! there loſe the horrors
That have diſtracted me! there loſe myſelf
In love's ecſtatic joys!

SCENE VII.

PERIANDER, LEONIDAS, ARISTON.

PERIANDER.

In happy time
Thou com'ſt, ARISTON. We were both deceiv'd;
And I revoke my order—But curſt PROCLES
Shall pay me dear for all.

ARISTON.

He has, my Lord:
And the ſad tale is terrible. I ſhrink
But to recount it. Slumbering Conſcience rous'd,
And flaſhing in his face the ſtartling proſpect
Of his paſt life, furious he daſh'd his head
Againſt his priſon walls. I found him fallen,
A piteous ſpectacle! rowling in blood,
Deform'd with pain; for agonizing death
Sate hideous on his brow. Faintly he drew
His parting breath: yet all that breath went forth
In blaſphemies, aſſaulting heaven with curſes,
The ravings of deſpair, for fruſtrating
His impious purpoſe on the Queen.

PERIANDER.

How dreadful
This period to a life like his! The hand
Of heaven is greatly juſt—But O my friends,
Theſe ſtrange events have well nigh overturn'd
This tottering brain. I feel I know not what
Of joy and terror, high amaze and tranſport,
All blended here, and working in wild tumult.

LEONIDAS.

LEONIDAS.

'Tis but the motion of a troubled ſea,
After ſore tempeſt ſinking to a calm.
All will be well, my Lord. Repoſe and health
Await you in her arms. What bliſs is yours?
A ſecond union of your meeting ſouls!
A better nuptial morn, with love new-riſing,
To ſhine for ever.

SCENE VIII.

PERIANDER, LEONIDAS, ARISTON, MELISSA.

O my royal Miſtreſs!
The dews of death are cold upon her brow!

PERIANDER.

What mean thy fatal words?

MELISSA.

Falſely accus'd
Of what her ſoul moſt loaths, and to deſpair
By your unkindneſs urg'd, the Queen alas!
Has drunk a deadly draught.

PERIANDER.

O heaven and earth!
Are theſe at laſt my hopes? 'Tis I—O horror!
'Tis I have murder'd her—

SCENE *the laſt.*

Scene opening diſcovers EURYDICE *ſitting,* POLYDORE *kneeling by her.*

PERIANDER.

Ye righteous Gods!
O give her back to life, and to your juſtice
I bow this guilty head—What's to be done?
LEONIDAS, ARISTON, fly, my friends,

Call,

Call, gather all our ſages; bid them try
Their ſovereign skill. My crown to him that ſaves her.

EURYDICE.

It cannot be. Already death invades
My ſhivering boſom. Yet a little moment,
And I ſhall be with thoſe that reſt for ever.
But here in this laſt awful hour I ſwear,
By that dread world whither my ſoul is parting,
I never knew pollution: I am ſtill
Your true and lawful wife.

PERIANDER.

I know thou art,
Thou dying innocence. My fatal blindneſs,
Deſtruction on my head! has ruin'd thee.
My life! my ſoul's beſt joy! and muſt I loſe thee?
Loſe thee for ever?—Wretch! raſh fool!—O yet
Forgive my madneſs.

EURYDICE.

Thus, in thy lov'd arms
Each unkind thought is loſt. Now I die pleas'd:
Now all is well.—Death! thou art here—

MELISSA.

Ah! ſhe expires. The laſt dim miſt ſwims o'er
Her cloſing eyes!

PERIANDER.

One moment, thou fair Spirit,
One moment tarry for me—Thus we join,
To part no more—

[he draws his ſword to ſtab himſelf.

ARISTON.

Ah! Sir—

LEONIDAS.

My Lord, what means
This fatal fury?

PERIANDER.

Cruel men, away.
And would you then detain me longer here

On

On this loath'd ſpot, to linger out old age
With darkneſs and deſpair! to curſe the hour
That gave a murderer birth! Would you, my friends,
Have me live thus?

ARISTON.

Ye Gods aſſwage his grief!

PERIANDER.

Theſe righteous Gods have caſt me off for ever.
My broken vow!—O terrible! it hangs,
A burſting thunder, o'er my head. I ſee—
And tremble at the ſight, th' inquiring Judge,
Beyond theſe heavens, high on his throne of terrors;
His fix'd and dread regard turn'd full upon me!
And look! behold! the Miniſter of vengeance
But waits his nod to ſtrike me thro' the centre.

POLYDORE.

Alas! my father—

PERIANDER.

O my ſon! my ſon!
I have undone thee too. How dare I look
On that dear face, where thy loſt Mother's ſweetneſs
Smiles ſtrong reproach, and charms me into madneſs?
Then, farewel reaſon! farewel human converſe!
Sun, day, and time, farewel!—All hail deſpair!
Eternal darkneſs hail!—Say'ſt thou I've loſt her?
No, no; we will not part. Thus let me preſs
Her clay-cold lips, thus weep my ſoul away
On her chaſte boſom here. O yet, my love!
My better life! O yet lift up thy eyes!
O ſpeak to me!

LEONIDAS.

Alas! ſhe hears you not.
The ſoul is fled for ever.

PERIANDER.

O my Queen!

[he throws himſelf by the body: the reſt ſtand weeping and ſilent.

[raiſing

[*raising himself up.*

Ha! there—ſave me! 'tis he, the King of terrors!
Lo how the ghaſtly viſion glares upon me
With his fix'd beamleſs eyes!—What path is this,
Dreary and deep, thro' which he drags me on?
Bleſs me!—look there—what ſhivering Forms are theſe,
Thin as the paſſing air, that skim around me?
And now th' infernal world hath ſhut me in!
But ſee the Furies arm'd! ſee their fell ſerpents
That rouſe themſelves to ſting me! Is there none,
No Power to ſcreen me from them?

LEONIDAS.

Gracious Sir,
Where is that patience—

PERIANDER.

Soft—I ſee her plain.
Yonder on high ſhe ſits amid the Gods,
Who wonder at her charms—And doſt thou ſmile
Upon thy murderer?—Thus let me kneel,
And weeping worſhip thee—Ha! ſeeſt thou there
Yon flaming pool? And what damn'd ſoul is that
Riſing from the mid deeps, that beckons me?
He wafts me ſtill—By hell, 'tis hated PROCLES,
The cauſe of all my ruine!—Traitor, yes,
I come, I fly, to plunge thee deeper ſtill
In this red ſea of tortures—O!

ARISTON.

He dies!

POLYDORE.

O matchleſs horror!

LEONIDAS.

Bear him gently hence.
Was ever ſight like this?—O Jealouſy!
This is thy dreadful work. May future times
Learn here thy power, and mark with heedful eyes,
From thy blind rage what mighty miſchiefs riſe.

THE END.

MUSTAPHA

MUSTAPHA.

A

TRAGEDY.

Acted at the

THEATRE-ROYAL

IN

DRURY-LANE,

By His Majesty's Servants.

LONDON:

Printed for A. Millar, at *Buchanan's Head*, over-against St. *Clement's* Church, in the *Strand.* M. DCC. XXXIX.

(Price 1 *s.* 6 *d.*)

TO HIS

ROYAL HIGHNESS

THE

PRINCE of *Wales*.

SIR,

I Should but ill deſerve the gracious permiſſion Your ROYAL HIGHNESS has given me to ſhelter the following Tragedy under your name; if a writer, ſo little known as I am, ſhould preſume to celebrate the great and good qualities, that equally adorn your public and private character. I will only ſay; (and it is the nobleſt praiſe:) they have endeared Your ROYAL HIGHNESS to the hopes and affections of a whole people.

May I have leave, at the ſame time, to congratulate every man of worth and genius, on that generous protection the politer arts now meet with from the Prince of WALES? and to join with them in wiſhing, from my heart, every bleſſing to Your ROYAL HIGHNESS? It is, in other words, to wiſh the future happineſs of GREAT BRITAIN.

I am, with the profoundeſt reſpect,

SIR,

Your ROYAL HIGHNESS'*s*

moſt devoted ſervant,

D. MALLET.

PROLOGUE.

By Mr. THOMSON.

Spoken by Mr. MILWARD.

SINCE Athens *first began to draw mankind,*
To picture life, and shew th'impassion'd mind;
The truly Wise have ever deem'd the stage,
The moral school of each enlighten'd age.
There, in full pomp, the Tragic Muse appears,
Queen of soft sorrows, and of useful fears.
Faint is the lesson reason'd rules impart:
She *pours it strong and instant thro' the heart.*
If virtue is her theme; we sudden glow
With generous flame: and, what we feel, we grow.
If Vice she paints; indignant passions rise;
The villain sees himself with loathing eyes:
His soul starts, conscious, at another's groan;
And the pale tyrant trembles on his throne.
To-night our meaning Scene attempts to show,
What fell events from dark suspicion flow;
Chief when it taints a lawless monarch's mind,
To the false herd of flattering slaves confin'd.
The soul sinks gradual to so dire a state;
Even excellence but serves to feed its hate:
To hate remorseless, cruelty succeeds,
And every worth, and every virtue bleeds.
Behold, our Author at your bar appears,
His modest hopes depress'd by conscious fears.
Faults he has many—But to ballance these,
His aim is honest: and he strives to please.
All slighter errors let indulgence spare;
And be his equal trial full and fair.
For this best British *privilege we call:*
Then—as he merits, let him stand, or fall.

EPI-

EPILOGUE.

By a Friend.

Spoken by Mr. QUIN.

WELL—for this once I'll undertake the part—
But, would have been excus'd with all my heart.
I come, good Sirs, to ſpeak an Epilogue;
I doubt, not ſeaſon'd to the taſte in vogue:
Nor was I made to ſimper, leer, and coax,
And torture meanings into wanton jokes.
Our author too avows himſelf unfit
To write ſuch ſtrains as but diſhonour wit.
Yet this, with humble hope, he bids me ſay:
If aught, leſs faulty, pleas'd you in his play;
If noble paſſions bade your boſoms glow;
If feeling pity taught a tear to flow;
If, while he try'd to make fair virtue ſhine,
You ſmil'd indulgent on the juſt deſign:
'Twere mean, thoſe bright impreſſions to efface,
That dignify the mind which gives 'em place:
And for the vain delight of ſome low jeſt,
Diſtaſte the wiſe, and pain the modeſt breaſt.
Behold, that circle of the liſt'ning Fair,
Their looks how open! how ſerene their air!
May no rude bluſh invade one ſmiling face,
That ſafe from inſult, they may veil no grace!
Be yours henceforth to ſave them from alarms,
And vindicate their violated charms.

Books printed for A. MILLAR.

THE Works of Mr. *Thomson*, in 2 vol. 8vo.—Vol. I. Containing Spring, Summer, Autumn, Winter; a Hymn on the Seasons; a Poem sacred to the Memory of Sir *Isaac Newton*; *Britannia*, a Poem; and *Sophonisba*, a Tragedy.

Vol. II. Containing ancient and modern *Italy* compared, *Greece*, *Rome*, *Britain*, and the Prospect; being the Five Parts of *Liberty*, a Poem: A Poem to the Memory of the Lord Chancellor *Talbot*; and *Agamemnon*, a Tragedy.

* Either Volume to be had separate.

N. B. There are a few Copies remaining of those printed on a superfine Royal Paper, in 2 Vol. 4to.

2. A Compleat Collection of the Historical, Political, and Miscellaneous Works of *John Milton*, correctly printed from the Original Editions; with an Historical and Critical Account of the Life and Writings of the Author; containing several Original Papers of his, never before publish'd; and a large Alphabetical Index, by *Thomas Birch*, A. M. F.R.S. in 2 Vol. Folio, beautifully printed on a fine Paper, and adorned with a curious Head of the Author, engraved by Mr. *Vertue*, from a Drawing by Mr. *Richardson*.

3. The *Oceana*, and other Works of *James Harrington* Esq; collected, methodiz'd, and review'd; with an exact Account of his Life prefix'd, by *Toland*. To which is added, an Appendix, containing all the Political Tracts wrote by this Author, omitted in Mr. *Toland's* Edition.

N. B. *There are a few of the last Two printed for the Curious, on a large Paper.*

4. The Mythology and Fables of the Ancients explain'd by History; translated from the *French* of the Abbé *Banier*, Member of the Royal Academy of *Inscriptions* and *Belles Lettres*, at *Paris*.

N. B. This Volume contains the Two Volumes of the *Paris* Edition in 12°.

5. The Tea-Table Miscellany; or a Collection of *Scots* Songs: the ninth Edition; being the compleatest and most correct of any yet publish'd. In three Volumes. By *Allan Ramsay*; with the Head of the Author, design'd by his Son, and engraven by Mr. *King*.

Next Month will be Publish'd,

Several Pieces, some of which never before printed; which, with this Play, and *Eurydice* a Tragedy, will compleat a Volume in Octavo of Mr. *Mallet's* Works.

N. B. They shall be printed in the same manner as the Plays, and to be had separate.

The Perſons repreſented.

SOLYMAN the Second, ſirnamed *The Magnificent*, Emperor of the *Turks*.	*Mr*. QUIN.
MUSTAPHA. } His Sons.	*Mr*. MILWARD.
ZANGER. } His Sons.	*Mr*. WRIGHT.
RUSTAN, Grand Vizir.	*Mr*. MILLS.
MUFTI.	*Mr*. WINSTON.
ACHMET, Friend of *Muſtapha*.	*Mr*. HAVARD.
OSMAN.	*Mr*. WOODBURN.
ROXOLANA, Empreſs.	*Mrs*. BUTLER.
EMIRA.	*Mrs*. GIFFARD.

Baſha, Attendants, Mutes.

SCENE, *the Sultan's Tent, in a large plain near* Aleppo, *where his army lies encamp'd.*

MUSTAPHA.

A TRAGEDY.

ACT I. SCENE I.

RUSTAN, MUFTI.

RUSTAN.

GUIDE of the faithful, oracle of truth,
Sage MUFTI, hail and welcome!

MUFTI.

Noble RUSTAN,
Be peace and benediction on the head
Of him, the wise and valiant, who supports
Th' imperial throne of earth's most potent Prince!

RUSTAN.

In happy hour you come. But sure, my Lord,
You travel'd on the spur.

MUFTI.

By duty wing'd,
True, I have glow'd beneath the noon-day beam,
And shiver'd in the midnight's dewy shade,

Unresting from the Porte. Such prompt dispatch
Great ROXOLANA's mandate had enjoin'd.
Inform me then what service she requires,
Whom I but live to serve.

RUSTAN.

Indeed you owe,
And I no less, all duty to her Highness.
I need not to your grateful thought recall,
How warm her love for our unerring law!
How liberal to its sages! Fir'd her self
With zeal for holy things, that zeal in others
Is title to her favour: and inspir'd
Her powerful mediation with the Sultan,
Great SOLYMAN, who rais'd your worth on high
To that prime station where it shines unenvy'd.

MUFTI.

Let her command me, Vizir. My obedience,
As most implicite, shall be most sincere.

RUSTAN.

Observe me then: and when your ear hath heard
Th' important tale, let caution lock it up
Deep in the darkest silence of your breast,
From all but heaven.

MUFTI.

Have I not liv'd in courts?
Been present where I would not trust a thought,
In whisper, even to things inanimate?

RUSTAN.

Th' attempt she meditates is arduous, great,
Involves her dearest happiness, her life;
Perhaps the lives of all she deigns to love.
Know then—the news will strike thee with amaze—
She holds Prince MUSTAPHA her deadly foe.

MUFTI.

Ha! say'st thou?—MUSTAPHA! the favourite son

Of

Of our redoubted Lord! his eldeſt hope!
Sole pledge the fair *Circaſſian* left his fondneſs!
How will ſhe root him from a father's love,
Who holds him dear for virtues that renown,
And dignify himſelf? The Prince has fought
His battels with ſucceſs: and is ſuſtain'd
By troops that know his worth; that idolize
His fame and fortune.

RUSTAN.

Thou haſt ſumm'd his crimes.
Theſe are, with reaſon are the mighty object
Of ROXOLANA's hate. But wouldſt thou know,
How ſhe may drive him from his father's boſom?
This boaſted courage ſhe admires! exalts!
With all th' inſidious artfulneſs of praiſe:
And will applaud the ſtripling into ruin.

MUFTI.

Nay, truſt a woman for ingenious ill.
Such foes indeed moſt ſurely aim their blow,
Who praiſe to wound, and honour to deſtroy.

RUSTAN.

My influence waits on hers. You know ſhe gave
Her daughter to my bed. Whate'er I hold,
Or graſp in diſtant hope, is hers alone.
And, as my faireſt fortunes, all my aims
With hers are blended intimate and deep.
If MUSTAPHA ſucceeds his Royal Sire,
She falls for ever! ſinks from what ſhe is,
Empreſs and conſort of unbounded ſway,
Dower'd and declar'd ſo—ſinks into a ſlave!
Her ſons too—can a parent bear the thought?
Her ſons muſt bleed! Her blooming ZANGER firſt,
Child of her love, th' unhappy victim falls
Of that dire policy, which founds the throne
Of each aſcending Prince in brother's blood.

She muſt deſtroy, or periſh. In ſuch caſe,
Neceſſity is juſtice.

MUFTI.

True, my Lord.
Cuſtom, the deity of half mankind,
All-powerful o'er the ſoul, on whom opinion
Waits with obſequious blindneſs, hath made ſacred
Such dreadful deeds; and bids our eaſtern world
Hold them in venerable eſtimation.
This, to your purpos'd vengeance, may give ſanction:
But what will give ſucceſs? The Prince, my Lord—
I tell it, with reluctance, of a foe—
By every title, by each filial tie,
Deſerves, and largely ſhares, his father's love.

RUSTAN.

What is the love our Sovereign bears his ſons?
'Tis coldneſs, 'tis averſion, to the flame
With which he burns for ROXOLANA's charms!
Not all the fabled power of herbs or ſpells
Could raiſe it to more height. He doats upon her
Beyond all vulgar paſſion. Age but ſtrengthens,
And each new day adds fervour to its warmth.
But as this great deſign requires much pauſe,
And gradual machination; I, at times,
Have thrown out hints, inſinuations, doubts,
Some dark and diſtant, ſome more plain and near:
And from ſuch fruitful ſeeds is ſpringing up
A harveſt to our hopes. The Sultan now,
Declining to th' infirmities of age,
Is lapſing to its vices; quick diſtruſt,
Umbrage at riſing excellence, but chief
At ſignal fame in arms. He fears his ſon:
And in the hearts of Kings, by years made gloomy,
From fear to hate the progreſs is not ſlow.
What ſays my friend?

MUFTI.

MUFTI.

Now, by the Prophet' tomb,
The happy news is gladneſs to my ſoul.
I hate the ſtripling—

RUSTAN.

Hark! The Sultan's voice—
He leaves his couch. I muſt attend him here.
You, haſten to th' apartment of the Empreſs.
Be wiſe, be ſecret: what ſhe gives in order,
Obey without reſerve.

The daily form
Of ſolemn ſalutation now begins;
Fram'd to remind him what a Monarch is,
And what he once muſt be.

SCENE II.

The back Scene opening, diſcovers the Sultan's pavilion: he ſitting; Officers and Slaves around him.

Firſt Officer, behind the throne.

The fragrant health
Of morning when it ſhines; the gentle calm
Of evening when its dewy ſhades deſcend,
Repoſe on SOLYMAN; and make his breaſt
A paradiſe of ſweets. To him, the King
Of Kings, the Lord of weſt and eaſt, belong
Juſtice and mercy; to chaſtiſe all vice,
And to reward all virtue.

Second Officer on the left.

Yet this Prince,
This firſt of Monarchs, mighty, and renown'd,
Shall die! ſhall die! ſhall die!

Third

Third Officer on the right.

Praiſe be to him
Who lives for ever.

SOLYMAN *riſing.*

Leave me——

SCENE III.

SOLYMAN, RUSTAN.

SOLYMAN.

What a Scene
Of ſolemn mockery is all human grandeur!
Thus worſhip'd, thus exalted by the breath
Of adulation, are my paſſions ſooth'd?
My ſecret pangs aſſuag'd? The peaſant-hind,
Who drives his camel o'er the burning waſte,
With heat and hunger ſmote, knows happier days,
And ſounder nights than I.

RUSTAN.

He ſeems diſturb'd.

SOLYMAN.

My couch is grown a bed of thorns: my ſleeps,
That ſhould repair frail nature, weigh her down
With viſionary terrors. This ſad dream,
Not ſuch as fancy in her ſhadowy workings
Amuſive raiſes and deſtroys at will,
Was on my brain with deep impreſſure ſtruck:
It ſeem'd the hand of ſome night-hovering power,
That meant to warn me—RUSTAN!

RUSTAN.

Health, my Lord,
And ever-growing honors! Dares your ſlave,

Your

Your trueſt ſervant, aſk what care invades
His Sovereign's peace of mind?

SOLYMAN.

Vizir, I bluſh
To think illuſions of the dark have power
To move me thus—Yet, wherefore, night by night,
Am I thus viſited with horrid ſhapes
And omens of impending ill?

RUSTAN.

Grant, heaven,
That in ſuch warnings be not ſhadow'd forth—
Pardon my zeal—th' unwelcome truths that oft
Alarm our ears, of dark and deep deſigns,
Thro' all thoſe bounds where MUSTAPHA preſides.

SOLYMAN.

Ha! Vizir—whither would'ſt thou lead my thought?

RUSTAN.

I know the perilous niceneſs of this theme;
'Tis cloath'd with death: and I am as a man
Who walks the ſummit of a fearful cliff,
Each motion hazards falling: And that fall
Is fate inevitable.

SOLYMAN.

Thou art ſafe.
When duty ſpeaks, its very error claims
Not only pardon: it deſerves applauſe.

RUSTAN.

What may not youth, my Lord, impetuous youth,
By factious armies heated and inflam'd,
By ſtrong ambition feaver'd into phrenzy,
Preſume to dare? Impatient of controul,
'Twould ſpurn at heaven itſelf, would ſcale the throne
Of him, the Sacred Power, who gave it being.

SOLYMAN.

Thou haſt arrous'd my ſoul. And if I doubt

I will prevent.—That were a tyrant's baseness;
Who kills—because he fears.—Away such thoughts.
Nor can this be. I have approv'd him faithful.
He still reveres the monarch in the father:
And love of one preserves him just to both.

RUSTAN.

So may it ever be. And you deserve
His most devoted service. For his sake,
You broke thro' all the rules of royal custom,
That buries in the dark seraglio's round,
And keeps at cautious distance, son or brother,
From knowledge and employment.

SOLYMAN.

True: my heart
Disdain'd those narrow forms which low suspicion,
Th' inglorious policy of mean-soul'd men,
Had render'd reverend to our barbarous world:
Beheld with scorn by wiser nations round us,
Whom reason and discernment have enlarg'd
With nobler views, and polish'd into honor.

RUSTAN.

A zeal well meant, tho' indiscreet, the King
Will sure forgive.—But does this son approve
The breach of ancient custom—in each instance?
There may be novelties—

SOLYMAN.

What wouldst thou say?

RUSTAN.

E'er since the time inhuman TAMERLANE,
In BAJAZET's insulted Queen, dishonor'd
The majesty of empire, future Sultans
Have shunn'd the marriage-tie.

SOLYMAN.

SOLYMAN has not:
Superior to that cowardice of pride,

Which

Which made it a ſtate-maxim—But ſay, who,
What ſlave of mine ſo lightly holds his life
As but to murmur at it?

RUSTAN.

All good ſubjects
Applaud your act with duteous veneration.
Fair ROXOLANA even adorns the name,
The honor'd name ſhe wears. The Prince too, Sir,
Is valiant, noble, rich in manly virtues,
And with theſe virtues, loyal—But his pride—

SOLYMAN.

His pride!—away—he does not, dares not blame—
Confuſion!—blame!—He muſt approve my act.
Reaſon inſpir'd, and honor boaſts it done.
She merits more than pomp and power can give:
Even all that love in his unbounded fondneſs,
Inventive to beſtow with taſte and grace,
Can find to crown the idol of his vow.—
I loſe my ſelf in fondneſs—Say, I wiſh
A moment's converſe with her.—Stay. Thy letters,
What ſay they of my ſon? Will he obey
My order? Does he come to vindicate
His queſtion'd loyalty?

RUSTAN.

To all but that
My letters ſpeak at large, and high extoll
His gentle manners, popular behavior,
And equal uſe of delegated ſway.

SOLYMAN.

My mandate was expreſs and abſolute:
And I expect him here, ere yonder orb
Has meaſur'd half its courſe—But ſhould he fail—
That popular behavior, priz'd ſo high,
May coſt him dear!—My ROXOLANA comes,
I would be left alone.

SCENE IV.

ROXOLANA, SOLYMAN.

ROXOLANA.

Alas, my Lord,
Thro' thoſe ſevere regards you dart around you,
Methinks I read ſome diſcontented thought.
Ah ſhould it point on me!

SOLYMAN.

My ROXOLANA!
That fear is vain, is cruel to us both.
No anger, no diſtaſte can dwell with love,
With love like ours, ennobled into friendſhip,
That, while it ſooths, invigorates the heart:
Union of wiſhes, harmony of wills,
Blended and loſt in one conſenting intereſt.
One undivided happineſs, beyond
The ſolitary, joyleſs pride of power,
That dazzles, not delights—A heart like mine
O'erflows its bounds, unheeding—I but meant
To pour into thy faithful breaſt the cares
That break upon my peace.

ROXOLANA.

Give me them all:
And I will charm them to repoſe, or ſhare
Their ſharpeſt pangs.

SOLYMAN.

A ſwarm of gloomy fears
Is waken'd here!

ROXOLANA.

What fears, my gracious Lord?

SOLYMAN.

SOLYMAN.

Now, ROXOLANA, ſpeak as in the ſight
Of that ſtern Angel who explores the grave,
And calls departed ſouls to ſtrict confeſſion.

ROXOLANA.

What do I hear?

SOLYMAN.

My favour'd MUSTAPHA,
So grac'd and ſo diſtinguiſh'd by my fondneſs,
Feels he for me that love a ſon ſhould feel
For ſuch a parent?

ROXOLANA.

Whence that doubt, my Lord?

SOLYMAN.

Aſk thy own heart. Has not thy love for me
Alarm'd thee to ſuſpicions of his conduct?

ROXOLANA.

What can a father wiſh, he not performs?
When your juſt vengeance ſends him forth to war,
Great in your power and glorious by your fame,
He hurls the dreadful thunder: then returns
Submiſſive to your nod, alike reſign'd,
Commanding or obeying. You the while,
To give this brave and boundleſs ſpirit ſcope,
Remain, my Lord, unactive in the ſhade,
Obſcuring your renown; that his may riſe
And ſhine, to dazzle your admiring ſubjects,
Who bleſs his brightneſs, dwell upon his ſight,
And hail their future Lord!

SOLYMAN.

Ha! heard I right?
Thou ſayſt I have been unactive—cruel truth!
The world has ceas'd to tremble at my name.
Once, Afric, Aſia, Europe, fled before it.
The Perſian loſt a kingdom to my arms:

I humbled *Egypt*; crush'd its daring rebels.
Proud *Rhodes*, defended by the chosen boast
Of Christian chiefs, sustain'd not my assault.
I shook the distant *Danube* with my thunder:
Struck terror to the heart of its bold ruler.
My threatning war hung o'er his capital,
A gather'd tempest; waiting but my nod
To burst in ruin on it.—Yes—this was.
But now—perdition!

ROXOLANA.

Moderate, my Lord,
This rising transport.

SOLYMAN.

'Tis a coward's vaunting:
And valour blushes at it.—ROXOLANA!
What am I now?—Sunk, lost in sloth and silence!
While MUSTAPHA has reign'd for SOLYMAN!
Poor and debasing!—Kings who cease to act,
Cease to be Kings.

ROXOLANA.

Yet MUSTAPHA's renown
Is yours, my Lord. The name of SOLYMAN
Bore terror in it, conquer'd where he fought not:
And, as the victory, the praise was yours.

SOLYMAN.

Thy virtuous tenderness for me deceives thee.
I see my fatal error, feel my danger.
We may oblige our children into foes,
Even till they hate as deep as we have lov'd.

ROXOLANA.

But then proceed, my Lord, by wary steps.
Observe him, if he leagues with men who screen
Their hate to you, their disappointed pride,
Behind the specious mask of public zeal.
Mark if the winning softness of his manners

Be native or aſſum'd. Humility
Is oft diſguis'd ambition. Note the means
By which he ſlides into the vulgar boſom;
Feign'd pity for their ſufferings, hinted hopes
Of better times. But chief remark the arts
He puts in uſe to court the ſoldiers' love;
A coarſe ſimplicity of taſte and life,
In their hard fare, groſs wit, and blunt demeanor,
Their fellow and companion. Miſchief oft,
And murderous treaſon lurk beneath ſuch plainneſs.

SOLYMAN.

O wretchedneſs of royalty! what thorns
Weave their ſharp points with empire's gaudy robe!
Now by my father's ſoul, thou haſt heard more——
I read it in that look——more than thy ſoftneſs
Dares truſt mine ear with——

SCENE V.

SOLYMAN, ROXOLANA, RUSTAN.

SOLYMAN.

RUSTAN!—whence this haſte?

RUSTAN.

My Lord, the Prince approaches——

SOLYMAN.

Ha! what ſay'ſt thou?

RUSTAN.

And enters now the camp.

SOLYMAN.

'Tis well.—The troops
How greet they his arrival?

RUSTAN.

With mad haſte
They pour by thouſands o'er the tented plain,

And

And ſwarm around him. 'Tis all wonder, fondneſs,
Each paſſion, every folly, of the vulgar
Expreſſing heart-felt joy.

SOLYMAN.

Indeed!

RUSTAN.

And hark!
That univerſal ſhout ſpeaks loud their tranſport.

SOLYMAN.

Again!——the traitors!

ROXOLANA.

What attendance brings he?

RUSTAN.

ACHMET will tell your Highneſs.

SOLYMAN.

Bid him enter.

SCENE VI.

SOLYMAN, ROXOLANA, RUSTAN,

ACHMET.

Prince MUSTAPHA——

SOLYMAN.

Is come!

ACHMET.

And by your ſlave,
Implores admiſſion to your royal preſence.

SOLYMAN.

I ſent thee to *Amaſia*, to his province:
Say how he was employ'd.

ACHMET.

As a Prince ſhould be:
In all the nobler cares of peaceful ſway,
That make the ruler lov'd, the people happy.

So-

SOLYMAN.

Didſt thou remark how he receiv'd my order?
How look'd he? what reply'd he?

ACHMET.

With ſubmiſſion
He kiſs'd th' imperial ſignet: then diſmiſs'd
His numerous court; on each with inſtance preſſing
Inviolable duty to their Sovereign.

SOLYMAN.

This more: with what attendance is he guarded?

ACHMET.

With only thoſe who wait about his perſon,
And one fair ſlave.

SOLYMAN.

Enough.—A croud of thoughts,
Doubting, diſcordant, tumult in my breaſt,
Unſettling my reſolves—What ſhould I think?—
Suſpicion may enquire, but muſt not judge.——
'Tis now devotion's hour: invoke we then,
To guide our councils, that unerring Mind,
Whoſe goodneſs guards the majeſty of Kings;
Whoſe juſtice each dark thought to judgment brings.

The End of the Firſt Act.

ACT

ACT II. SCENE I.

MUSTAPHA, ACHMET, HELI, OSMAN, *Soldiers.*

MUSTAPHA, *at the door of the tent, to the ſoldiers who had followed him.*

MY friends and fellow-ſoldiers, I accept
Well pleas'd, theſe kind expreſſions of your love;
As meant in honor of our common Lord,
While thus you grace his ſon, But leave me now,
And each attend his duty.——HELI, go,
Watch near EMIRA; bid her be of comfort:
Say all is well.——Good OSMAN, find my brother,
My ZANGER: I would meet him here.—Oh ACHMET!
Faithful inſtructor of my youth in arms,
Theſe ſhouts, this honeſt tranſport of the army,
That had been muſic in the front of battle,
Is diſcord here!

ACHMET.

Now by fair faith and honor!
I felt my heart ſpring high within my boſom,
And anſwer to th' effuſions of their joy.
Their ſhouts, their acclamations ſwell'd to paſſion.

MUSTAPHA.

Ah, friend——theſe acclamations will undo me!

ACHMET.

What ſays my Prince?

MUSTAPHA,

MUSTAPHA.

For thoſe, whom ſovereign power
Beholds with jealous eye, to be belov'd
Is to be guilty!

ACHMET.

What can malice forge
To raiſe a doubt againſt you? Have you not
Fulfill'd all duties of a ſon and ſervant?
In peace, moſt true and loyal to your father:
In war, your ſword has ever been employ'd,
And ever with ſucceſs, againſt his foes.
What would he more?—Suſpected? no, my Lord,
The Sultan truely loves you.

MUSTAPHA.

Bred in camps,
Train'd in the gallant openneſs of truth
That beſt becomes a ſoldier; thou, my friend,
Art happily a ſtranger to the baſeneſs,
The infamy of courts.——ACHMET, the *Caſpian*,
When terrible with tempeſt, is leſs fatal
To the frail bark that plows it, than a court
To innocence and worth. A ſtepdame's hatred,
Hatred implacable, becauſe unjuſt;
A Vizir, meanly cunning, coolly cruel,
Grown old in arts of treachery and ruin,
Purſue me, hunt me down! And what can I,
Unpractis'd in all guile, oppoſe to dark
And deadly rage?——the breath of public praiſe!
An empty name——that will but ſpeed my ruin!

ACHMET.

Why ſhould they be your foes? why hate the worth
That never injur'd them?——Forgive me, heaven!
Could I believe ſo baſely of mankind,
I would renounce their fellowſhip, and ſeek
The ſilvan wild, to herd with nobler brutes.

How can this be? All things around us wear
A face of peace and silence.

MUSTAPHA.

Such the silence,
The fearful stillness, ere the thunder bursts!
Else whence this boding solitude? this tent
By all forsaken, even the meanest slaves?
As we had sent the pestilence before,
Our mortal harbinger!——But be it so.
True valor, friend, on virtue founded strong,
Meets all events alike.

ACHMET.

Ah, Prince, 'twas cruel——
Forgive my honest love——'twas most unkind
To hide these apprehensions from your friend:
And now, too late, disclose the fatal secret.
But was it not most rash, if such your fears,
Most wilful, unsupported by your troops,
To meet this danger?

MUSTAPHA.

ACHMET——I can die:
But dare not disobey a father's orders.

ACHMET.

The Vizir moves this way.

MUSTAPHA.

Then, O my soul!
Wake all thy powers, and arm me strong within;
That honesty and honor, bravely plain,
May strike confusion through his hollow smile,
And vizor'd malice.

SCENE

SCENE II.

MUSTAPHA, RUSTAN, ACHMET, BASHA.

RUSTAN.

May the Power we ſerve,
Moſt merciful and gracious, crown my Lord,
Thro' length of years, with brightneſs and renown!
To ſee your Highneſs here my ſoul has long,
Has warmly wiſh'd.

MUSTAPHA.

Becauſe——thou art my friend.

RUSTAN.

Heaven knows with what fond warmth my willing tongue,
Still prompted from the heart, has painted forth
Your matchleſs virtues; that exalted courage,
That generous prudence, rival of your courage,
Which aged warriors wonder at with envy!
But my applauſe is poor, and ſinks beneath
The mighty ſubject: Fame herſelf is proud
To celebrate that hero, whoſe ſole arm
Suſtains the throne of godlike SOLYMAN,
His glory and defence!

MUSTAPHA.

Thou know'ſt me not.
He who can liſten, pleas'd, to ſuch applauſe,
Buys at a dearer rate than I dare purchaſe,
And pays for idle air with ſenſe and virtue.
Art thou indeed my friend? then ſhew it nobly;
As man, by deeds like theſe thy tongue extols:
As ſubject, in true duty to thy Sovereign.

RUSTAN.

What amiable modesty! The Sultan
Must needs, my Lord——

MUSTAPHA.

Conclude this prefacing:
And to your business.

RUSTAN.

Sir, your Royal Father——

MUSTAPHA.

Proceed.

RUSTAN.

'Tis only——

MUSTAPHA.

What?

RUSTAN.

The Emperor orders
This Basha may receive your sword.

MUSTAPHA.

My sword!

RUSTAN.

Such his command.

MUSTAPHA.

And, as he knows this RUSTAN
My kindest advocate, my warmest friend,
The man who sounds my praise aloud to heaven,
He sends him on this errand!

RUSTAN.

Born to serve,
With absolute obedience to perform
My master's will, his faithful slave presumes not
To ask a reason for it.

MUSTAPHA.

Heaven and earth!
My sword?

RUSTAN.

I

RUSTAN.

What would your Highneſs have me ſay
In anſwer to this order?

MUSTAPHA.

Take it, Vizir—
And tell my Lord and Father, that a ſon
Who loves his perſon, venerates his virtues,
Durſt ne'er diſpute his pleaſure—nor does now.
Say, this good ſword has truly been employ'd
Againſt his foes.—ACHMET, it was the gift
With which his fondneſs grac'd my early hand!
Which I had hop'd to part with but in death!
Stay. If thou art a friend, add this one truth,
Add boldly—when his ſacred will demands
The life he gave me; this unhappy ſon,
Suſpected as he is, will yield that life
With equal reſignation. Thou wilt ſay ſo?

RUSTAN.

By heaven, I will.

MUSTAPHA.

So, in thy lateſt hour,
That heaven, who ſees us both, deal with thy ſoul!

SCENE III.

MUSTAPHA, ACHMET.

MUSTAPHA.

Oh friend!

ACHMET.

Perdition on the doubling traitor!
Was it by arts like theſe he roſe to greatneſs?
To envy'd power? How low beneath all ſcorn
This court-diſſimulation ſinks mankind!

MUSTAPHA.

MUSTAPHA.

Fly, ACHMET, to EMIRA; greet her from me
With love's moſt ſacred vows—But ſmooth this news
With all the kind deceit, the virtuous falſhood,
That friendſhip bids us uſe, to ſave from anguiſh
The tender boſom of the fair we love.

SCENE IV.

MUSTAPHA, ZANGER.

ZANGER.

MUSTAPHA!

MUSTAPHA.

ZANGER!

ZANGER.

Brother of my love——
O greatly, dearly welcome!

MUSTAPHA.

O my ZANGER!
My heart has ſicken'd to transfuſe it ſelf
Into thy faithful boſom. Friendſhip mourn'd,
And found himſelf unbleſt for want of thee,
Thou ſoul of tenderneſs, to wake anew
His holy flame, and light it into rapture.

ZANGER.

O more than brother! O my nobler ſelf!
I ſwear by honor, by the ſacred inſtinct
That nature kindled in my infant breaſt,
That taſte improv'd, and reaſon makes immortal;
My ſoul that languiſh'd for thee, finds her powers
Reſtor'd to health and vigor in thy preſence:
Nor more refreſhing are the dews of heaven
To *Araby*'s dry deſart, than to me
Thy ſight and wiſh'd return!

MUSTAPHA.

May fame renounce

And ſcorn my name, if I not prize thy love
Beyond renown; beyond th'applauding ſhouts
Of myriads in the lawrel'd front of war.

ZANGER.

O thou haſt fir'd my ſoul! thy voice recalls
The days of glory, when I trac'd thy ſteps
Thro' honor's rugged paths to noble danger!
The watch by night; the weary march by day;
The battle's open rage; the dark aſſault,
Where unknown perils dwelt; the ſum of toils,
That fame impoſes, and ambition courts!

MUSTAPHA.

Ah, ZANGER—thoſe bleſt days are fled for ever!

ZANGER.

What ſays my Friend?

MUSTAPHA.

Alas! I am no more
That brother of the war, whoſe honeſt name
Thy partial love has laviſhly adorn'd.
ZANGER, in me thine eyes behold a ſlave,
Diſgrac'd! diſarm'd!

ZANGER.

O my preſaging heart!
The Vizir——

MUSTAPHA.

He.

ZANGER.

Blue plagues upon him!—yes,
I have of late, I have obſerv'd his viſage
O'ercaſt with dark reſerve; his ſpeech ambiguous,
Broken, and ſhifting quick, or pauſing ſhort.
Even when he talk'd no more, fell miſchief lour'd
And boded in his ſilence. But I thought not—
How could fair Honor think, his hell-born arts
Took aim at you?—It is not, cannot be.
Our father loves you to your worth's extent:
Then who dares be your foe?

MUSTAPHA.

MUSTAPHA.

I have not learnt
By what pernicious tales the Sultan's ear
Hath been abus'd: nor can thy plainneſs think,
Thy honeſt ſoul, what arrows of the dark
Cloſe Hatred ſhoots with; various, ſecret, ſudden,
And fatal every ſhaft. Some three moons paſt,
A preſent of delicious fruit was brought me;
The firſt and faireſt of the bounteous year;
Seaſon'd with complements of high regard;
And profer'd love. I bade the bearer taſte
What ſeem'd moſt exquiſite. 'Twas ſure my genius
That gave the ſtrong alarm. Th'unwary ſlave
Ate freely—But, O heaven! the lightning's flaſh
Scarce ſwifter kills. His ghaſtly eye-balls roll'd;
Convulſions ſhook his frame—he groan'd! he died!
Expir'd before mine eyes!—O noble ZANGER,
The hand from whence that mortal preſent came
I muſt not, will not gueſs!

ZANGER.

Do not, my brother:
Leſt I ſhould ſpurn all human ties, and curſe
Whom nature bids me reverence. Filial virtue!
Forgive the direful thought that wakens here—
Away—to harbor it were parricide—
Alas! my brother, friendſhip makes me impious!
And now, thy ſight, whence I had hop'd all joy—
Thy ſight diſtreſſes me—Why didſt thou come?
O cruel raſhneſs!—wherefore art thou here?
To heap damnation on their heads! on mine
Horror and ſure deſpair!

MUSTAPHA.

Look on me, ZANGER.
Thy virtuous ſoftneſs, while it charms, diſtracts me.
Let me not ſee thy tears—they melt away

My

My firmer heart—Indeed I am to blame
To wound thy gentle nature with this tale—
I am, by heaven—I ſhould have lock'd it up
Even from my own reflection for thy ſake.
Turn this way, hear me, friend.—Had I not come,
Not paid obedience to a father's order,
I had avow'd a guilt that fled the light,
And merited the fate I meanly ſhun'd:
Nay more, had furniſh'd to my honor's foe
Sure arms againſt my ſelf; to ſtab me, ZANGER,
Thro' all ſucceeding ages, in my fame?
And what are thouſand temporary deaths
To one, one cureleſs wound that bleeds for ever?
Well, OSMAN.

SCENE V.

MUSTAPHA, ZANGER,

OSMAN.

Sir, the Emperor approaches.
His orders are, Prince ZANGER ſhould retire:
He would confer with you in private.

ZANGER.

Brother!

MUSTAPHA. [*Embracing.*

ZANGER! heaven only knows or when or where
We meet again—Find ACHMET out: the ſecret
That moſt imports my ſoul, he can diſcloſe.
Friendſhip will teach thee how to act.—Farewel.

SCENE VI.

MUSTAPHA.

He comes. A nameleſs terror ſtirs my ſoul,

And ſpreads ſevere diſquiet thro' my boſom.
Why ſhould I fear? The man of guilt alone
Should feel diſorder—'Tis but nature's frailty;
Th' unbidden trembling of the various heart,
Where hopes and fears ariſe, and paſs by turns.

SCENE VII.

SOLYMAN, MUSTAPHA.

SOLYMAN.

MUSTAPHA, ſit——My order is obey'd:
And thou art come.

MUSTAPHA.

While life informs this frame,
Your will, my Lord—

SOLYMAN.

It now enjoins thee ſilence.
Attentive mark my words, till I command
An anſwer.—When that Power, whoſe will is fate,
Firſt call'd me to the cares of royalty;
And when thoſe cares had waken'd me to thought,
To grave reflection; Ignorance, I found,
Black, heavy, total, had o'erſpread my realms.
Her ſteril darkneſs, to a people rude
As nature at the birth of human-kind,
Seem'd venerable; ſeem'd the proper ſtate
Of greatneſs: and as blindneſs is moſt vain,
The proud Barbarians, all they knew not, ſcorn'd.
Amid this general night, I turn'd my view
Back to th' enlighten'd times of *Greece* and *Rome*;
The times of ſcience and of glorious deed:
And ſaw, with pleaſing wonder, to what heights
Inſtruction and example lift the mind!
Their ſtory I revolv'd; and reverent own'd

Their

Their polifh'd arts of rule, their human virtues;
The luftre and the dignity of man.
Till, what I long admir'd, at laft I try'd
To emulate: nor found the trial vain.
Hence was my foul with nobler aims enlarg'd
In war and peace. Heaven feconded my cares:
My neighbours fear'd, my fubjects bleft, my fway:
But chief my family, where blood-ftain'd Rage
No longer rioted in fcenes of death.
Thee, of my fons the eldeft, beft belov'd,
I cherifh'd with diftinguifh'd fondnefs; rear'd
In arts and arms; with morals and with honor
Seafon'd thy tender thought: whence, to my felf
I hop'd a worthy fon; and to mankind,
When fate fhould fummon me, an equal mafter.
This have I done: but where is my reward?
What hope, what comfort to my age remains,
If thou, impatient to afcend my throne,
Wouldft rather, now, invade it, than await
Till time and right have made it fairly thine?
Speak: thou haft leave.

MUSTAPHA.

For this indulgence, Sir,
To heaven and you I bend my heart in thanks:
And as I would deferve it, all my words
Shall be to holy truth feverely juft.
E'er fince reflection beam'd her light upon me,
You, Sir, have been my ftudy. I have plac'd
Before mine eyes, in every light of life,
The Father and the King. What weight of duty
Lay on a fon from fuch a parent fprung;
What virtuous toil to fhine with his renown;
Has been my thought by day, my dream by night.
True to the fair example in my view—
Forgive the boaft of youth—my aim has been

To merit rather than to wear a crown.
I courted fame, but as a ſpur to brave,
To honeſt deeds: and who deſpiſes fame,
Will ſoon renounce the virtues that deſerve it.
But firſt, and ever neareſt to my heart,
Was this prime duty; ſo to frame my conduct
Toward ſuch a father, as, were I a father,
My ſoul would wiſh to meet with from a ſon.
And may Reproach tranſmit my name abhor'd
To lateſt time—if ever thought was mine
Unjuſt to filial reverence, filial love!

SOLYMAN.

But yet, the genius of imperial rule,
All-incommunicable, knows no equal;
Nay knows no ſecond. Thou haſt borne thy ſelf
Above a ſubject's ſtate: by ſecret arts,
By dangerous popularity, haſt dar'd
To taint my armies, and divide their homage.
Too well I know the native bent of man:
From towering thoughts to traitorous deſigns
He climbs apace. If I at laſt muſt fear
A rival in my ſlave (for ſuch thou art)
Thy virtues all are crimes. And were there none,
Not one of OTHMAN's blood to heir his empire;
By that eternal Mind who form'd my ſoul!
If guilt is found upon thee—true, thy father
Will be unhappy—but thou art undone!

MUSTAPHA.

And may that Power, whoſe ever-waking eye
Explores the depth of human hearts, and ſees
Each wiſh, each ſecret purpoſe, riſing there,
Diſcloſe all mine before you!—O my father,
Source of my being, ever lov'd and honor'd,
Yes, let Inquiry, rigorous Inquiry,
Call the whole tenor of my life to tryal,

Severe,

Severe, impartial tryal. If ſuch crimes
Have ſtain'd me but in thought; let open ſhame.
Let tortures ſuch as wait the wretch accurs'd,
The parricide, attone their guilt.

SOLYMAN.

This wears
A face of virtue.—MUSTAPHA—the father
Would favor thee: the judge muſt know no biaſs:
Their differing titles call me ſeparate ways;
And each would have its due.

MUSTAPHA.

My failings, Sir,
Will want th' indulgence of a father's love:
My honeſty of heart dares well abide
The judge's ſearching eye.—O think, my Lord;
Why am I here alone? Had my own thoughts
Borne evidence againſt me, would I thus
Provoke examination? thus embrace
Perhaps the nobler, but th' unſafer, part?
For I have foes———

SOLYMAN.

What foes? Be warn'd, and know,
By charging others, guilt would ſcreen himſelf.

MUSTAPHA.

Look on me, Sir. Suſpected tho' I be,
I am your ſon: I ſtill inherit from you
A generous pride that cannot ſtoop to baſeneſs,
The baſeneſs of a lye. Moſt true, my foes
Had form'd a dark deſign againſt my life.

SOLYMAN.

Ha! what deſign?

MUSTAPHA.

By poiſon to deſtroy me.

SOLYMAN.

Poiſon? aſtoniſhment!

MUSTAPHA.

And of a kind
Exalted to ſuch power, ſuch deadly keenneſs,
That he, the ſlave who firſt aſſay'd its rage,
Taſted at once and died!

SOLYMAN.

Merciful heaven!

MUSTAPHA.

My people ſaw, and trembled to behold
The horrid ſcene!

SOLYMAN.

I tremble too——O Nature!
A parent cannot baniſh thee for ever——
Was no enquiry made? Canſt thou not gueſs
This cruel foe?

MUSTAPHA.

I can forgive, my Lord.

SOLYMAN.

What ſhould I think?—Thy brothers are thy friends.
My ROXOLANA——but 'tis profanation
To mention her. She never was thy foe.

MUSTAPHA.

I never gave her cauſe.

SOLYMAN.

Her faith to me
I oft have prov'd, and ever found ſincere.
Her tongue too has been laviſh in thy praiſe:
By heaven, it has.

MUSTAPHA.

Betwixt my foes and me
Let heaven be judge.—But if their arts can win
On him, a father whom my ſoul reveres
With all the ſanctity of truth and love,
To think me baſe, ungrateful and unjuſt:
Hear, Honor! and approve me while I ſwear—[*Kneels.*

I

I envy that poor ſlave! I would be now
As he is—Pangs like mine were well exchang'd
For death's ſhort agonies——

SOLYMAN.

Forbid it, Virtue!
Thou muſt not talk thus.

MUSTAPHA.

Had I periſh'd then,
I ſhould have clos'd mine eyes in peace—convinc'd,
You never thought me falſe—convinc'd, my fate,
Unmerited, untimely, would have drawn
A tear of pity from a parent's eye——
Alas! my Lord——

SOLYMAN.

O MUSTAPHA—my ſon!—
For ſuch again thou art, belov'd! endear'd!
I mix my tears with thine.

MUSTAPHA.

My king and father!
'Tis joy, 'tis bliſs too powerful clouds my ſight
With this ſoft moiſture.

SOLYMAN.

Hence each doubt and fear,
Children of dark diſtruſt. My ſoul receives thee
To love and confidence.—And now, my ſon——
But whence theſe horrid ſhouts?—OSMAN, what news?

SCENE VIII.

SOLYMAN, MUSTAPHA,

OSMAN.

My Lord, a ſudden mutiny ſpreads ſwift
Among the troops. The Janizaries chief
Croud from their tents, and cry to arms.

SOLY-

SOLYMAN.

Confuſion!
To arms?—Speak, MUSTAPHA, what may this mean?

MUSTAPHA.

So heaven befriend my ſoul as I am loſt
In horror and amaze——But haſte, my Lord,
And meet bold treaſon in its mid career.

SCENE IX.

SOLYMAN, MUSTAPHA, OSMAN,

RUSTAN.

Appear, great Emperor, or all is loſt.
The traitors arm'd, and furious in their rage,
Surround your tent——

SOLYMAN.

How!—MUSTAPHA, I will not
Pronounce thee guilty——But this hour muſt fix
The name of ſon or parricide upon thee.

MUSTAPHA.

Sir, I provoke the tryal.

SCENE X.

RUSTAN.

Curſt event!
The danger imminent and ſure is mine.
Should they demand my head—By hell! 'tis theirs.
To ſave himſelf, the Sultan will reſign
His miniſter: that fatal policy
Long cuſtom has made ſacred——Dire Ambition!
By following thee, I headlong urge my fate,
And change ſecure repoſe for wretched ſtate.

The End of the Second Act.

ACT III. SCENE I.

ROXOLANA, MUFTI.

ROXOLANA.

WHERE will this fearful revolution end?
And who muſt fall the ſacrifice of fate,
RUSTAN or MUSTAPHA?

MUFTI.

Their fury ſeems
As if inflam'd, and chequ'd, by one ſole will,
Unlike the wavering multitude.

ROXOLANA.

That ſhows
Moſt terrible!

MUFTI.

It would be——but for him,
Their idol MUSTAPHA, whoſe pride of ſoul——
Or call it loyalty——will ſurely prompt him,
With oſtentation, to repreſs at once
The ſtorm his fancy'd danger has arrous'd.

ROXOLANA.

Doſt thou believe ſo, MUFTI?

MUFTI.

Hold it, Madam,
A moſt undoubted truth: and that on you
No other labour lies, but to perplex
By ſtudy'd doubts and fears the Sultan's ſpirit;
To hint his certain ruin from a ſon

So dangeroufly powerful o'er the paffions
Of men inur'd to turbulence and treafons.

ROXOLANA.

My better angel warns me from thy lips:
And, MUFTI, thou fhalt find me nobly grateful.
RUSTAN, what news?

SCENE II.

ROXOLANA, MUFTI, RUSTAN.

RUSTAN.

This tumult threaten'd more
Than even my fears furmiz'd. Already were
Thofe daring traitors pour'd around the grove
That fhades this tent; a mighty hoft in arms,
Outragious, clamouring high for MUSTAPHA,
And menacing perdition to his foes;
But chief to me.

ROXOLANA.

Audacious flaves!——but on.

RUSTAN.

In that nice moment, SOLYMAN appear'd
Superior and unmov'd. At fight of him,
A fpace they ftood confounded and appall'd.

MUFTI.

The multitude unaw'd is infolent;
Once feiz'd with fear, contemptible and vain.

RUSTAN.

Yet, MUFTI, when they caft their eyes abroad
On their own gather'd ftrength, rekindled rage
Spoke loud their madnefs in tempeftuous fhouts,
And mingled uproar. I beheld from far
The various horror; how at once they rag'd,
At once kept filence: and, as thwarting paffions

By turns prevail'd, were dreadful and dismay'd!

ROXOLANA.

What follow'd this?

RUSTAN.

Just then——but I could wish
To leave that part untold——the Prince rush'd in;
His look with grief and anger deep impress'd,
His bosom naked to their swords——" Strike here;
" Here point your rage, he cry'd. I, only I
" Am guilty——if your impious arms have dar'd,
" In violation of th' allegiance due
" From subjects, chief from me, to menace him
" Who reigns supreme o'er all."

MUFTI.

Why did they not,
O Prophet! fairly take him at his word?

RUSTAN.

This, with strong transport utter'd, and enforc'd
By bursting tears, which indignation shed,
Amaz'd, abash'd them into fear and shame.
At once they crouded round the rais'd tribunal;
Threw down their arms at once, and prostrate begg'd
For pardon, or for death.——I would not dwell
Upon the sequel. MUSTAPHA's demeanor
Has won anew his father's heart, and wrought
A firmer reconcilement.

ROXOLANA.

Wrought our ruin;
If this be so.

MUFTI.

An enterprize like ours,
Rais'd to this fateful point, must be accomplish'd,
Or crush its authors.

RUSTAN.

There is no return.
No; we must on, must pass the perilous flood:

To venture backward from this depth, we risque
Inevitable sinking.

ROXOLANA.

Ha!———it dawns:
Thy counsel, MUFTI, breaks upon my thought,
Like morning o'er the shades of night. We yet
Shall counterwork our fate. This paper too,
Even from the friends of MUSTAPHA procur'd,
May serve to urge his fate.—The Sultan comes.
Retire, my Lords—Stay, RUSTAN: I may want
Thy present aid. Now recollect thy soul,
And second what I say.

SCENE III.

SOLYMAN, ROXOLANA, RUSTAN.

SOLYMAN.

Presumptuous slaves!———
These accidents in such a state as this is,
By laws unfix'd, are ever to be fear'd,
Are often fatal.——This alarming storm
Is past, my love: and tho' the rage of tumults
Has from old time shook sore our empire's frame,
Nay buried monarchs in the general wreck,
This last I can forgive. It shew'd me plain
The soul of MUSTAPHA. With care I watch'd
Th' emotions springing from his inmost breast,
There where no art has power: and found them true
To virtue and to me. I know this news,
To her whose dearest happiness is mine,
Will be most welcome.

ROXOLANA.

You are just, my Lord;
Just to us both. I triumph in your joy,
And wish it all sincere.

SOLYMAN.

SOLYMAN.

Long peace, I find,
But nurses dangerous humours up to strength,
Licence and wanton rage; which war alone
Can purge away. I will resume my arms.
The *Persian*, whom I deadly hate, must down.
Some slight advantage by his troops obtain'd——
I fought not there——has swell'd his inborn pride
Above all equal bounds. But ere the sun
Lights up another morn, my powers shall hence
To scourge that pride. A rougher season now,
My ROXOLANA, must divide the hearts,
It shall not change.

ROXOLANA.

Mine is not in the power
Of time or accident. This faithful breast
Will know no hour of joy, till favouring heaven
Restore you, bright with conquest, to these arms.
But——is all well, my Lord?

SOLYMAN.

All well!

ROXOLANA.

Alas!

SOLYMAN.

Ha! what alarms thee?

ROXOLANA.

Does my Lord believe,
His lowly handmaid loves him?

SOLYMAN.

Most unkind!
Why dost thou kneel, and hang upon my robe?

ROXOLANA.

O SOLYMAN——But wilt thou then forgive
The woman's softness? those presaging thoughts
That wish, yet doubt thy safety?

SOLYMAN.

SOLYMAN.

Safety! what,
What wouldst thou say?

ROXOLANA.

O may my fears be vain!
But when my thought recalls this horrid tumult;
Recalls th' unbounded insolence that spread
So fast, and rag'd so high; when I revolve
The cause that spirited those factious men
To such bold outrage——can I chuse but weep,
And tremble for thy life?

SOLYMAN.

My life!

RUSTAN, *aside.*

Well said.
Exquisite woman!

ROXOLANA.

Have they not presum'd
On idle rumors——rumors too that fix
The name of murderer on you——here to judge
Betwixt you and your son? to give you laws?
As if the sovereign power was in their hands!
And you their slave!

SOLYMAN.

Ha!—ROXOLANA—RUSTAN!

RUSTAN.

She speaks a dreadful truth! Power is no more;
Authority is lost, when rebel subjects dare,
With curious boldness, scan their master's right,
Control his royal pleasure, and rejudge
His highest acts. Contempt unkings a sovereign.

SOLYMAN.

Contempt!——perdition!—Am I vilely fallen
To that dishonor?

RUSTAN.

RUSTAN.

You are ſtill yourſelf,
Great, valiant, glorious: but ungrateful ſubjects,
Wanton with wealth and eaſe, may wiſh to change
The happy preſent for th' uncertain future———
Alas, I go too far; you droop, my Lord.

SOLYMAN.

Away——What ſhould I fear? My ſon's known virtue
Forbids a doubt of him.

ROXOLANA.

How I have lov'd,
How oft with rapture dwelt upon his name,
You, SOLYMAN, beſt know. But duty now
Shall triumph o'er that fondneſs——This wild ſtorm
He with a breath appeas'd.

SOLYMAN.

He did.

ROXOLANA.

Grant heaven
I be miſtaken!—That ſame breath can raiſe
A ſecond, wilder far; and bid it burſt
On me——would that were all!—alas on you!
Even on your ſacred head——for who will then
Bid the rous'd ocean peace? or drive its ſurge
With govern'd fury?

SOLYMAN.

Hold I then a crown
Precarious and dependent on the nod,
The caprice of another?——ROXOLANA!
Thou doſt not think ſo.

ROXOLANA.

Would I could not think it.
O who can ſound the ſecret heart of man?———
Pardon my anxious love——His thoughts are hid,
His real aims unſeen: his power is known,
Is evident and felt.

SOLY-

SOLYMAN.

Woman, by heaven!
Thy words dart light into my darken'd ſoul——
There muſt be treachery. Who told thoſe rebels
I ſought his life? What friend of mine would ſay,
That danger threaten'd him?

RUSTAN.

O juſtly thought.
Did ROXOLANA, did your ſlave, whoſe head
They loudly call'd for, bid the traitors riſe,
To plunge their daggers in our breaſts?

SOLYMAN.

'Tis plain.——
Who, who would be a father?—Friends, you weep
In pity of my fate!——I too could pour
A breaking heart in tears.

ROXOLANA.

O may the news,
This paper holds, be falſe as Calumny,
As Malice can deviſe.

SOLYMAN.

What news? what paper?
Whence comes it?

RUSTAN.

From *Amaſia*, Sir: a ſlave
Deliver'd it but now.

SOLYMAN.

I dread to look
Upon this fatal paper——Ha! it ſpeaks
" Of peace at hand; of terms the *Perſian* offers."——
" That monarch courts with ardent love and ſervice
" My favourite ſon"—Why trembles thus my frame?
What dire ſuggeſtions, conjur'd up at once
In fiend-like ſhapes, ſpread horror thro' my breaſt?
Where am I?—What?—depos'd? plung'd in a dungeon,
To drag out weary life to its laſt verge,

A

A ſlave! a nameleſs reptile!——Theſe ſtrong warnings
Are heaven's impreſſive hand.——But how reſolve?
How ſatisfy my vengeance and my fame?
My ſtormy ſoul yet knows not, dares not yet
Acknowledge to itſelf.

ROXOLANA *looking after him.*

The Mufti ſoon
Shall clear that doubt.

SCENE IV.

RUSTAN.

We are not yet ſecure.
Fond nature may return, and baffle all
Our labour'd ſchemes.——Ambition! deadly tyrant!
Inexorable maſter! what alarms,
What anxious hours, what agonies of heart,
Are the ſure portion of thy gaudy ſlaves?
Cruel condition! Could the toiling hind,
The ſhivering beggar, whom no roof receives,
Wet with the mountain ſhower, and crouching low
Beneath the naked cliff, his only home;
Could he but read the ſtateſman's ſecret breaſt,
But ſee the horrors there, the wounds, the ſtabs,
From furious paſſions and avenging guilt:
He would not change his rags and wretchedneſs,
For gilded domes and greatneſs!

SCENE V.

ZANGER, RUSTAN.

ZANGER.

RUSTAN! yes,
Alone and musing——Soft: I will repress
Th' indignant rage my honest bosom swells with,
And speak him fair.

RUSTAN.

I heard a noise—Prince ZANGER!

ZANGER.

You seem wrapt up in meditation, Vizir.

RUSTAN.

I have been thinking what sweet peace attends
The homely shepherd's life.

ZANGER.

Can such a life
Provoke a great man's envy?

RUSTAN.

Sir, forgive me:
I must attend the Sultan.

ZANGER.

Vizir, stay:
The Sultan is retir'd. I saw and mark'd
His visage, ruffled with tempestuous passions.
I know the dreadful cause: thou too must know,
Some instant peril menaces a life
That mine but lives in. RUSTAN, by the names,
The sacred names of honor and renown!
Now join thy influence with mine, and save
The noblest of his race.

RUSTAN.

RUSTAN.

Save whom, young Prince?

ZANGER.

Whom! holds the world a ſecond MUSTAPHA?
Vizir, believe me, this one glorious deed,
Were thy life ſtain'd and foul with every crime,
Would waſh out all.

RUSTAN.

You much amaze me, Prince.
Is it for me to trace the ſecret ſprings
That act my ſovereign's will? or croſs its workings?
Be far that curious raſhneſs from my thought.
But what alarms you thus? I have not learnt
What fate impends o'er MUSTAPHA—and yet
Suppoſe——'twere death.

ZANGER.

Ha! Vizir——

RUSTAN.

Yours, my Lord,
Is all the gain.

ZANGER.

O Prophet!

RUSTAN.

He remov'd,
You are this empire's heir.

ZANGER.

By that ſole Being
Who governs all events! I would not reign,
In wrong to him, the maſter of mankind.

RUSTAN.

Fine air-built notions, Prince. The wiſe have thought,
That power, howe'er acquir'd, is ſovereign good.
Devoted to your ſervice, let me ſpeak
With uſeful freedom. Be adviſ'd in time;

Renounce a friendſhip that avails not him,
And may to you prove fatal.

ZANGER.

Sure thou doſt not,
All-ſtateſman as thou art, thou canſt not mean
The horrors thou haſt utter'd? Were I, Vizir,
This empire's lord, my firſt, my deareſt care,
Should be rewarding thee, even to the full,
For giving righteous counſel.

RUSTAN.

My advice
Beſpeaks my hearty love, and merits not
Such harſh and proud return.

ZANGER.

Thou earth-born ſlave!——
I thought to have reſtrain'd me———but thy baſeneſs
Arrouſes me beyond diſſembling.———No:
Thy counſel periſh with thee———Heaven! is he,
Are ſuch as he the men whom princes truſt?
And muſt the fate, the ſafety or deſtruction
Of millions, each leſs guilty than himſelf,
Hang on the breath of one whom thou muſt hate?
O providence! is human race no more
The object of thy care?———Why end I not,
Even here, his life and crimes?

RUSTAN.

Prince, have a care;
Nay handle not your ſword. Theſe ſtarts of youth,
Swelling and frantic, touch not, move not me.
Yet know———that but for her, my royal miſtreſs,
Who loves thee, and to whom my duty bends———
This threat might coſt thee dear.

SCENE

SCENE VI.

ZANGER.

How could I hope
To melt a heart like his? What now remains?
Said he, my mother loves me? then I know
Where even her breaſt is vulnerab'e. Yes;
It is determin'd—If my friend muſt fall;
This righteous ſword, thro' mine, ſhall reach her heart.

SCENE VII.

MUSTAPHA, ZANGER.

ZANGER.

Nature and friendſhip!—how they tear my boſom?
How wound my inmoſt ſoul?

MUSTAPHA.

What means my brother?

ZANGER.

I know not what has wrought this fatal change:
Some moments paſt, the Sultan croſs'd my walk;
His brow was knit in frowns, his eye look'd ruin—
This villain-ſtateſman too has talk'd ſuch things!—
Thy ruin is reſolv'd on.

MUSTAPHA.

Be it ſo.
Life is beneath my care; nor can I wiſh
To wear it longer, if a father deems me
Unworthy to partake the common bleſſing,
All creatures ſhare in.

ZANGER.

MUSTAPHA, no more.

Self.

Self-preſervation is heaven's eldeſt law,
Impreſt upon our nature with our life
In characters indelible. Who ſhrinks
From this great cauſe is wanting to his reaſon:
But when our honor is traduc'd and ſtab'd at,
'Tis virtue, 'tis heroic fortitude,
Then to encounter violence with force.

MUSTAPHA.

What force, my ZANGER, ſhall a ſon employ
Againſt the ſacred life that gave him being?
In me, reſiſtance would be parricide:
That guilt I dread; I cannot fear to die.

ZANGER.

Fly then: prevent th' enormous guilt of others
By timely flight.

MUSTAPHA.

And ſo avow the crime
My foes would fix, in all its blackneſs, on me?
Such cowardice were treaſon to my ſelf.
Think, ZANGER, for us both.

ZANGER.

What can I think,
But that you charm th' unhappy breaſt you wound?
O MUSTAPHA!—yet can your virtue bear
To ſee our father ſtain himſelf with blood?
The blood that Nature, Honor, bid him ſpare?
He is no more the Monarch, Europe, Aſia,
Have trembled at. His amorous weakneſs grows
To dotage: and has robb'd him of himſelf.
Slave to a woman's will—I would forget
She gave me birth—and to a miniſter,
Familiar with all guilt; behold his ſword,
That ſhould be drawn for juſtice, turn'd to murder!
To perpetrate th' offence it ſhould revenge!
And will not you by honeſt flight prevent

His

His ſin and ſhame? prevent the ſure reproach
That muſt deſcend for ever on his name?
The brand of murderer?

MUSTAPHA.

ZANGER, ſhould I fly—
No other choice is mine—I muſt unſheathe
The all-devouring ſword. Then what enſues?
Revolt, inteſtine broils, the baneful train
Of crimes and miſeries that wait on war.
Shall I, good heaven! to breathe this idle air
A few years longer, load me with the ſins
And blood of thouſands? ſhake an empire's peace,
Unhinge its frame, and rend it with convulſions?
Is life worth ſaving at ſuch mighty coſt?
Compar'd with this, can death be terrible?

ZANGER.

The crime is theirs who force you into arms.
On them alone, the rapines that ſhall waſte,
The flames that ſhall devour, our fields, our towns,
The blood that ſhall be ſpilt, for ever reſts.
Yet more; a Prince's life is not his own:
Not for himſelf, he lives for human race.
This univerſal duty to your kind
Cancels all private bonds. The future bliſs,
Or woe of millions, you were born to rule,
Hangs on your great reſolve.

MUSTAPHA.

I hear with wonder
The glorious counſel which I muſt not take.
No end is noble where the means are baſe.
What? violate allegiance, duty, nature?
Wade on thro' cruelty, rebellion, ruin?
Thro' all the varied guiltineſs of war?
And riſe to empire by ten thouſand horrors,
That ſubjects may, at laſt, have cauſe to bleſs

A

A ſovereign, thus exalted?—No, my friend;
Heaven means not me its inſtrument of good,
If but by ways like theſe I muſt effect it.
Brother—farewel: I leave the world with joy,
Leaving it thee!

ZANGER.

O cruel—godlike friend!
Canſt thou reſolve on death, and bid me live?

MUSTAPHA.

Yes, live, my brother, live to bleſs mankind.
Shew wondering nations what a Monarch ſhould be;
Heaven's true Vicegerent, whoſe ſuperior ſoul,
Rais'd high above the tyrant's ſelfiſh poorneſs,
Pants but for power of doing good, rejects
All power of doing ill; who makes no war
But to revenge his people's wrongs, no peace
But what ſecures their ſafety; courts no fame
But from their happineſs: a parent he,
The public parent; they not ſlaves, but ſons.

ZANGER.

Thou ſhalt not go. This moment yet remains;
Perhaps the laſt—Does friendſhip plead in vain?
Yet if thine ear is deaf to ZANGER's call——
Think of EMIRA! think of her, my brother,
To whom thy ſoul has wedded all its wiſhes!
Canſt thou abandon her? be deaf to love?
The pleading voice of love, and youth, and beauty,
Deſpairing, dying in thy death?

MUSTAPHA.

Ah friend,
What haſt thou done? Why doſt thou ſound my heart,
To ſhew me I am man? frail, fearful man?
Why, ZANGER, haſt thou brought to light a weakneſs,
I would have kept in darkneſs from all eyes?
Even from my ſelf? or wept in ſilence o'er it,
My laſt unconquerable fondneſs?

ZANGER.

ZANGER.

See !——
She comes. What grace, what noble ſweetneſs ſhines,
Victorious, in her opening ſpring of charms !

MUSTAPHA.

O go, my brother ; leave me to my ſelf :
My heart runs o'er with paſſion, nor can bear
Even a friend's eye ſhould read its tender follies.

SCENE VIII.

EMIRA, MUSTAPHA.

MUSTAPHA.

EMIRA !

EMIRA.

Prince !—what mean theſe eager tremblings ?
This troubled ſilence ?

MUSTAPHA.

O my ſoul's beſt joy !
At ſight of thee, I feel—I know not what :
My beating heart is all a ſoft confuſion
Of fears and wiſhes, tenderneſs and tears—
Bleſt heaven !

EMIRA.

My Lord !—why are you thus alarm'd ?
Ah ! have you then deceiv'd me ? Was the peace,
The reconcilement with your royal father
But feign'd to ſoothe me with betraying hopes ?
Cruel—

MUSTAPHA.

EMIRA, I am much to blame :
And manhood murmurs at the fond conſent
That has expos'd thee, in this doubtful journey,
To danger and alarms. Love made me weak,

Even made me cruel!

EMIRA.

Prince, why am I yours
But to divide your cares? to ſhare your fortunes?
I feel no danger, MUSTAPHA, but thine;
No fears but for thy ſafety.

MUSTAPHA.

Knowing that,
I know too much, and therefore am moſt wretched!

EMIRA.

Ha! thou art pale—why doſt thou hide thee from me?
What fatal change has happen'd?

MUSTAPHA.

Dear EMIRA!
Thou amiable goodneſs! ſtop theſe tears.
There is no preſent danger; none, my love.
But let me place thee ſafe beyond the din,
Beyond the rage of war—for war is threaten'd.
Now while the friendly ſhades of night deſcend,
Let ACHMET guide thee hence.

EMIRA.

Inhuman! oh—
You hide ſome horrid ſecret from mine ear.
What leave thee? fly with ACHMET at this hour?
Muſt then EMIRA be the laſt to know,
She is for ever wretched?

MUSTAPHA.

No, my Love:
Our parting ſhall be ſhort—Nay hang not on me:
Reſiſt not with thy tears. I muſt a while,
Refuſing thee, deny my ſoul its comfort—
See ACHMET comes.—'Tis well. Retire at once.

[Achmet *whiſpers him.*

Angels conduct thy ſteps!

EMIRA.

O loſt EMIRA!

SCENE IX.

MUSTAPHA, OSMAN.

OSMAN.

The Sultan, on whoſe head be peace and bleſſing!
Commands, my Lord, you ſhould expect his pleaſure
Alone in that pavilion.

MUSTAPHA.

I obey.
O heaven-born patience! ſource of peace and reſt,
Deſcend; infuſe thy ſpirit thro' my breaſt;
That I may calmly meet the hour of fate,
My foes forgive and triumph o'er their hate.
This body let their engines tear and grind;
But let not all their racks ſubdue my mind.

The End of the Third Act.

ACT IV. SCENE I.

RUSTAN, MUFTI.

RUSTAN.

THE night looks black and boding. Darkneſs fell
Precipitate and heavy o'er the world;
At once extinguiſhing the ſun: and lo!
What clouds aſcending deepen ſhade on ſhade.
Some ruffling ſtorm is nigh. But are we ſafe?
Are we alone? I would be ſhrouded cloſe
From mortal eye and ear. Liſt—

MUFTI.

All is ſtill.

RUSTAN.

Then tell me—for my ſoul impatient longs
To hear the news—What has our dreaded Lord
At laſt reſolv'd?

MUFTI.

I follow'd to his tent.
The ſcene was terrible. His mind appear'd
A mighty ocean ſtir'd by fighting winds.
His pace uncertain, fury in his aſpect,
His boſom heaving with convulſive thoughts,
By turns he caſt his eyes ſevere on heaven;
By turns he bent them gloomy on the ground:
A pauſe of ſilence where dumb horror reign'd,
More wild and more expreſſive to the ſight,
Than on the ear the ſtorm of words can pour.

RUSTAN.

RUSTAN.

Proceed, my Lord.

MUFTI.

At laſt, in broken ſounds
By paſſion render'd vehement and low;
"MUFTI, he cry'd, how ſays our ſacred law?
"What doom inflicts it on a truſted ſlave,
"Who plots deſtruction to his maſter's houſe?
"In cloſe conjunction with their foe profeſt,
"A rancorous heretic—"

RUSTAN.

He meant the *Perſian*;
Who long has courted MUSTAPHA in private.
Well, you reply'd—

MUFTI.

His blood be on my head.
Thus ſtain'd and black with complicated guilt,
He merits more than death; chief for his league
With heretics, a race on earth abhor'd,
Accurſt of heaven.

RUSTAN.

Ay, that was well, my Lord;
And after SOLYMAN's own heart. I hope
You urg'd it home with weight of argument.

MUFTI.

I did: and prov'd all hereſy more black,
More peſtilent, than even the falſe belief
Of Chriſtian dogs. He bow'd his head profound,
Invoking heaven, atteſting MAHOMET:
And cry'd—"This ſon muſt periſh. Not a world,
"A pleading world ſhould ſave him from my juſtice."
Then order'd his confinement.

RUSTAN.

Ha! confinement?
By AZRAEL, the angel that muſt ſever
His ſoul and mortal part! I was in hopes,

His

His execution, MUFTI, had been order'd.
This tardy vengeance dashes half my joys:
'Tis dangerous, and may be deadly to us.
Would I had ne'er embarqu'd on this wild sea,
Where tempest ever rages!—conscience too
Now sharpens all her stings—

MUFTI.

Away, my Lord;
What are you doing but what thousand statesmen,
Who liv'd and died in fame, have done before you?
He shall not scape. I have fresh accusations,
That with the Sultan's piety will weigh
More strong than all his crimes. This MUSTAPHA
Is a rank unbeliever.

RUSTAN.

How, my Lord?
This news revives my heart.

MUFTI.

Inflam'd with zeal,
And holy hatred to the foes of heaven,
Jews, Christians, who pollute our pious land,
I would have wrought that boy to prompt his father
In giving to the sword those infidels.
What was his answer, think you?

RUSTAN.

I can guess:
Some libertine reply.

MUFTI.

'Twas most profane!
He pointed to a plain that lay before us,
Profusely gay with flowers—" Admire, he cry'd,
" Wise nature's various hand: a thousand colors
" A thousand odors, greet the sight and smell.
" Fair suns arise, and genial dews descend
" To foster all alike: and in return,
" They waft their mingled incense to the sky,

" A grateful offering there. Perhaps 'tis ſo
" With difference in opinions : this at leaſt,
" They have their uſe ; nor ſhall they want protection,
" While thoſe who hold them live, as ſubjects ſhould,
" In amity and peace, promoting each
" The general wealth, obſervant of the laws,
" And to their ſovereign true."—He ſaid : and turn'd
Abruptly from me, frowning ſcorn and anger.

RUSTAN.

I thank thee for this news : but go, my Lord,
Watch near the Sultan's door. I will the while
Walk here and meditate.

SCENE II.

RUSTAN.

Uncertainty !
Fell demon of our fears ! the human ſoul,
That can ſupport deſpair, ſupports not thee !
The ſon yet lives—the father may relent :
What then becomes of RUSTAN ?—By the night !
By this dead darkneſs that involves the world !
The murderer, in ſome loneſome dungeon ſunk,
Not with more dread, more ſhaking apprehenſion,
Awaits the hour, the midnight hour that brings
Back from his tomb, in hideous viſitation,
The bleeding Shadow of the ſlain—than I
The iſſue of this thing.—Huſh—

SCENE III.

ROXOLANA, RUSTAN.

ROXOLANA.

RUSTAN ! ſpeak,
Say, is it done ?

RUSTAN.

O would to heaven it were!
Or ne'er had been attempted!

ROXOLANA.

Be of courage.
Expect the fatal mandate that at once
Will end all fears.

RUSTAN.

I wait it with the dread,
The agoniz'd impatience of a man
Who liſtens for the ſentence that muſt ſave,
Or end his being—Sure I heard a noiſe!

ROXOLANA.

Let not vain terrors of the night deſtroy
Thy ſtrength of reaſon. Arm thee for th' event.
Where is Prince ZANGER?

RUSTAN.

Madam, we are obſerv'd.
'Tis he—

ROXOLANA.

Leave us.—I ſee him much diſturb'd.

SCENE IV.

ROXOLANA, ZANGER.

ROXOLANA, *after a pauſe.*

Why art thou ſilent? What hath mov'd thee thus?

ZANGER.

I would have read my ſentence in your eyes;
Whether they doom your ſon to life or death.

ROXOLANA.

What wouldſt thou ſay?

ZANGER.

O hear me; hear and ſave:
Screen my lov'd brother from the ſhameful fate

That

That hovers o'er him. Fly, prevent a father—
You only can—from plunging into blood:
And from the ſting of conſcience that will goad him
To his laſt hour.

ROXOLANA.

ZANGER, I know thy follies.
Deaf to ambition's glorious call, and blind
To ſovereign power that ſpreads its dazling charms,
The ruling ſceptre, ſtarry diadem,
Before thy ſight and now within thy reach;
Unſpirited and poor! thou wouldſt depend
For food and raiment on another's nod:
Grow baſely old, unactive, loſt to fame,
Nor know the peaſant's privilege, to eat
Thy wretched meal ſecure: but ſtill unſafe,
And trembling ſtill, each fearful hour expect,
As rage or caprice guides thy tyrant's will,
The bowl or poniard.

ZANGER.

Be more juſt to both.
Nor would I ſuffer, nor will he impoſe,
Such brutal treatment. O you know him not:
A ſoul with every goodneſs, every worth,
Enrich'd, accompliſh'd—

ROXOLANA.

I will hear no more.
A mother's fondneſs for thee bids me pity
What elſe my heart would ſcorn: and leave thy blindneſs
To its due portion of contempt and wrongs.
Shake off this dull ſimplicity of ſoul,
Unworthy me, defeating all my ſchemes
For empire and for glory. Every aim,
Th' important travel of my thoughts, is all
For thee alone. Awake, expand thy views
To greatneſs, and deſerve my noble cares.

ZANGER.

O ſacred honor! does ſome dire illuſion

Dazle my ſenſe?—I view my ſelf with horror!
Heaven! was I born to be the bane of virtue?
To baniſh from her heart, who gave me life,
All human thoughts? all goodneſs?

ROXOLANA.

Thou haſt learnt
Of MUSTAPHA! and art, I find, right apt
To profit by ſuch leſſons!—yet—be wiſe:
He who adopts his crimes may ſhare his fate!

ZANGER.

What are his crimes?

ROXOLANA.

His birth-right. He was born
To reign thy maſter: he might live to ſee
A ſlave in ROXOLANA.

ZANGER.

Yet, 'tis heaven,
Not MUSTAPHA, you ſhould accuſe.

ROXOLANA.

Accuſe?
No; fruitleſs, fond complaining ſuits not me.
I will prevent, and puniſh.

ZANGER.

Then ſtrike here:
I am the criminal.

ROXOLANA.

Thy folly is;
Thy milky ſoftneſs uninform'd, unwarm'd
By brave ambition.

ZANGER.

Rather ſay, not ſear'd
By hate, not ſavag'd by remorſeleſs rage.

ROXOLANA.

How! does thy madneſs loſe all reverent ſenſe
Of love and duty to a parent due?
Unnatural and ingrate!

ZANGER.

ZANGER.

What is my fault?

ROXOLANA.

All I am doing for thee.

ZANGER.

Have I wiſh'd?
Have I contriv'd that guilt?

ROXOLANA.

Yet is it thine.
The guilt is his who profits by it.

ZANGER.

No:
Such gains my ſoul renounces. Can a world
A purchas'd world advantage him, who pays
His virtue for the purchaſe?——Yet recall,
My mother, O recall your better mind, [*he kneels.*
That feeling pity, that ſoft ſenſe of goodneſs,
The grace and glory of the gentler ſex.
Now, Madam, while the Sultan's awful will
Yet wavers unreſolv'd; addreſs his mercy,
His juſtice, ſave him from the worſt of crimes!
Theſe moments are moſt precious————

ROXOLANA.

ZANGER, riſe,
And heedful mark me——'tis my laſt advice,
My kindeſt—Rouſe thee from this dreaming fondneſs,
This ſoul-debaſing narrowneſs of purpoſe.
Reſolve to ſecond me, to aid my views;
Or ſhare thy brother's fate.

ZANGER.

His fate I envy.
He dies with all his virtue, all his fame:
Nor is his parting ſoul inſulted, poiſon'd,
By ſuch dire offers—Gracious heaven!

ROXOLANA.

Go on.

ZANGER.

I dare not: nature, honor, cheque my tongue.

ROXOLANA.

'Tis well—thou voluntary wretch! henceforth
I hold thee as an alien to my love.
Tremble. This hand may ſend thee——

ZANGER.

Should it prove
Another murderous preſent——

ROXOLANA.

Ha!

ZANGER.

'Twould be
More welcome than an empire on ſuch terms.

ROXOLANA.

Thy choice be thine. I caſt thee from my heart;
Renounce thee; know thee for no ſon of mine.
Thou ſlave in ſoul! this moment is thy laſt:
This moment joins thee to thy brother's doom!

[*returning*.

ZANGER—be warn'd.—I feel I love thee ſtill——
The mother riſes o'er the woman's rage,
And bids me ſpare thee——'Tis thy cauſe I plead——
Inhuman! why are all my cares, my labors,
If not for thee!——Reply not: but obey————
Thou ſeeſt my tears: in them the parent ſee—
Diſtract me not: my life is in thy hands,
My fame, my all on earth!——Remember too,
That from this hour my bleſſing, or my curſe,
Is thine for ever!

SCENE V.

ZANGER.

O there needs not that:
'Tis curſe enough that I was born of thee.

Supreme

Supreme Difpofer of the world!——But no;
I dare not imprecate thy vengeance here!
What can I more? My thoughts are one wild whirl
Of horror and defpair——Ah Princefs!

SCENE VI.

EMIRA, ZANGER.

EMIRA.

Brother!
Where is my Lord?—They would have torn me hence;
Have carried me to fafe inglorious diftance:
Love would not hear of parting!

ZANGER.

Heaven and earth
Confpire againft us! Whither fhall I turn me?
What fhall I counfel thee——But fee——the Sultan!

EMIRA.

Ah where?

ZANGER.

EMIRA——on this moment hangs
Our laft, our only hope.——Fall at his knees,
Befeech, adjure him. Youth and grace like thine
May reach his foul, and melt him into nature.
Difclofe thy ftory: tell him with thy tears,
With all the moving foftnefs of diftrefs,
The fecret of your hearts. Who knows but heaven
May greatly interpofe its fovereign aid
For injur'd virtue and imploring love——
But I muft hence unfeen.

EMIRA.

Alarming tryal!

SCENE

SCENE VII.

SOLYMAN, EMIRA.

SOLYMAN.

In change of place there is no change of pain.
Contending paſſions urging each its claim,
Tear up my boſom with inteſtine war.
Shall treaſon go unpuniſh'd? Shall I dip
My hands in filial blood? O fatal choice!
O cruel conflict! Have I liv'd till now
A parent——not a murderer? Muſt I late,
When my white age is bending to the grave,
Pollute me with that ſtain?——O MUSTAPHA!
Thou haſt undone my fame————
What bright unknown
Attracts my eyes, and charms away my rage.
Fancy not fairer paints thoſe heaven-born maids,
Daughters of paradiſe, for ever young,
For ever blooming; who on beds of flowers,
By ſtreams of living waters, ſoft repoſe
To crown th' immortal bliſs of happy ſouls
With raptures unconceiv'd——She kneels! and weeps!

EMIRA.

O royal SOLYMAN————

SOLYMAN.

Say, beauteous maid,
What may this poſture mean?

EMIRA.

Supreme of monarchs,
Renown'd for virtues, greatly good and juſt,
Let not a helpleſs ſtranger plead in vain!
I beg for mercy.

SOLYMAN.

Mercy? Can thy youth,

Can

Can charms like thine want honor? want protection?
You must not kneel.

EMIRA.

Unhappy MUSTAPHA——

SOLYMAN.

Ha! what of him?

EMIRA.

Is innocent, my Lord;
Is clear of every crime against a father,
Whom more than life he loves.

SOLYMAN.

This would be scan'd.
You know him then.

EMIRA.

Believe these streaming eyes;
Truth is not fairer, nor is faith more loyal.
O by your just renown, by all your hopes
Of peace on earth, of paradise on high
Be timely warn'd: revoke the dreadful doom,
That, giving him to death, will ruin you!
Will kill your sweet repose of heart for ever!

SOLYMAN.

Amazement all!—Thy words, thy mournful action
Confound my thought. Say, speak, how is the fate
Of MUSTAPHA thy care?

EMIRA.

O SOLYMAN!
O father of th'unhappy————

SOLYMAN.

O my soul!
What can she mean?——Go on.

EMIRA.

O pardon him!
Have pity on us both!—I am——his wife————

SOLYMAN.

Confusion!——wife!

EMIRA.

Arm not your eye with anger.

If

If 'tis a crime——revenge it all on me:
And in my gushing blood———

SOLYMAN.

Rack me no more.
Resume thy senses: tell me who thou art.

EMIRA.

Alas, my Lord, you tremble with your passion.
But hear me with indulgence——By the love
I bear your son; th' observant faith we both
Profess for SOLYMAN———all may be well.
I bring the noblest dowry to his arms;
Peace to your realms, a potent monarch's friendship
On happy terms obtain'd.

SOLYMAN.

Am I awake?
Speak, speak, and ease my soul.

EMIRA.

I am———

SOLYMAN.

Well, say.

EMIRA.

The Sophy's daughter.

SOLYMAN.

Ha!

EMIRA.

The eldest born
Of *Persia*———

SOLYMAN.

Hell and horror! heard I true?
Of *Persia*? daughter of my mortal foe?———
At length his treasons all are come to light———
Perfidious! lying slave!

EMIRA.

O no, my Lord:
By him who sees the soul, he is not false.
He never knew a thought———

SOLYMAN.

Away——he dies!

Should

Should I and all my kingdoms perifh with him.
What hoa——Conduct her to the womens' tent:
Let ROXOLANA keep her fafe.——'Tis done.
The conflict's ended. OSMAN—

SCENE VIII.

SOLYMAN, OSMAN.

SOLYMAN.

Art thou privy
To this confpiracy?

OSMAN.

My Lord?

SOLYMAN.

I ftood
Even on the verge, th' extremeft verge of fate:
And one ftep more——I doubted her I love,
Her who has fav'd me—OSMAN, he fhall die!
Call RUSTAN; bid the mutes be ready——Stay.
This cool diffembler, this fmooth hypocrite,
What can he now alledge?——Bring him before me.

OSMAN.

Whom, gracious Sir?

SOLYMAN.

Him.—Doft thou linger, flave?
This rage difturbs my reafon.——MUSTAPHA.
O wretched SOLYMAN!

SCENE IX.

SOLYMAN, MUSTAPHA.

MUSTAPHA.

You fpeak not, Sir;
You fee me not. If I appear before you,
Tho' guiltlefs, with confufion; not thefe bonds,
Nor what more fatal may enfue alarms me:

The man who knows no crime ſhould know no fear;
And yet a father's frown can ſhake my heart.
Sir, if I may be heard; if innocence
Thus wrong'd and ſuffering——

SOLYMAN.

I will cheque the ſtorm
That heaves within, and would o'erflow all bounds.
Juſtice alone ſhall try him and condemn.
And yet——ſhall treaſon thus, detected treaſon,
Profane the language of fair loyalty?

MUSTAPHA.

Treaſon! O by my ſoul's immortal life,
This curſt ſedition leſs offended you,
Than it afflicted your unhappy ſon.

SOLYMAN.

Of that my heart has labour'd to acquit thee.
Turn this way: raiſe thine eyes aloft to mine,
And fix their beams with ſteady gaze upon me——
"Who knows no crime, thou ſayſt, ſhould know no fear."
Now anſwer me——Art thou not join'd in league?
In helliſh compact with thy father's foes?
Art thou not—married?

MUSTAPHA.

Heaven!

SOLYMAN.

Ha! does this truth
Flaſh juſt conviction on thee? ſtrike thee dumb?
Now, whither is thy confidence of tongue,
Thy daring licence fled?

MUSTAPHA.

Then—farewel, Hope!
Yet—let me die the ſame I ſtill have liv'd,
Above all falſehood, all diſſimulation.
I am, my Lord: and but for that mad tumult,
Which broke our evening's talk abruptly off,
(So angry heaven decreed) I had even then,
In all the plainneſs of diſcovery, laid

The ſecret at your feet; from full belief,
My action, try'd by candor as by juſtice,
Muſt have procur'd forgiveneſs to my ſelf;
And to EMIRA, crown'd with every grace,
With every virtue bright, your tendereſt love.
May I proceed!

SOLYMAN.

Proceed? What canſt thou add,
What can I hear, but riſing proofs on proofs,
That I am miſerable, thou moſt baſe?

MUSTAPHA.

I plead not now for life: nor would I hold it
Diſhonor'd by a father's deep diſtruſt,
Embitter'd by his hate. I would but lighten
Th' imputed guilt that weighs upon my name.
My foes, I knew, my unrelenting foes
Were high in your regard, truſted, belov'd;
Attach'd with no leſs faith to you, than fix'd
And in cloſe league combin'd—to ruin me.
Their power in all its dark extent I ſaw;
Its baleful influence felt. The law of heaven,
The voice of reaſon, urg'd me to preſerve
My ſelf from death, my father from a crime.
Againſt inveterate, unabating hate,
I ſought protection, ſought a ſure retreat:
And found it in the *Perſian* monarch's love.
Weary of war's fell ravage, wiſhing reſt,
He gave his blooming daughter to my arms,
And with her thoſe fair provinces your ſword
Had won and loſt by turns; to be annex'd
For ever to your empire, on ſuch terms
Of peace, as you and juſtice might approve.
Behold, my Lord, even in its laſt receſs,
The heart of MUSTAPHA!

SOLYMAN.

Well—thou hast said.

Is there aught more?

MUSTAPHA.

My Lord, to life or death
Indifferent, as impatient of dishonor,
Resign'd, unfearing, I expect my fate.
But oh—EMIRA!—On my knee, for her,
Who but for being mine had been most happy,
I beg a father's dear regard.

SOLYMAN.

Retire.

SCENE X.

SOLYMAN.

[RUSTAN *enters at a distance.*

Why does my straining eye pursue his steps?
Out, foolish nature; leave me to the thoughts
That suit a monarch. He, or I must fall.
'Tis rage no more: 'tis reason's deep alarm,
Abruptly waken'd o'er the startling view
Of precipice and ruin full before her:
May I believe my senses? How! a son
Aspiring, popular, belov'd and brave,
His very virtues formidably great,
Combin'd, confederate with my mortal foe?
Even wedded to his daughter? young and fair,
And mighty o'er a husband's ductile heart!
To drive his passions, and inflame his will
With each curst purpose of her father's hate.
And shall a tale by smooth-tongu'd cunning fram'd
Stagger my heart, or soothe me to false peace?
No, rouse thee, SOLYMAN, and shew mankind,
Imperial justice knows no ties of blood.

RUSTAN,

RUSTAN, approach. Prepare thy band of mutes;
The ſterneſt of the tribe. The night is diſmal,
And dreadful deeds ſhall cloſe it.

SCENE XI.

RUSTAN.

That were well.
They ſhall be ready: ROXOLANA too
Shall fix the great reſolve. Ariſe, ye powers,
Who aid conſpiracy in her ſad muſings;
Engage his head, his heart, till this be done,
And crown the work of fate your ſelves begun.

The End of the Fourth Act.

ACT

ACT V. SCENE I.

ZANGER, ACHMET.

ACHMET.

THE hour grows more tempeſtuous.

ZANGER.

Not a ſtar
Remains unquench'd ; but total blackneſs fills
The vault of night.

ACHMET.

Look, from the turbid ſouth
What floods of flame in red diffuſion burſt,
Frequent and furious, darted thro' the dark
And broken ridges of a thouſand clouds,
Pil'd hill on hill: and hark, the thunder rous'd
Groans in long roarings thro' the diſtant gloom.

ZANGER.

'Tis well : and we, O heaven ! revere thy voice,
Thy voice of terror, meant to ſhake the hearts
Of guilty men. What withers their reſolves,
Lends force to ours. ACHMET, if honor lives
Within thy breaſt ; if this tremendous call
Can wake thee to a deed of noble daring,
Now ſave thy maſter.

ACHMET.

Prince, command my ſervice.
Be life or death the ſequel, I have learnt,
When honor calls, undoubting to obey.
This worthy part is ours: th' event we leave
To heaven's all-ruling care.

ZANGER.

I need not ſay,

In

In ſaving MUSTAPHA, we ſave the friend
Of virtue, of mankind. But how? alas!
For I have ſounded all a mother's heart,
Each ſource of tenderneſs profeſs'd for me,
In favor of this brother—and in vain!
The Sultan too, inexorable, deaf
Even to EMIRA's voice! has ſeal'd his doom.
Amid the ſilence of the midnight hour,
A ſhameful death awaits him!

ACHMET.

Judge ſupreme!
Is ſuch the lot for innocence decreed?
What can we do?

ZANGER.

Brave ACHMET, true, the camp
Lies plung'd in ſlumber: but the troops adore
This injur'd virtue. Rouſe the neareſt bands:
Then, on a ſignal given, ruſh we at once
Into the guilty room; and bear him thence
Among th' expecting ſoldiers.

ACHMET.

By the ſtorm
That thunders round us with redoubling peals!
The brave deſign has fir'd me: I will ſave,
Or periſh greatly with him. Knows the Prince
Of our intention?

ZANGER.

No; nor were it ſafe
To truſt his ſcrupulous virtue with the ſecret.
Above all fear of death, he would not riſque
A life this way, to make his own immortal.
Then give we honor ſtrict as his no cauſe
To diſavow our action; let no blood,
Even of his executioners, be ſpilt.

ACHMET.

We will not ſtain an enterprize of juſtice

With

With deeds of cruelty. That care be mine.
What ſhall the ſignal be?

ZANGER.

A blazing torch
Wav'd thrice amid the trees that ſhade this tent,
My watch is there.

ACHMET.

Enough.

ZANGER.

Farewel.

ACHMET.

Yet ſay,
Where do we meet?

ZANGER.

Behind the blaſted pine
That bounds the laſt pavilion.

ACHMET.

Prince, remember,
My ſervice ſhall not linger: if I fall,
'Tis as a ſoldier ſhould.

ZANGER.

Away—the Vizir
Is coming towards us.

SCENE II.

ROXOLANA, MUFTI, RUSTAN.

ROXOLANA.

MUFTI, what a night
Is roaring o'er us! My frail woman's heart
Quakes at the loudning horror of the ſtorm?
What mean the angry ſkies?

MUFTI.

I have obſerv'd,
When the ſoul labors with ſome mighty purpoſe
That dread and danger uſher into birth,

Fancy

Fancy alarm'd ſees in each accident
A heaven-ſent omen; of her own vain fears
Shapes fiends or ghoſts; embodies empty ſpace,
Pours terror on th' unreal form: then ſhrinks
Appall'd and trembling from her own creation.
Why, this tempeſtuous time reſpects not us;
Or it befriends our purpoſe.

RUSTAN.

True, great Princeſs.
The ſoldiers all are huſh'd: the camp is now
Still as the midnight deſart. Even the factious,
Whoſe prying curioſity had elſe
Been buzzing round us, tremble in their tents,
Awe-ſtruck; nor dare aſſemble while the heavens
Are blazing round their heads.

MUFTI.

Madam, ſee here—
And give full ſcope to joy—behold the ſcroll
That numbers MUSTAPHA among the dead!

ROXOLANA.

Yet, Mufti, was it hardly gain'd. The combat
'Twixt love and vengeance in his father's breaſt,
Like agonizing nature ere it yields
To death's laſt dart, held ſtrong and terrible.

MUFTI.

Nor had the ſon's accumulated crimes
Met their due puniſhment, but for your ſkill,
Your known aſcendant o'er the Sultan's heart,
All-open to your influence.—Take it, Vizir,
Th' important ſchedule; and ſee juſtice done
On this our enemy.

RUSTAN.

O I could give
A looſe to rapture!—But the time forbids.
When muſt he die?

MUFTI.

Deſtruction hovers o'er him,

Theſe moments are his laſt. So wills the Sultan:
And has ſhut up his tent from all acceſs,
Till this be done.

ROXOLANA.

Now, now indeed I live!
Now am I bleſt! O friends, you both ſhall taſk
Henceforth my deareſt intereſt in your ſervice.
Fly, RUSTAN, plant ſtrong watch at every gate,
At every avenue: let none go forth,
None enter, till the morning ſhines abroad.

RUSTAN.

All is prepar'd. The ſlaves are ready arm'd,
A numerous band: and I will poſt them ſtrait
With watchful ſecreſy.—Now, MUSTAPHA,
Thy boaſted victories, the courted love
Of giddy multitudes that hail'd, this morn,
Thy ſhort-liv'd triumph—what avail they now?
That pageant ſhow will but embitter thought,
But aid thy foes to torture thee in death.
Come, Mufti: to our taſk.

SCENE III.

ROXOLANA.

I am alone!
My boſom pants with ardent expectation,
And dreadful hope! O wou'd this hour were paſt!
The ſolitary horror of my thoughts
Diſmays me—Who goes there?—His wife!—I would not
Now hear her fond complainings.

SCENE

SCENE IV.

EMIRA, ROXOLANA.

EMIRA.

Fly not, Madam:
For misery has sure a mournful right
To pity, even to reverence. If your soul
Is truly royal, and adorns the height
Of your imperial fortune, you will weep
The woes you have not known. If mercy lives,
If gentleness yet holds her softest seat,
Where once she joy'd to dwell, a woman's breast;—
O ROXOLANA—by these melting eyes!
By this imploring posture! now exert
Your thousand ways of charming him you love!
Wake nature, reason, in his heart; to save
A hero who supports his throne, a son
Who fears no death but from a father's frown.
Think, for this noble act, how fair your name,
How bright with praise, to nations yet unborn
All-lovely will descend!—You hear me not.
Ah, Madam, this way bend your sight: in me
No common suppliant kneels. I once believ'd—
O groundless pride!—that but to heaven alone
I could have bow'd me thus!

ROXOLANA.

My wonder, Princess,
Has kept me silent: let it plead my pardon
That you have knelt so long. Nay, dry your tears;
My self will send the Prince to your embrace,
And end for ever all your doubts and fears.

SCENE V,

EMIRA.

What insolence of cruelty, what cold,
Unfeeling pride sate mocking in her eye!
O man! what savage bears a heart like thine,
Till thy own ills have taught thee social sense!
And soften'd thee to goodness!—MUSTAPHA!

SCENE VI.

EMIRA, MUSTAPHA.

MUSTAPHA.

Am I so blest once more to see thy face?
Once more to press thee in my faithful arms?
O transport even in death!

EMIRA.

Death! guard me, Love,
Defend me, heaven, from that distracting thought!
O most inhuman Queen!—What! lose thee then?
Thus lose thee—in thy flowering spring of life?
With all thy honors green and fragrant on thee?

MUSTAPHA.

If I have right employ'd this scanty span,
'Tis life's full measure: honor is old age.
Were I not torn from thee, from thy lov'd bosom
To die is to be happy. Gracious heaven
In mercy to mankind has made life short;
Else wrongs and sufferings, our sure portion here,
Would be supportless load!

EMIRA.

O heaven and earth!
Shall ruffians, mercenary slaves, enur'd
To murders, recent from the basest crimes,

Attempt

Attempt thy ſacred life?

MUSTAPHA.

The cauſe alone
For which we ſuffer makes death terrible.
What can he more, with all his terrors arm'd,
When we oppoſe fair virtue to his blow,
But firſt enlarge the ſoul to liberty?
And then to bliſs immortal? I will meet him,
This foe of nature, with the ſame calm brow
I oft have ſeen and ſought him thro' the ranks
Of raging war—To ſpare a father's crime,
Would I had found him there!

EMIRA.

Are then my hopes
All fled for ever?—Have I liv'd to this?
O MUSTAPHA—yet let me ſhare thy fate:
Yes, periſh with thee. From thy firmer heart
My weakneſs will draw ſtrength, and meet the doom,
That muſt involve us both, ſerene and fearleſs.

MUSTAPHA.

Thou angel-virtue! this is death's ſharp pang,
This tenderneſs that pains me into agony.
Thy lover and thy huſband who ſhould ſhield,
Should cover thee from every fear, alas!
Is trembling with thy ſoftneſs!

EMIRA.

My lov'd Lord!
Soul of my wiſhes! glory of my thoughts!
Your father—has he then renounc'd that name?
Caſt from his heart humanity and honor?
Can it be poſſible?———Yet let me fly,
Aſſault him, pierce him with my tears, and wake
The god within his breaſt!

MUSTAPHA.

My gentle love,
It will not be. The ſecret of our nuptials

Untimely

Untimely told, betray'd I know not how,
Has fix'd my doom irrevocable.

EMIRA.

Oh!——
My Lord! my life!

MUSTAPHA.

Why doſt thou tremble? why
With this convulſive ardor graſp my hand?

EMIRA.

Ah MUSTAPHA——

MUSTAPHA.

What woulſt thou ſay? My hour
Is haſting forward.

EMIRA.

Wouldſt thou know—O horror!
The cruel, killing foe, the deadly tongue
That has undone thee?

MUSTAPHA.

So may heaven receive
My parting ſoul, as anger and revenge,
As every paſſion is extinguiſh'd here——
All but my love for thee.

EMIRA.

O grief of heart——
When injur'd virtue not upbraids our crime,
But pities, but forgives; the bitter pang
Our ſoul then feels is every death in one!
Strike here, my Lord.

MUSTAPHA.

Ha! what? My ſenſes all
Recoil to hear thee talk thus.

EMIRA.

Yet ſhew mercy:
If you not loath me, ſtrike. 'Twas I, alas!
'Twas curſt EMIRA's tongue proclaim'd thy ſecret.

MUSTAPHA.

Thou deareſt! thou unequal'd tenderneſs!
Now am I moſt prepar'd to lay down life.

My

My heart——I bluſh to think it could be baſe——
Was liſtning to ſuſpicions of ſome friend,
Whoſe falſeneſs had undone us. Thou haſt ſav'd me
From dying with that guilt upon my ſoul.

EMIRA.

Thy friends are innocent. Even SOLYMAN,
Even fatal ROXOLANA, both were friends
To me———EMIRA was thy only foe.

MUSTAPHA.

Thy words diſtract me. I ſhall die a coward,
Forgetful of my name, unworthy thee.
It was the ſweet exceſs of tendereſt love,
Led thee to plead a daughter's ſacred claim
In SOLYMAN: and ſure if aught on earth,
If human influence could have found his heart,
Thy tears, thy truth, thy charms, muſt have prevail'd.

EMIRA.

O ſpare me, MUSTAPHA. Each piercing accent
Is a keen ſword, and ſtabs into my heart.
Were I to live after this dear forgiveneſs,
What were it but to hear, each lingring hour,
Th' upbraiding voice of honor, virtue, duty,
Condemning, laſhing my diſtracted ſoul
With their ſevereſt ſcorpions. No, EMIRA,
No farther thought of life————

MUSTAPHA.

Yes, you muſt live;
Or ſee me die, the laſt of human race:
O if my fair renown thro' life preſerv'd,
And meant a brave example now in death,
Be dear to my EMIRA; ſhe will live
To plead my virtue's cauſe before a father:
And reconcile him to a ſon's juſt fame,
Who living honor'd, and who dying bleſt him.

EMIRA.

What ſays my Lord? For all the promis'd joys

Of

Of paradiſe, I would not ſee his face:
Nor will I part from thee.

MUSTAPHA.

My hour is come!
I heard th' inexorable Angel call!
His potent voice ſounds awful in mine ear!
EMIRA!——Oh——farewel!

EMIRA.

Ha! who are theſe?

MUSTAPHA.

The miniſters of fate. [OSMAN *and Mutes enter*.

EMIRA.

Ye bleſſed powers!
Save, ſhield me from their ſight!

MUSTAPHA.

Alas—ſhe faints!
O ZANGER! O my friend! where now is he?
Whoſe hand ſhould comfort and ſupport my love?
Look on her, heaven: I leave her in thy care.

[*The Mutes make ſigns for him to retire.*

I come, my friends. A few tears will have way
At this eternal parting——Dear EMIRA!
OSMAN, look here—and let my father know
What thou haſt ſeen!—One kiſs—Her cheek is cold—
One more—O bitter ſweet!—And now the pangs
Of death are paſt. [EMIRA *is carried off.*

OSMAN.

My heart weeps blood
At this ſad ſight!

SCENE VII.

SOLYMAN, OSMAN.

SOLYMAN.

Protect me, heaven!

OSMAN.

My Lord?

SOLYMAN.

SOLYMAN.

OSMAN, it vanish'd here!

OSMAN.

My gracious sovereign,
What moves you thus? What do your eyes pursue
With such transported gaze?

SOLYMAN.

If parted souls
Can leave the midnight caverns dark and damp,
Where sleeps their mouldering dust, to walk on earth;
This very now, the spectre of a man———
It bore the semblance of my buried father———
Stalk'd pale and terrible athwart my sight!
And glar'd a look of anger as it pass'd!

OSMAN.

Can this be possible?

SOLYMAN.

I saw it plain.
In my lone tent, deaf murmurs struck mine ear,
From airy voices whispering thro' the gloom.
I listen'd: when at once a wave of flame
Burst, dimly flashing round me, and disclos'd
The hideous vision—Look, it bends this way—
Behold it, OSMAN!

OSMAN.

'Tis illusion all.

SOLYMAN.

O night of horrors!——MUSTAPHA! thy fate,
Thy pangs are yet less terrible than mine!
OSMAN, I am most wretched———

OSMAN.

Hark! my Lord,
What shouts! what furious outcries!

SCENE VIII.

SOLYMAN, OSMAN, RUSTAN.

SOLYMAN.

RUSTAN! ha————
Bleeding and pale!

RUSTAN.

Prince ZANGER————

SOLYMAN.

What of him?

RUSTAN.

To ſave his brother——But my ſtrength forſakes me—
I die————

SOLYMAN.

Confuſion!——raiſe him up—ſay on.

RUSTAN.

To ſave his brother, rous'd the ſleeping camp——
I threw my ſelf, with all your gather'd ſlaves,
To bar their paſſage————

SOLYMAN.

Is my ſon eſcap'd?

RUSTAN.

I faint—my heart pants thick——Too late I ſee
Th' avenging hand of heaven!—too late I find,
All wickedneſs is miſery!———But yet,
I will not die with unrepented guilt
Upon my parting ſpirit——MUSTAPHA——
Prophet! forgive me——was moſt innocent:
And ROXOLANA————

SOLYMAN.

Slave!—thou dy'ſt too ſoon:
And haſt eſcap'd my juſtice————ROXOLANA—
Thou wouldſt have ſaid—is falſe as hell, or thee!

SCENE IX.

Back Scene opening discovers the mutes and soldiers in attitudes of grief round the body of MUSTAPHA. *They bring it forward.*

ZANGER, *entering.*

Alas! my brother—dead!—Look here, just heaven!
I could not save—but I can perish with thee.

[*stabs himself.*

SOLYMAN.

What hast thou done? —Wert thou too leagu'd against me?
Yet live: my heart forgives, and bids thee live.

ZANGER.

Not universal rule should bribe me now
Longer to breathe this tainted air —My Lord—
By those soft tears of pity and remorse
You shed o'er this sad scene———Support me, friends—
To dying friendship grant this last request———
Beneath one marble let us rest together:
In the same social tomb our human part
Sleep safe and undisturb'd——Now, MUSTAPHA—
Now, I am thine——for ever!

SOLYMAN.

O my sons!
Did ever age produce such god-like worth?
Such matchless friendship?—Ah—what then am I—
Their murderer!—Hide, hide me from that thought.
O let me plunge into profoundest night!
Let her broad wing with ever-during shade
Involve my memory! lest fame should tell,
Should publish to remotest time——I clos'd
A life of glory——thus!

SCENE

SCENE X.

To them ROXOLANA.

Ah—ZANGER!

SOLYMAN.

Look!
See, sorceress——woman, see—the curst effects
Of thy dire arts!

ROXOLANA.

Recall not to my thought
What I have done—O give me instant death!

SOLYMAN.

Death—were reward and mercy. Thou shalt live
To prove the pangs, the heart-destroying horrors,
Even all that love betray'd and chang'd to gall
Can pour upon thee. Yes, we both shall live,
Two demons, hourly to upbraid and curse
Each other's crime—Ha! drag her from the corpse.
She shall not breathe a sigh, or drop a tear,
O'er my unhappy sons——* Hark! righteous heaven
Rolls deep th' avenging thunder o'er our heads.
[* *here the thunder is heard*
Justice divine! discharge it here—on me—
On her. It cannot err: we both are guilty.

O dire example, known and felt too late,
Of amorous weakness, and of woman's hate!
O curs'd prerogative of boundless sway!
That gives the deadly passions scope to play;
Hate, anger, rage, to coward-fear succeed:
And worth must perish, tho' a son should bleed.

The End of the Fifth Act.

ALFRED

with James Thomson, 1740

ALFRED:

A

MASQUE.

Si velimus cum priorum temporum *necessitate certare, vincemur. Ingeniosior est enim ad* excogitandum *simulatio, Veritate; servitus, Libertate; metus, Amore.* Plin. Pan. Trajan.

[Price One Shilling.]

ALFRED:

A
MASQUE.

Represented before

Their ROYAL HIGHNESSES

THE

PRINCE and PRINCESS of *WALES*,

At *CLIFFDEN*,

On the First of *August*, 1740.

LONDON:

Printed for A. MILLAR, over-against St. *Clement's* Church in the *Strand*. M DCC XL.

The ARGUMENT.

After the Danes *had made themſelves maſters of* Chippenham, *the ſtrongeſt city in the Kingdom of* Weſſex; Alfred *was at once abandoned by all his ſubjects. In this univerſal defection, that Monarch found himſelf obliged to retire into the little iſle of* Athelney *in* Somerſetſhire; *a place then rough with woods and of difficult acceſs. There, habited like a peaſant, he lived unknown, for ſome time, in a ſhepherd's cottage. He is ſuppoſed to be found in this retreat by the Earl of* Devon; *whoſe caſtle, upon the river* Tau, *was then beſieged by the* Danes.

Persons.

ALFRED.	Mr. MILWARD.
ELTRUDA.	Mrs. HORTON.
HERMIT.	Mr. QUIN.
EARL of *Devon*.	Mr. MILLS.
CORIN, a ſhepherd.	Mr. SALWAY.
EMMA, his wife.	Mrs. CLIVE.

A Bard, Soldiers, Spirits.

The SCENE *repreſents a plain, ſurrounded with woods. On one ſide, a cottage: on the other, flocks and herds in diſtant proſpect. A Hermit's cave in full view, overhung with trees, wild and grateſque.*

ALFRED:

A

MASQUE.

ACT I. SCENE I.

CORIN, EMMA.

EMMA.

SHEPHERD, 'tis he. Beneath yon aged oak,
All on the flowery turf he lays him down.

CORIN.

Soft: let us not diſturb him. Gentle EMMA,
Poor tho' he be, unfriended and unknown,
My pity waits with reverence on his fortune.
Modeſt of carriage, and of ſpeech moſt gracious,
As if ſome ſaint or angel, in diſguiſe,
Had grac'd our lowly cottage with his preſence,
He ſteals, I know not how, into the heart,
And makes it pant to ſerve him. Truſt me, EMMA,
He is no common man.

EMMA.

EMMA.

Some lord, perhaps,
Or valiant chief, that from our deadly foe,
The haughty, cruel, unbelieving *Dane*,
Seeks ſhelter here.

CORIN.

And ſhelter he ſhall find.
Who loves his country is my friend and brother.
Behold him well. Fair manhood in its prime,
Even thro the homely ruſſet that conceals him,
Shines forth, and proves him noble. Seeſt thou, EMMA,
Yon weſtern clouds? The ſun they ſtrive to hide,
Yet darts his beam around.

EMMA.

Your thought is mine:
He is not what his preſent fortunes ſpeak him.
But, ah! the raging foe is all around us:
We dare not keep him here.

CORIN.

Content thee, wife:
This iſland is of ſtrength. Nature's own hand
Hath planted round a deep defence of woods,
The ſounding aſh, the mighty oak; each tree
A ſheltering grove: and choak'd up all between
With wild encumbrance of perplexing thorns,
And horrid brakes. Beyond this woody verge,
Two rivers broad and rapid hem us in.
Along their channel ſpreads the gulphy pool,
And trembling quagmire, whoſe deceitful green
Betrays the foot it tempts. One path alone
Winds to this plain, ſo roughly difficult,
This ſingle arm, poor ſhepherd as I am,
Could well diſpute it with twice twenty *Danes*.

EMMA.

Yet think, my CORIN, on the ſtern decree

Of that proud foe; "Who harbours or relieves
"An *English* captain, dies the death of traitors:
"But who their haunts discovers, shall be safe,
"And high rewarded."

CORIN.

Now, just heaven forbid,
A *British* man should ever count for gain,
What villainy must earn. No: are we poor?
Be honesty our riches. Are we mean,
And humbly born? The true heart makes us noble.
These hands can toil, can sow the ground and reap,
For thee and thy sweet babes. Our daily labour
Is daily wealth: it finds us bread and raiment.
Could *Danish* gold give more?

EMMA.

Alas the while,
That loyal faith is fled from hall and bower,
To dwell with village-swains!

CORIN.

Ah look! behold!
Where, like some goodly tree by wintry winds
Torn from the roots and withering, our sad guest
Lies on the ground diffus'd.

EMMA.

I weep to see it.

CORIN.

Thou hast a heart sweet pity loves to dwell in.
Dry up thy tears; and lean on this just hope:
If yet to do away his country's shame,
To serve her bravely on some blest occasion;
If for these ends this stranger sought our cottage,
The heavenly hosts are hovering here unseen,
To watch and to protect him.—But oh! when—
My heart burns for it—shall I see the hour
Of vengeance on those *Danish* infidels,

That war with heaven and us?

EMMA.

Alas, my love!
These passions are not for the poor man's state.
To heaven and to the rulers of the land
Leave such ambitious thoughts. Be warn'd, my CORIN:
And think our little all depends on thee.

SONG.

O peace! the fairest child of heaven,
To whom the sylvan reign was given,
The vale, the fountain and the grove,
With every softer scene of love:
Return, sweet peace! and chear the weeping swain;
Return, with ease and pleasure in thy train.

CORIN.

Hush: break thee off—For see, our mournful guest
Has rais'd his head—and lo! who comes to greet him;
His friend, the woodman of the neighbouring dale,
Whom late, as yester evening-star arose,
At his request I found, and hither brought.

SCENE II.

ALFRED, *Earl of* DEVON.

ALFRED.

How long, sweet heaven! how long
Shall red war desolate this prostrate land?
All, all is lost—And ALFRED lives to tell it!
His cities laid in dust! his subjects slaughter'd!
Or into slaves debas'd! the murderous foe

Proud

Proud and exulting in the general ſhame!——
Are theſe things ſo? and He without the means
Of great revenge? caſt down below the hope
Of ſuccouring thoſe he weeps for? O deſpair!
O grief of griefs!

DEVON.

Old as I am, my Liege,
In rough war harden'd, and with death familiar,
Theſe eyes have long forgot to melt with ſoftneſs:
But O, my gracious maſter, they have ſeen—
All-pitying heaven!—ſuch ſights of ruthleſs rage,
Of total deſolation—

ALFRED.

O my people!
O ruin'd *England!*—DEVON, thoſe were bleſt,
Who dy'd before this time. Ha! and thoſe robbers,
That violate the ſanctity of leagues,
The reverend ſeal of oaths; that baſely broke,
Like nightly ruffians, on the hour of peace,
And ſtole a victory from men unarm'd,
Thoſe *Danes* enjoy their crimes! Dread vengeance! ſon
Of power and juſtice! come, array'd in terrors,
Thy garment red with blood, thy keen ſword drawn:
O come, and on the heads of faithleſs men
Pour ample retribution; men whoſe triumph
Upbraids eternal juſtice.—But no more:
Submiſſion is heaven's due.—I will not launch
Into that dark abyſs where thought muſt drown.
Proceed, my lord: on with the mournful tale,
My griefs broke off.

DEVON.

From yonder heath-crown'd hill,
This iſland's eaſtern point, where in one ſtream
The *Thone* and *Parret* roll their blending waves,

I look'd, and ſaw the progreſs of the foe,
As of ſome tempeſt, ſome devouring fire
That ruins without mercy where it ſpreads.
The riches of the year, the golden grain
That liberal crown'd our plains, lies trampled wide
By hoſtile feet, or rooted up and waſte
Deforms the broad high-way. From ſpace to ſpace,
Far as my ſtraining eye could ſhoot its beam,
Trees, cottages, and caſtles, ſmoak to heaven
In one aſcending cloud. But Oh for pity!
That way, my lord, where yonder verdant height,
Declining, ſlides into a fruitful vale,
Unſightly now and bare; a few poor hinds,
Grey-hair'd, and thinly clad, ſtood and beheld
The common ravage: motionleſs and mute
With hands to heaven uplift, they ſtood, and wept—
My tears attended theirs—

ALFRED.

If this ſad ſight
Could pain thee to ſuch anguiſh, what muſt I
Their king and parent feel?—Thou ſacred ſhade
Of my lov'd father! all ye parted ſpirits
Of my fam'd anceſtors! be men once more,
To know my pangs, and weep for *England*'s ſhame—
Why end I not at once this wretched being?
The means are in my hand.—But ſhall a prince
Thus poorly ſhroud him in the grave from pain,
And ſenſe of ſhame? The madman, nay the coward,
Has often dar'd the ſame. A monarch holds
His life in truſt for others. I will live then:
Let heaven diſpoſe the reſt.

DEVON.

Thrice-noble ALFRED,
And *England*'s only hope, whoſe virtues raiſe
Our frail mortality, our human duſt,

Up to angelic ſplendor and perfection;
With you to bear the worſt of ills, the ſpoil
Of waſteful war, the loſs of life or freedom,
Is happineſs, is glory.

ALFRED.

Ah, look round thee:
That mud-built cottage is thy ſovereign's palace.
Yon hind, whoſe daily toil is all his wealth,
Lodges and feeds him. Are theſe times for flattery?
Or call it praiſe: ſuch gaudy attributes
Would miſbecome our beſt and proudeſt fortunes.
But what are mine? what is this high-prais'd ALFRED?
Among ten thouſand wretches, moſt undone.
That prince who ſees his country laid in ruins,
His ſubjects periſhing beneath the ſword
Of foreign rage; who ſees and cannot ſave them,
Is but ſupreme in miſery!

DEVON.

My Liege,
Who has not known ill fortune, never knew
Himſelf, or his own virtue. Be of comfort:
We can but die at laſt. Till that hour comes,
Let noble anger keep our hopes alive.
A ſudden thought, as if from heaven inſpir'd,
Darts on my ſoul. One caſtle ſtill is ours,
Tho cloſe begirt and ſhaken by the *Danes*.
In this diſguiſe, my chance of paſſing on,
Of entering there unknown, is promiſing,
And wears a lucky face. 'Tis our laſt ſtake,
And I will play it like a man whoſe life,
Whoſe honor hangs upon a ſingle caſt.
Mean while, my Lord—

ALFRED.

ALFRED.

Ha! DEVON, thou haſt rous'd
My ſlumbering virtue. I applaud thy thought.
The praiſe of this brave daring ſhall be thine;
The danger ſhall be common. We will both
Strait tempt the *Daniſh* camp, and gain this fort;
To animate our brothers of the war,
Thoſe *Engliſhmen* who yet deſerve that name.
And hear, eternal Juſtice! if my life
Can make atonement for them, King of Kings!
Accept thy willing victim. On my head
Be all their woes: To them be grace and mercy.
Come on, my noble friend.

DEVON.

Ah, good my Liege,
What fits a private valor, and might grace
The ſimple ſoldier's venture, would proclaim
His general's raſhneſs. You are *England*'s king:
Your infant children, and your much-lov'd queen;
Nay more, the public weal, ten thouſand ſouls,
Whoſe hope you are, whoſe all depends on you,
Forbid this enterprize. 'Tis nobler courage
To cheque this ardor, to reſerve your ſword
For ſome great day of known and high import;
That to your country, to the judging world
Shall juſtify all hazards you may run.
This trial ſuits but me.

ALFRED.

Stay thee, raſh man—
Deſpair and indignation wing his ſteps.
May that good angel, who inſpir'd thy thought,
Throw round thy ſteps a veil of cloudy air,
That thou mayſt walk inviſible and ſafe.—
Now for reflection— Ha! this ſylvan ſcene,
The broad wild umbrage of theſe pendant ſhades

That

That murmur in the breeze, and deep embrown,
As evening ſpreads the holy Hermit's cave:
Theſe ſcenes that muſing Melancholy loves,
Breathe their ſtill influence on me. O bleſt lot
Of calm obſcurity—But, liſt. Ha! whence
Theſe air-born notes that ſound in meaſur'd ſweetneſs
Thro this vaſt ſilence?

SCENE III.

Solemn muſic is heard at a diſtance. It comes nearer in a full ſymphony: after which a ſingle trumpet ſounds a high and awakening air. Then the following ſtanzas are ſung by two aërial ſpirits unſeen.

First SPIRIT.

Hear, ALFRED, *father of the ſtate,*
Thy Genius heaven's high will declare!
What proves the hero truly great,
Is never, never to deſpair:
Is never to deſpair.

Second SPIRIT.

Thy hope awake, thy heart expand
With all its vigor, all its fires.
Ariſe! and ſave a ſinking land!
Thy country calls, and heaven inſpires.

Both SPIRITS.

Earth calls, and heaven inſpires.

SCENE.

SCENE IV.

ALFRED *alone.*

All hail, ye gentle miniſters of heaven!
Your ſong inſpires new patience thro my breaſt,
And generous hope: it wings my mounting ſoul
Above th' entangling maſs of earthly paſſions,
That keep frail man, tho ſtruggling to be free,
Still fluttering in the duſt.

SCENE V.

ALFRED, *the* HERMIT *advancing from his cave.*

ALFRED.

Thrice-happy Hermit!
Whom thus the heavenly habitants attend,
Bleſſing thy calm retreat; while ruthleſs war
Fills the polluted land with blood and crimes.
In this extremity of *England*'s fate,
Led by thy ſacred character, I come
For comfort and advice. Thy aged wiſdom,
Purg'd from the ſtormy cloud of human paſſions,
And by a ray from heaven exalted, ſees
Deep thro' futurity. Say what remains,
What yet remains to ſave our proſtrate country?
Nor ſcorn this anxious queſtion even from me,
A nameleſs ſtranger.

HERMIT.

HERMIT.

ALFRED, *England's* king,
All hail! and welcome to this humble cell.

ALFRED.

Whence doſt thou know me, venerable father?

HERMIT.

Laſt night, when with a draught from that cool fountain,
I had my wholeſome, ſober ſupper crown'd;
As is my ſtated cuſtom, forth I walk'd,
Beneath the ſolemn gloom and glittering ſky,
To feed my ſoul with prayer and meditation.
And thus to inward harmony compos'd,
That ſweeteſt muſic of the grateful heart,
Whoſe each emotion is a ſilent hymn;
I to my couch retir'd. Strait on mine eyes
A pleaſing ſlumber fell, whoſe myſtic power
Seal'd up my ſenſes, but enlarg'd my ſoul.
At once, diſclos'd amid the dark waſte night,
A viſion to my phantaſy appear'd.
For know, this ample element contains
Unnumber'd ſpiritual beings, or malign,
Or good to man. Theſe, when the groſſer eye
Of nature ſleeps, oft play their ſeveral parts,
As on a ſcene, before th' attentive mind,
And to the favour'd man diſcloſe the future.
Led by theſe ſpirits friendly to this iſle,
I liv'd thro' future ages; felt the virtue,
The great, the glorious paſſions that will fire
Diſtant poſterity: when guardian laws
Are by the patriot, in the glowing ſenate,
Won from corruption; when th' impatient arm
Of liberty, invincible, ſhall ſcourge
The tyrants of mankind— and when the Deep,
Through all her ſwelling waves, ſhall proudly joy
Beneath the boundleſs empire of thy ſons.

I ſaw thee, ALFRED, too—But o'er thy fortunes
Lay clouds impenetrable.

ALFRED.

Ah, good Hermit,
That ſcene is dark indeed! Ye awful powers!
To what am I reſerv'd? Still muſt I roam
A wanderer here, inglorious and unknown?
Or am I deſtin'd thy great inſtrument,
From fierce oppreſſion to redeem this land?

HERMIT.

Perhaps, the laſt.—But, prince, remember, then,
The vows, the noble uſes, of affliction.
Preſerve the quick humanity it gives,
The pitying, ſocial ſenſe of human weakneſs:
Yet keep thy ſtubborn fortitude entire,
The manly heart that to another's woe
Is tender, but ſuperior to its own.
Learn to ſubmit; yet learn to conquer fortune.
Attach thee firmly to the virtuous deeds
And offices of life: to life itſelf,
With all its vain and tranſient joys, ſit looſe.
Chief, let devotion to the ſovereign mind,
A ſteady, chearful, abſolute dependance
On his beſt, wiſeſt government, poſſeſs thee.
In thoughtleſs, gay proſperity, when all
Attends our wiſh; when nought is ſeen around us,
But kneeling flattery, and obedient fortune;
Then are blind mortals apt, within themſelves
To fix their ſtay, forgetful of the giver.
But when thus humbled, ALFRED, as thou art,
When to their feeble natural powers reduc'd,
'Tis then they feel this univerſal truth—
That heaven is all in all—and man is nothing.

ALFRED.

ALFRED.

I thank thee, father, for thy pious counſel.
And witneſs, thou dread power! who ſeeſt my heart;
That if not to perform my regal taſk,
To be the common father of my people,
Patron of honor, virtue and religion;
If not to ſhelter induſtry, to guard
His honeſt portion from oppreſſive pride,
From waſtful riot, and the ſons of rapine,
Who baſely raviſh what they dare not earn;
If not to deal out juſtice, like the ſun,
With equal light; if not to ſpread thy bounty,
The treaſures truſted to me, not my own,
On all the ſmiling ranks of nouriſh'd life;
If not to raiſe our drooping *Engliſh* name,
To clothe it yet with terror; make this land
Renown'd for peaceful arts to bleſs mankind,
And generous war to humble proud oppreſſors:
If not to build on an eternal baſe,
On liberty and laws, the public weal:
If not for theſe great ends I am ordain'd,
May I ne'er idly fill the throne of *England!*

HERMIT.

Still may thy breaſt theſe ſentiments retain,
In proſperous life.

ALFRED.

Proſperity were ruin,
Could it deſtroy or change ſuch thoughts as theſe.
When Thoſe whom heaven diſtinguiſhes o'er millions,
Profuſing on them honors, riches, power,
Whate'er th' expanded heart can wiſh; when they,
Accepting the reward, neglect the duty;
Or worſe, pervert theſe gifts to deeds of ruin:
Is there a wretch they rule ſo mean as they?
Guilty, at once of ſacrilege to heaven,

And of perfidious robbery to men——
But hark! methinks I hear a plaintive voice
Sigh thro the vale, and wake the mournful echo.

SONG.

I.

Sweet valley, say, where, pensive lying,
For me, our children, England, *sighing,*
The best of mortals leans his head.
Ye fountains, dimpled by my sorrow,
Ye brooks that my complainings borrow,
O lead me to his lonely bed:
Or if my lover,
Deep woods, you cover,
Ah whisper where your shadows o'er him spread!

2.

'Tis not the loss of pomp and pleasure,
Of empire, or of tinsel treasure,
That drops this tear, that swells this groan:
No; from a nobler cause proceeding,
A heart with love and fondness bleeding,
I breathe my sadly-pleasing moan.
With other anguish
I scorn to languish:
For Love will feel no sorrows but his own.

SCENE

SCENE VI.

ALFRED, HERMIT, ELTRUDA, *advancing*.

ALFRED.

Sure, by the voice, and purport of the ſong,
This generous mourner is my queen, ELTRUDA.
And yet how can that be ?—O all good powers !
'Tis ſhe ! 'tis ſhe !

ELTRUDA.

My lord, my life, my ALFRED !
Oh take me to thy arms ; with toil o'ercome,
And ſudden tranſport, thus at once to find thee,
In this wild foreſt, pathleſs and perplext !

ALFRED.

Come to my ſoul, thou deareſt, beſt of women !
Come, and repoſe thy ſorrows in my boſom.
O all my paſſions mix in doubtful ſtrife !
If pain or joy prevail, I ſcarce can ſay,
While thus I claſp thee, yet recall the perils
To which thy trembling ſteps have been expos'd.
Why haſt thou left the convent where I plac'd thee ?
Why, unprotected truſt thee to a land,
A barbarous land where rages *Daniſh* war ?
Our hoſpitable *England* is no more !

ELTRUDA.

Dire was the cauſe, my ALFRED. The rous'd country,
All hurl'd in breathleſs terror and confuſion,
Inform'd us, a near party of the *Danes*,
Whoſe brutal fury ſpares no ſex, no age,
No place however privileg'd or holy,
Were on full march that way. Inſtant I fled,

In this difguife, with only thefe attendants:
But in our way oft chear'd by airy voices,
To bear to this retreat our helplefs children.

ALFRED.

Ah wanderers too young! ah haplefs children!
But more unhappy Sire! who cannot give,
To thofe he loves, protection.

ELTRUDA.

Thou too, ALFRED,
Art thou not unattended? None to ferve thee,
To foothe thy woes, to watch thy broken flumbers!
And when the filent tear o'erflows thy eye,
None, with the warm and cordial lip of love,
To kifs it off! There is in love a power,
There is a foft divinity, that draws
Even tranfport from diftrefs; that gives the heart
A certain pang, excelling far the joys
Of grofs unfeeling life. Befides, my ALFRED,
Even had the fury of this barbarous foe
Not forc'd me from the convent, life is fhort;
And now it trembles on the wing of danger:
Why fhould we lofe it then? One well-fav'd hour,
In fuch a tender circumftance, to lovers,
Is better than an age of common time.

ALFRED.

Oh 'tis too much! thy tendernefs o'ercomes me!
Nay, look not on me with that fweet dejection,
Thro tears that pierce my foul!—Chear thee, my love:
Hope ftill the beft; that better days await us,
And fairer from remembrance.—Thou, ELTRUDA,
Thou art a pledge of happinefs!—On thee
Good angels wait; they led thy journey hither:
And I have heard them, in this wild retreat,
Warbling immortal airs, and ftrains of comfort.—
But ah the foe is round us: and this ifle

Now

Now holds my ſoul's beſt wealth, the treaſur'd ſtore
Of all my joys.—I go to ſkirt it round,
To viſit every creek and ſedgy bank,
Where ruſtles thro the reeds the ſhadowy gale;
Or where the bending umbrage drinks the ſtream.
And now, by ſlow degrees, ſolemn and ſad,
Wide-falling o'er the world, the nightly ſhades
Huſh the brown woods, and deepen all their horrors:
While humbled into reſt, and aw'd by darkneſs,
Each creature ſeeks the covert. To that cell
Retire, my life. I will not long be abſent.

End of the firſt Act.

ACT II.

SCENE I.

ALFRED *alone*.

'TIS now the depth of darkneſs and repoſe.
Now walks mute *Midnight* ſhadowy o'er the plain,
To rule the ſolitary hour; and ſheds
His ſlumbery influence o'er the peaceful world.
All nature ſeems to reſt: while ALFRED wakes
To think, and to be wretched.—My brave friend,
I fear me, has miſcarry'd.—Where yon oak
With wide and duſky ſhade o'erhangs the ſtream,
That glides in ſilence by, I took my ſtand:
What time the glow-worm thro' the dewy path
Firſt ſhot his twinkling flame. Attent I ſtood,
Liſtening each noiſe from twilight hill and dale:
But all was huſh'd around. Nor trumpet's clang,
Nor ſhout of roving foe, nor haſty tread
Of evening paſſenger, diſturb'd the wide
And awful ſtillneſs. Homeward as I ſped,
O'er many a delve, thro many a path perplext,
Maze running into maze; ill-boding thoughts
Haunted my ſteps.—Perhaps my gallant friend,
Diſcover'd to the *Danes*, this moment bleeds
Beneath their ſwords! or lies a breathleſs corſe,
The prey of midnight wolves.—Some mournful ſound
Struck ſudden on my ſenſe.

SCENE

SCENE II.

ALFRED, ELTRUDA.

ELTRUDA.

Here will I lean
On this green bank, to wait the wiſh'd return
Of morning, and my lord.

ALFRED.

My gentle love,
ELTRUDA, why to this untimely ſky
Expoſe thy health? The dews of night fall faſt:
The chill breeze ſighs aloud.

ELTRUDA

I could not reſt.
Can Love repoſe when Apprehenſion wakes,
And whiſpers to the heart all fearful things,
That walk with night and ſolitude? Methought,
In each deaf murmur of the woods, I heard
The dreadful foe—or heard my ALFRED groan!
Our tender infants too—their fancy'd cries
Still ſound within my ears!

ALFRED.

ELTRUDA, there
I am a woman too: I who ſhould cheer,
And ſhelter thee from every care. My children!
The thought of what may chance to them compleats
Their father's ſum of woes. O what ſafe ſhade
Can ſkreen their opening bloſſom from the ſtorm
That beats ſevere on us! Not ſweeter buds

The primrose in the vale, nor fooner fhrinks
At winter's churlifh blaft—

ELTRUDA.

Behold, my Lord—
Good Angels fhield us—What a flood of brightnefs
Waves round our heads!

ALFRED.

The Hermit moves this way.
That wondrous man holds converfe with the hoft
Of higher natures. Thefe far-beaming fires
Were doubtlefs kindled up at his command.
Be filent and attentive.

SCENE III.

ALFRED, ELTRUDA, HERMIT.

HERMIT.

I have heard
Thy fond complainings, ALFRED.

ALFRED.

You have then,
Good father, heard the caufe that wrings them from me.

HERMIT.

The human race are fons of forrow born:
And each muft have his portion. Vulgar minds
Refufe, or crouch beneath their load: the Brave
Bear theirs without repining.

ALFRED.

Who can bear
The fhaft that wounds him thro an infant's fide?
When whom we love, to whom we owe protection,
Implore the hand we cannot reach to fave them?

HERMIT.

HERMIT.

Weep not, ELTRUDA.—Yet thou art a king,
All private paſſions fall before that name.
Thy ſubjects claim thee whole.

ALFRED.

Can public truſt,
O reverend ſage! deſtroy the ſofter ties
That twine around the parent's yearning heart?
That holy paſſion heaven itſelf infus'd,
And blended with the ſtream that feeds our life.

HERMIT.

You love your children, Prince—

ALFRED.

Lives there on earth,
In air, or ocean, creature tame or wild
That has not known this univerſal love?
All nature feels it intimate and deep,
And all her ſons of inſtinct or of reaſon.

HERMIT.

Then ſhew that paſſion in its nobleſt form.
Seaſon their tender years with every virtue,
Social or ſelf-retir'd; of public greatneſs,
Or lovely in the hour of private life;
With all that can exalt, or can adorn
Their princely rank.

ALFRED.

Alas, their hope muſt ſtoop,
Such my unhappy fate, to humbler aims:
Affliction and baſe want muſt be their teachers.

HERMIT.

Affliction is the wholeſome ſoil of virtue:
Where patience, honor, ſweet humanity,
Calm fortitude take root, and ſtrongly flouriſh.
But proſperous fortune, that allures with pleaſure,

Dazles with pomp, and undermines with flattery,
Poisons the soil, and its best product kills.
Should'st thou regain thy throne—

ALFRED.

My throne? What glimpse,
What smallest ray of hope—

HERMIT.

That day may come—
What do I feel? My labouring breast expands
To give the glorious inspiration room.
And now the cloud that o'er thy future fate,
Like total night, lay heavy and obscure,
Fades into air: and all the brightening scene
Dawns gay before me! A long line of kings,
From thee descending, glorious and renown'd,
In shadowy pomp I see!

Genius of *England!* hovering near,
In all thy radiant charms appear.

O come and summon, from the world unknown,
Those mighty chiefs, those sons of future fame,
Who, ages hence, this island shall renown,
And spread to distant realms her dreaded name.
Slow let the visionary forms arise,
And solemn pass before our wondring eyes.

[*Music grand and awful. The Genius descending sings the following*

SONG.

SONG.

From those eternal regions bright,
Where suns, that never set in night,
Diffuse the golden day:
Where spring unfading pours around,
O'er all the dew-impearled ground,
Her thousand colors gay:
O whether on the fountain's flowery side,
Whence living waters glide,
Or in the fragrant grove,
Whose shade embosoms peace and love,
New pleasures all your hours employ,
And rapture every sense with every joy!
Great heirs of empire! yet unborn,
Who shall this island late adorn;
A monarch's drooping thought to chear,
Appear! appear! appear!

Spirits of EDWARD III. PHILIPPA *his queen, and the* Black Prince *his son, arise.*

HERMIT.

ALFRED, look; and say,
What seest thou yonder?

ALFRED.

Three majestic shapes:
Two habited like mighty warriors old;
A third in whose bright aspect beauty smiles
More soft and feminine. A lucid veil,
From her fair neck dependent floats around,
Light-hovering in the gale.

HERMIT.

O ALFRED, man

Belov'd

Belov'd of heaven, behold a King *indeed*;
Matchless in arms; in arts of peaceful rule,
A sovereign's truest glory, yet more fam'd,
England's third EDWARD!—At his fear'd approach,
Proud *France*, even now, thro all her dukedoms quakes.
Her Genius sighs: and from th' eternal shore,
The soul of her great CHARLES, a recent guest,
Looks back to earth, and mourns the distant woes,
His realms are doom'd to feel from EDWARD's wrath.
Beneath his standard, *Britain* shall go forth,
Array'd for conquest, terrible in glory:
And nations shrink before her. O what deaths,
What desolation shall her vengeance spread,
From engines yet unfound; whose lightnings flash,
Whose thunders roar, amazing, o'er the plain:
As if this King had summon'd from on high
Heaven's dread artillery to fight his battle!
 Nor is renown in war his sole ambition:
A nobler passion labours in his breast———
ALFRED attend——to make his people blest!
The sacred rights that Reason loudly claims
For free-born men——these, ALFRED, are his care:
Oft to confirm, and fix them on the base
Of equal laws.——O father of mankind!
Successive praises from a grateful land
Shall saint thy name for ever!

ALFRED.

Holy sage,
Whom angels thus enlighten and inspire,
My bosom kindles at thy heaven-born flame.
Great EDWARD! Be thy conquests and their praise
Unrival'd to thy self. But O thy fame
For care paternal of the public weal;
For *England* blest at home—my rapt heart pants

To

To equal that renown!

HERMIT.

Know farther, ALFRED;
A ſovereign's great example forms a people.
The public breaſt is noble, or is vile,
As he inſpires it. In this EDWARD's time,
Warm'd by his courage, by his honor rais'd,
High flames the *Britiſh* ſpirit, like the ſun,
To ſhine o'er half the globe: and where it ſhines,
The cheriſh'd world to brighten and enrich.
Laſt ſee this monarch in his hour of leiſure;
Even ſocial on a throne, and taſting joys
To ſolitary greatneſs ſeldom known:
As friend, as huſband, and as father bleſt.
That god-like *Youth* remark, his eldeſt hope,
Who gives new luſtre to the name he bears;
A hero ere a man.—I ſee him now
On *Creſſy*'s glorious plain! The father's heart,
With anxious love and wonder at his daring,
Beats high in mingled tranſport. Great himſelf,
Great above *jealouſy*, the guilty mark
That brands all meaner minds, ſee, he applauds
The *filial excellence*, and gives him ſcope
To blaze in his full brightneſs!—Lo again,
He ſends him dreadful to a nobler field:
The danger and the glory all his own!
A *captive King*, the rival of his arms,
I ſee adorn his triumph! Heaven! what grace
What ſplendor from his gracious temper mild
That triumph draws! As gentle Mercy kind,
He chears the hoſtile prince whoſe fall he weeps!

ALFRED.

A ſon ſo rich in virtues, and ſo grac'd
With all that gives thoſe virtues fair to ſhine,

When

When I would aſk of heaven ſome mighty boon,
Should claim the foremoſt place.

HERMIT.

Remember then,
What to thy infant ſons from thee is due,
As parent and as prince.

ELTRUDA.

Forgive me, Hermit,
Forgive a queen and wife her anxious fondneſs.
Yon beauteous ſhade, that, as I gaze her o'er,
My wonder draws, eſcapes your graver thought.

HERMIT.

O bright ELTRUDA! thou whoſe blooming youth,
Whoſe amiable ſweetneſs promiſe bleſſings
To ALFRED and to *England!* ſee, and mark,
In yonder pleaſing form, the beſt of wives,
The happieſt too, repaid with all the faith,
With all the friendſhip, love and duty claim.
She, powerful o'er the heart her charms enſlave—
O virtue rarely practis'd!—uſes nobly
That happy influence; to prompt each purpoſe
Fair honor kindles in her EDWARD's breaſt.
Amid the pomps, the pleaſures of a court,
Humble of heart, ſeverely good: the friend
Of modeſt worth, the parent of the poor.
ELTRUDA! O tranſmit theſe nobleſt charms
To that fair *daughter*, that unfolding roſe,
With which, *as on this day*, heaven crown'd your loves.

The ſpirit of ELIZABETH *ariſes.*

ALFRED.

Say, who is ſhe, in whom the noble graces,
Th' engaging manner, dignity and eaſe,
Are join'd with manly ſenſe and reſolution?

HERMIT.

The great ELIZA. She, amid a world
That threatning ſwells in high commotion round her;
Each dangerous ſtate her unrelenting foe,
And chief a proud enormous empire ſtretch'd
O'er half mankind; with not one friendly power,
But what her kind creating hand ſhall raiſe
From out the marſhes of the branching *Rhine*;
And min'd, at home, her ever-tottering throne
By reſtleſs bigots, who, beneath the maſk
Of mild religion, are to every crime
Set looſe, the faithleſs ſons of barbarous zeal:
Yet ſhe ſhall crown this happy iſle with peace,
With arts, with riches, grandeur and renown;
And daſh, by turns, the madneſs of her foes.
As when the winds, from different quarters, urge
The tempeſt on our ſhore: ſecure, the cliffs
Repel its idle rage, and pour it back,
In broken billows, foaming to the main.

ALFRED.

How ſhall ſhe, Hermit, gain theſe glorious ends?

HERMIT.

By ſilent wiſdom, whoſe informing power
Works unperceiv'd: that ſeems in council ſlow;
But, when reſolv'd and ripe for execution,
That parts like lightning from the ſecret gloom.
By ever ſeizing the right *point* of view,
Her trueſt intereſt; which ſhe firm purſues,
With ſteady patience, thro the maze of ſtate,
The ſtorm of oppoſition, the mixt views,
And thwarting manag'd paſſions of mankind.
By healing the diviſions of her people,
And ſowing that fell peſt among her foes.
By ſaving, from the vermin of a court,
Her treaſure; which, when fair occaſion calls,

She knows to lavish, in protecting arts,
In guarding nations, and in nursing states.
By calling up to power, and public life,
Each virtue, each ability: yet *she*,
Amid the various worthies glowing round her,
Still shines the first; the central sun that wakes,
That rules their every motion: not the slave,
And passive property of her own creatures.
But the great soul that animates her reign,
That lights it to perfection, is the love,
The confidence unbounded, which her wisdom,
Her probity and justice, shall inspire
Into the public breast. Hence cordial faith,
Which nought can shake; hence unexhausted treasure:
And hence, above all mercenary force,
The hand that by the freeborn heart is rais'd,
And guards the blended weal of prince and people
She too shall rouse *Britannia*'s naval soul;
Shall greatly ravish, from insulting *Spain*,
The world-commanding scepter of the deep.

ELTRUDA.

O matchless queen! O glory of her sex!
The great idea, father, fills my soul,
And bids it glow beyond a woman's passions.

Spirit of WILLIAM III. *arises.*

HERMIT.

Once more, O ALFRED, raise thine eyes, and mark,
Who next adorns the scene, yon laurel'd *shade*.
Ere yet the age that clos'd this female reign
Hath led around its train of circling years,
Shall *Britain* on the verge of ruin stand.
A *monarch*, lost to greatness, to renown,
The slave of dreaming monks, shall fill her throne.
Weak and aspiring; fond of lawless rule,

The

The lawleſs rule his mean ambition covets
Unequal to acquire. Yon prince thou ſaw'ſt,
To glory tutor'd by the hand ſevere
Of ſharp Adverſity, ſhall heaven upraiſe,
And injur'd nations with joint call invoke,
Their laſt, their only refuge. Lo! he comes:
Wide o'er the billows of the boundleſs deep
His navy rides triumphant: and the ſhores
Of ſhouting *Albion* echo with his name.
Immortal WILLIAM! from before his face,
Flies Superſtition, flies oppreſſive Power,
With vile Servility that crouch'd and kiſs'd
The whip he trembled at. From this great hour
Shall *Britain* date her rights and laws reſtor'd:
And one high purpoſe rule her ſovereign's heart;
To ſcourge the pride of *France*, that foe profeſs'd
To *England* and to freedom. Yet I ſee,
From diſtant climes in peaceful triumph borne,
Another KING ariſe! His early youth
With living laurel crown'd, for deeds of arms
That Reaſon's voice approves; for courage, rais'd
Beyond all aid from paſſion, greatly calm!
Intrepidly ſerene!—In days of peace,
Around his throne the human virtues wait,
And fair adorn him with their mildeſt beams;
Good without ſhow, above ambition great;
Wiſe, equal, merciful, the friend of man!
O ALFRED! ſhould thy fate, long ages hence,
In meaning ſcenes recall'd, exalt the joy
Of ſome glad feſtal day, before a *prince*
Sprung from that king belov'd—Hear, gracious heaven!
Thy ſoft humanity, thy patriot heart,
Thy manly virtue, ſteddy, great, reſolv'd,
Be his ſupreme ambition! and with theſe,

The happineſs, the glory, that await
Thy better days—be ſhower'd upon his head!

ALFRED.

O Hermit! thou haſt rais'd me to new life!
New hopes, new triumphs ſwell my bounding heart—

HERMIT.

It comes! it comes!—The promis'd ſcene diſcloſes!
Already the great work of ſate begins!
The mighty wheels are turning, whence will ſpread,
Beyond the limits of our narrow world,
The fair dominions, ALFRED, of thy ſons,
Behold the warrior bright with *Daniſh* ſpoils!—
The *raven* droops his wings—and hark! the trumpet,
Exulting, ſpeaks the reſt.

SCENE IV.

Symphony of martial muſic.

ALFRED, ELTRUDA, HERMIT, *Earl of* DEVON, *followed by ſoldiers.*

ALFRED.

Welcome, my lord
I ſee true courage lags not in its courſe;
It ſtands not weighing actions, with cold wiſdom
That borders near on cowardice.

DEVON.

My Liege,
Your troops have been ſucceſsful.—But to heaven
Aſcend the praiſe! For ſure th'event exceeds
The hand of man.

ALFRED.

How was it, noble DEVON?

DEVON.

You know my caſtle is not hence far-diſtant,
Thither I ſped: and in a *Daniſh* habit
The trenches paſſing, by a ſecret way,
Known to myſelf alone, emerg'd at once
Amid my joyful ſoldiers. There I found
A generous few, the veteran, hardy gleanings
Of many a hapleſs fight. They with a fierce
And gloomy joy inſpirited each other;
Reſolv'd on death, diſdaining to ſurvive
Their deareſt country.—" If we fall, I cry'd,
" Let us not tamely fall like paſſive cowards!
" No: let us live—or let us die, like men!
" Come on, my friends: to ALFRED we will cut
" Our glorious way; or, as we nobly periſh,
" Will offer to the genius of our country
" Whole hecatombs of *Danes*."—As if one ſoul
Had mov'd them all, around their heads they flaſh'd
Their flaming faulchions—" Lead us to theſe *Danes!*—
" Our country!—vengeance!" was the general cry.
Strait on the careleſs drouſy camp we ruſh'd:
And rapid, as the flame devours the ſtubble,
Bore down the heartleſs *Danes*. With this ſucceſs
Our enterprize encreas'd. Not now contented
To hew a paſſage thro the flying herd;
We, unremitting, urg'd a total rout.
The valiant HUBBA bites the bloody field,
With twice ſix hundred *Danes* around him ſtrow'd.

ALFRED.

My glorious friend!—this action has reſtor'd
Our ſinking country.—What reward can equal
A deed ſo great?—Is not yon pictur'd *Raven*
Their famous magic ſtandard—Emblem fit

To ſpeak the ſavage genius of the people—
That oft has ſcatter'd on our troops diſmay,
And feeble conſternation?

DEVON.

'Tis the ſame.
Wrought by the ſiſters of the *Daniſh* king,
Of furious IVAR, in a midnight hour:
While the ſick moon, at their enchanted ſong,
Wrapt in pale tempeſt, labour'd thro' the clouds
The *Demons* of deſtruction then, they ſay,
Were all abroad, and mixing with the woof
Their baleful power: The ſiſters ever ſung;
"Shake, ſtandard, ſhake this ruin on our foes!"

HERMIT.

So theſe infernal powers, with rays of truth
Still deck their fables, to delude who truſt them.

ALFRED.

But where, my noble couſin, are the reſt
Of your brave troops?

DEVON.

On t'other ſide the ſtream,
That half encloſes this retreat, I left them.
Rous'd from the fear, with which it was congeal'd
As in a froſt, the country pours amain.
The ſpirit of our anceſtors is up,
The ſpirit of the Free! and with a voice
That breathes ſucceſs, they all demand their king.

ALFRED.

Quick, let us join them, and improve their ardor.
We cannot be too haſty to ſecure
The glances of occaſion.

SCENE

SCENE *the laſt.*

To them CORIN, EMMA, *kneeling to* ALFRED.

CORIN.

Good my Liege,
Pardon the poor unequal entertainment,
Which we, unknowing—

ALFRED.

Riſe, my honeſt ſhepherd.
I came to thee a peaſant, not a prince :
And, what exalts a king o'er other men,
Stript of the toys of royalty? Yet more,
Thy rural entertainment was ſincere,
Plain, hoſpitable, kind : ſuch as, I hope,
Will ever mark the manners of this nation.
You friendly lodg'd me, when by all deſerted :
And ſhall have ample recompenſe.

CORIN.

One boon,
Is all I crave.

ALFRED.

Good ſhepherd, ſpeak thy wiſh.

CORIN.

Permiſſion, in your wars, to ſerve your Grace :
For tho here loſt in ſolitary ſhades,
A ſimple ſwain, I bear an *Engliſh* heart :
A heart that burns with rage to ſee thoſe *Danes*,
Thoſe foreign ruffians, thoſe inhuman pirates,
Oft our inferiors prov'd, thus lord it o'er us.

ALFRED.

ALFRED.

Brave countryman, come on. 'Tis ſuch as thou,
Who from affection ſerve, and free-born zeal,
To guard whate'er is dear and ſacred to them,
That are a king's beſt honor and defence.

EMMA *ſings the following ſong.*

1.

If thoſe, who live in ſhepherd's bower,
Preſs not the rich and ſtately bed:
The new-mown hay and breathing flower
A ſofter couch beneath them ſpread.

2.

If thoſe, who ſit at ſhepherd's board,
Soothe not their taſte by wanton art;
They take what Nature's gifts afford,
And take it with a chearful heart.

3.

If thoſe, who drain the ſhepherd's bowl,
No high and ſparkling wines can boaſt;
With wholeſome cups they chear the ſoul,
And crown them with the village toaſt.

4.

If thoſe, who join in ſhepherd's ſport,
Gay-dancing on the daizy'd ground,
Have not the ſplendor of a court;
Yet Love adorns the merry round.

ALFRED.

ALFRED.

My lov'd ELTRUDA! thou ſhalt here remain,
With gentle EMMA, and this reverend Hermit.
Ye ſilver ſtreams, that murmuring wind around
This duſky ſpot, to you I truſt my all!
O cloſe around her, woods! for her, ye vales,
Throw forth your flowers, your ſofteſt lap diffuſe!
And *Thou!* whoſe ſecret and expanſive hand
Moves all the ſprings of this vaſt univerſe:
Whoſe government aſtoniſhes; who here,
In a few hours, beyond our utmoſt hope,
Beyond our thought, yet doubting, haſt clear'd up
The ſtorm of fate: preſerve what thy kind will,
Thy bountiful appointment, makes ſo dear
To human hearts! preſerve my queen and children!
Preſerve the hopes of *England!* while I go
To finiſh thy great work, and ſave my country.

ELTRUDA.

Go, pay the debt of honor to the public.
If ever woman, ALFRED, lov'd her huſband
More fondly than herſelf, I claim that virtue,
That heart-felt happineſs. Yet, by our loves
I ſwear, that in a glorious death with thee
I rather would be wrapt, than live long years
To charm thee from the rugged paths of honor:
So much I think thee born for beauteous deeds,
And the bright courſe of glory.

ALFRED.

Matchleſs woman!
Love, at thy voice, is kindled to ambition.
Be this my deareſt triumph, to approve me
A huſband worthy of the beſt ELTRUDA!

HERMIT.

Behold, my Lord, our venerable Bard,

Aged and blind, him whom the Muses favour.
Yet ere you go, in our lov'd country's praise,
That noblest theme, hear what his rapture breathes.

An ODE.

1.

When Britain *first, at heaven's command,*
Arose from out the azure main;
This *was the charter of the land,*
And guardian Angels sung this *strain:*
" *Rule* Britannia, *rule the waves;*
" Britons *never will be slaves.*"

2.

The nations, not so blest as thee,
Must, in their turns, to tyrants fall:
While thou shalt flourish great and free,
The dread and envy of them all.
" *Rule*, &c.

3.

Still more majestic shalt thou rise,
More dreadful, from each foreign stroke:
As the loud blast that tears the skies,
Serves but to root thy native oak.
" *Rule*, &c.

4.

Thee haughty tyrants ne'er shall tame:
All their attempts to bend thee down,
Will but arrouse thy generous flame;
But work their woe, and thy renown.
" *Rule, &c.*

5.

5.

To thee belongs the rural reign ;
Thy cities ſhall with commerce ſhine :
All thine ſhall be the ſubject main,
And every ſhore it circles thine.
" *Rule*, &c.

6.

The Muſes, ſtill with freedom found,
Shall to thy happy coaſt repair :
Bleſt iſle! with matchleſs beauty crown'd,
And manly hearts to guard the fair.
" *Rule*, Britannia, *rule the waves :*
" Britons *never will be ſlaves.*

HERMIT.

ALFRED, go forth! lead on the radiant years,
To thee reveal'd in viſion.—Lo! they riſe!
Lo! patriots, heroes, ſages, croud to birth:
And bards to ſing them in immortal verſe!
I ſee thy commerce, *Britain*, graſp the world:
All nations ſerve thee; every foreign flood,
Subjected, pays its tribute to the *Thames*.
Thither the golden South obedient pours
His ſunny treaſures: thither the ſoft Eaſt
Her ſpices, delicacies, gentle gifts:
And thither his rough trade the ſtormy North.
See, where beyond the vaſt *Atlantic* ſurge,
By boldeſt keels untouch'd, a dreadful ſpace!
Shores, yet unfound, ariſe! in youthful prime,
With towering foreſts, mighty rivers crown'd!
Theſe ſtoop to *Britain*'s thunder. This new world,
Shook to its centre, trembles at her name:

And

And there, her ſons, with aim exalted, ſow
The ſeeds of riſing empire, arts, and arms.

Britons, proceed, the ſubject Deep command,
Awe with your navies every hoſtile land.
In vain their threats, their armies all in vain:
They rule the balanc'd world, who rule the main.

The END.

ALFRED

revised, 1751; textual markings by John Genest

ALFRED.

A

MASQUE.

ACTED at the

THEATRE-ROYAL

IN

DRURY-LANE,

By His MAJESTY's Servants.

Price One Shilling and Six-pence.

ALFRED:

A

MASQUE.

Acted at the

THEATRE-ROYAL

IN

DRURY-LANE,

By His Majesty's Servants.

LONDON:

Printed for A. Millar, oppoſite to Catharine-Street, in the Strand.

M. DCC. LI.

Advertisement.

HAving been obliged to discontinue the Duke of MARLBOROUGH'*s History for a few months past, till I could receive from a foreign country some papers of importance; that I might not be quite idle in the mean while, I read over, in order to improve, this* MASQUE; *the first draught of which had been written by the late Mr.* THOMSON, *in conjunction with me, several years ago. But, to fit it for the stage, I found it would be necessary to new-plan the whole, as well as write the particular scenes over again; to enlarge the design, and make* ALFRED, *what he should have been at first, the principal figure in his own* MASQUE. *This I have done; but, according to the present arrangement of the Fable, I was obliged to reject a great deal of what I had written in the other: neither could I retain, of my friend's part, more than three or four speeches, and a part of one song. I mention this expresly; that, whatever faults are found in the present performance, they may be charged, as they ought to be, entirely to my account.*

D. Mallet.

PROLOGUE.

By a FRIEND.

Spoken by Mr. GARRICK.

IN arms renown'd, for arts of peace ador'd,
ALFRED, the nation's father, more than lord,
A British *author has presum'd to draw,*
Struck deep, even now, with reverential awe;
And sets the godlike figure fair in view—
O may discernment find the likeness true.
When Danish *fury, with wide-wasting hand,*
Had spread pale fear, and ravage o'er the land,
This prince arising bade confusion cease,
Bade order shine, and blest his isle with peace;
Taught liberal arts to humanize the mind,
And heaven-born science to sweet freedom join'd.
United thus, the friendly sisters shone,
And one secur'd, while one adorn'd, his throne.
Amidst these honors of his happy reign,
Each Grace and every Muse compos'd his train:
As grateful servants, all exulting strove,
At once to spread his fame, and share his love.
To night, if aught of fiction you behold,
Think not, in Virtue's cause, the bard too bold.
If ever angels from the skies descend,
It must be—truth and freedom to defend.
Thus would our author please—be it your part,
If not his labors, to approve his heart.
True to his country's, and to honor's cause,
He fixes, there, his fame, and your applause;
Wishes no failing from your sight to hide,
But, by free BRITONS, *will be freely try'd.*

PERSONS.

ALFRED.	*Mr.* GARRICK.
Earl of DEVON.	*Mr.* LEE.
EDWIN.	*Mr.* BURTON.
HERMIT.	*Mr.* BERRY.
CORIN.	*Mr.* BLAKES.
DANISH *King*.	*Mr.* SOWDON.
First DANE.	*Mr.* PALMER.
Second DANE.	*Mr.* MOZEEN.
ELTRUDA.	*Miss* BELLAMY.
EMMA.	*Mrs.* BENNET.
SHEPHERDESS.	*Miss* MINORS.

The Vocal Parts by

Mrs. CLIVE, *Miss* NORRIS, *Mr.* BEARD, *Mr.* REINHOLD, *Mr.* WILDER, *Master* VERNON, *&c.*

Shepherdesses, Soldiers, Attendants, Spirits.

The SCENE *represents a Plain, surrounded with woods. On one side, a cottage; on the other, flocks and herds in distant prospect. A Hermit's cave in full view, over-hung with trees, wild and grotesque.*

ALFRED:

A

MASQUE.

ACT I. SCENE I.

CORIN *and* EMMA *appear at the door of their cottage.*

Two SHEPHERDESSES.

First SHEPHERDESS *sings.*

O PEACE, the fairest child of heaven,
To whom the sylvan reign was given,
The vale, the fountain, and the grove,
With every softer scene of love;
Return, sweet Peace, to chear the weeping swain:
Return, with Ease and Pleasure in thy train.

EMMA, *coming forward.*

Shepherd, 'tis he. Againſt yon aged oak,
Penſive and loſt in thought, he leans his head.

CORIN.

Soft: let us not diſturb him. Gentle EMMA,
Poor tho he be, unfriended and unknown,
My pity waits with reverence on his fortune.
Modeſt of carriage, and of ſpeech moſt gracious,
As if ſome ſaint or angel in diſguiſe
Had grac'd our lowly cottage with his preſence,
He ſteals, I know not how, into the heart,
And makes it pant to ſerve him. Truſt me, EMMA,
He is no common man.

EMMA.

Some lord, perhaps,
Or valiant chief, that from our deadly foe,
The haughty, cruel, unbelieving *Dane*,
Seeks ſhelter here.

CORIN.

And ſhelter he ſhall find:
Who loves his country, is my friend and brother.
Behold him well. Fair manhood in it's prime,
Even thro the homely ruſſet that conceals him,
Shines forth, and proves him noble.

EMMA.

'Tis moſt like,
He is not what his preſent fortunes ſpeak him.
But, ah! th' inhuman foe is all around us:
We dare not keep him here.

CORIN.

CORIN.

Thou haſt not weigh'd
This iſland's force; the deep defence of woods,
Nature's own hand hath planted ſtrong around;
The rough encumbrance of perplexing thorns,
Of intertwining brakes that riſe between,
And choak up every inlet from abroad.
Yet more; thou know'ſt, beyond this woody verge
Two rivers broad and rapid hem us in;
Along whoſe border ſpreads the gulphy pool,
And trembling quagmire to betray the foot
It's treacherous greenſword tempts. One path alone
Winds to this plain, ſo difficult and ſtrait,
My ſingle arm, againſt a band of foes,
Could long, perhaps, defend it.

EMMA.

Yet, my CORIN,
Revolve the ſtern decree of that fierce tyrant,
The *Daniſh* king: "Who harbours, or relieves
" An *Engliſh* captain, dies the death of traitors:
" But who their haunts diſcovers, ſhall be ſafe,
" And high rewarded."

CORIN.

Now, juſt heaven forbid,
An *Engliſhman* ſhould ever count for gain
What villainy muſt earn. No: are we poor?
Be honeſty our riches. Are we mean,
And humbly born? The true heart makes us noble.
Theſe hands can toil; can ſow the ground and reap
For thee and thy ſweet babes. Our daily labour

Is daily wealth: it finds us bread and raiment.
Could *Danish* gold give more?

EMMA.

Alas the while!
That loyal faith is fled from hall and bower,
To dwell with village-swains!

CORIN.

Ah look! behold,
Where EDITH, all-abandon'd to despair,
Hangs weeping o'er the brook.

Second SHEPHERDESS *approaches slowly to soft music.*

Is there not cause?

all the above in the Ed of 1740 -
alterations are slight

She

She sings.

I.

A youth adorn'd with every art,
To warm and win the coldest heart,
In secret mine possest:
The morning bud that fairest blows,
The vernal oak that straitest grows,
His face and shape exprest.

II.

In moving sounds he told his tale,
Soft as the sighings of the gale
That wakes the flowery year.
What wonder he could charm with ease!
Whom happy nature form'd to please,
Whom love had made sincere.

III.

At morn he left me—fought, and fell;
The fatal evening heard his knell,
And saw the tears I shed:
Tears that must ever, ever fall;
For ah! no sighs the past recall,
No cries awake the dead!

CORIN.

CORIN.

Unhappy maid! yet not alone in woe:
For look, where our ſad gueſt, like ſome fair tree
Torn from the root by winter's cruel blaſt,
Lies on the ground o'erthrown.

EMMA.

I weep, to ſee it!

CORIN.

Thou haſt a heart ſweet pity loves to dwell in:
But, dry thy tears, and lean on this juſt hope——
If yet to do away his country's ſhame,
To ſerve her bravely on ſome bleſt occaſion;
If for theſe ends this ſtranger ſought our cottage,
The heavenly hoſts are hovering here unſeen,
To guard his ſacred life, and bleſs us all.
But let us hence: he riſes to embrace
His friend, a woodman of the neighbouring dale,
Whom late, as yeſter-evening ſtar aroſe,
At his requeſt I bid to meet him here.

SCENE

SCENE II.

ALFRED, *Earl of* DEVON.

ALFRED.

How long, juſt heaven! how long
Shall war's fell ravage deſolate this land?
All, all is loſt—and ALFRED lives to tell it!
Are theſe things ſo? and he without the means
Of great revenge? caſt down below the hope
Of ſuccouring thoſe he weeps for?

DEVON.

Gracious ALFRED,
England's laſt hope, whoſe feeling goodneſs ſhews
What angels are; to bear, with ſuch a prince,
The worſt of ills, exile, or chains, or death,
Is happineſs, is glory.

ALFRED.

Ah! look round thee—
That mud-built cottage is thy ſovereign's palace.
Yon hind, whoſe daily toil is all his wealth,
Lodges and feeds him. Are theſe times for flattery?
Or call it praiſe: ſuch gaudy attributes
Would miſbecome our beſt and proudeſt fortunes.
But what are mine? What is this high-priz'd ALFRED?
Among ten thouſand wretches moſt undone!

1740

That prince who ſees his country laid in ruins,
His ſubjects periſhing beneath the ſword
Of foreign war; who ſees and cannot ſave them,
Is but ſupreme in miſery!—But on,
Proceed, my lord; compleat the mournful tale,
My griefs broke off.

DEVON.

From yonder heath-clad hill,
Far as my ſtraining eye could ſhoot it's beam
I look'd, and ſaw the progreſs of the foe,
As of ſome tempeſt, ſome devouring tide,
That ruins, without mercy, where it ſpreads.
The riches of the year, the bread of thouſands
That liberal crown'd our plains from vale to hill,
With intermingled foreſts, temples, towers,
Now ſmoak to heaven, one broad-aſcending cloud.
But oh for pity! on each mountain's height,
Shivering and ſad the pale inhabitants,
Gray-headed age and youth, all ſtood and mark'd
This boundleſs ravage: motionleſs and mute,
With hands to heaven up-rais'd, they ſtood and wept—
My tears attended theirs—

ALFRED.

If this ſad ſight
Could pain thee to ſuch anguiſh, what muſt I
Their king and parent feel?

DEVON.

Sir, be of comfort.
Who has not known ill fortune, never knew
Himself, or his own virtue.

ALFRED.

Well—no more—
Complaint is for the vulgar: kings must act;
Restore a ruin'd state, or perish with it.
Despair shall be our strength—

DEVON.

Behold, my lord,
From yonder hazle copse, who issues forth,
And moves this way—a stranger—but his look
Speaks haste and apprehension—

ALFRED.

Ha! beyond
My utmost hope!—'Tis EDWIN—

SCENE III.

ALFRED, DEVON, EDWIN.

ALFRED.

Hast thou ought
Of joyful to impart? or is the soul
Of *England* dead indeed?

EDWIN.

My gracious maſter,
This journey has been fruitful to our wiſh.
Awak'd, as from the laſt and mortal trance,
That ſoul, which ſeem'd extinguiſh'd, lives again.
By me aſſur'd, their ſovereign ſtill ſurvives,
Survives to take due vengeance on thoſe robbers,
Who violate the ſanctity of leagues,
The reverend ſeal of oaths; who baſely broke,
Like midnight ruffians, on the hour of peace,
And ſtole a victory from men unarm'd;
Of this aſſur'd, your people breathe once more.
The ſpirit of our anceſtors is up!
The ſpirit of the free! and, with one voice
Of happy omen, all demand their king.

ALFRED.

Then, heaven who knows our wrongs will deign to guide
The virtue it inſpires—My lord, how ſound
Theſe tidings in your ears?

DEVON.

As the ſure omen
Of better fate, my heart receives and hails them.
For know, my liege, the fury of thoſe *Danes*,
This laſt dire ſcene of total deſolation,
Will kindle up the flame to ſeven-fold fierceneſs;
New-wing each ſhaft, edge every lifted ſword,
And drive—

ALFRED.

A moment—EDWIN, yet inform me
What numbers have you gather'd? how diſpos'd,
Where poſted them?

EDWIN.

In theſe ſurrounding woods,
Soon as the ſhade of night deſcends to veil them,
A generous few, the veteran hardy gleanings
Of many a well-fought field, all at one hour,
Behind the ruſhy brook from hence due eaſt,
By different paths, and in ſmall parties meet,
Accoutred at all points: and, as I judge,
Their numbers count twelve hundred.

ALFRED.

Ha! twelve hundred—
Incredible—ſoft—let me duly weigh
What I, unhoping, ſcarce believing, hear.
Something muſt, now, be done—Ay, that attempt
Is great—but greatly hazardous—why then,
Neceſſity, our juſt plea, muſt excuſe
The deſperate daring her hard law impoſes.
Hear, my brave friends. One caſtle ſtill is ours,
Tho cloſe begirt and ſhaken by the *Danes*.
DEVON, ſpeed thither: find out that cloſe path,
By EDWIN's eye and aid, which from the midſt,
The central point of *Kinwith-foreſt* winds
In deep deſcent; and, under ground prolong'd,
Safe in the fortreſs ends.

DEVON.

Suppoſe me there:
What follows this, my lord?

ALFRED.

Be it your part
To animate our brothers of the war,
Thoſe *Engliſhmen*, who yet deſerve that name.
The foe—dwell much on this—by our known weakneſs
Made daring and ſecure, will now the rein
Of diſcipline relax, and to looſe revel
Indulge the midnight hour. Therefore, at three—
O count the clock with more than lovers' vigilance—
At three, that choſen band ſhall from behind,
Riſing at once, with ALFRED at their head,
Aſſail the hoſtile camp: while your warm ſally,
That very moment, pours upon it's front.
Hence; and ſucceſs be thine.

DEVON.

On this our purpoſe,
The ſacred cauſe of liberty and vengeance,
Smile, righteous heaven!

ALFRED.

O urge it home, my friend,
That each man's ſword now wears upon it's point
The preſent age, and laſt poſterity!
Farewell. EDWIN, within the hour return,
And find me here.

SCENE IV.

ALFRED.

Ha! day declines apace.
What anxious thoughts, in this wild ſolitude,
My darker hours muſt know? And now, the veil
Of evening, o'er theſe murmuring woods around,
A lonely horror ſpreads—But ſoft: the breeze
Is dumb! and more than midnight ſilence reigns!
Why beats my boſom?—Muſic! Shield me, heaven!
Whence ſhould it come?—Hark!—now the meaſur'd ſtrains,
In awful ſweetneſs warbling, ſtrike my ſenſe,
As if ſome wing'd muſician of the ſky
Touch'd his ethereal harp.

SCENE V.

Solemn music is heard at a distance. It comes nearer in a full symphony: after which a single trumpet sounds a high and awakening air. Then the following stanzas are sung by two aëreal Spirits.

First SPIRIT.

Hear, ALFRED, *father of the state,*
Thy genius heaven's high will declare!
What proves the hero truly great,
Is never, never to despair.

Both SPIRITS.

Is never to despair.

Second SPIRIT.

Thy hope awake, thy heart expand
With all its vigour, all its fires:
Arise, and save a sinking land!
Thy country calls and heaven inspires.

Both SPIRITS.

Earth calls and heaven inspires.

SCENE

SCENE VI.

ALFRED.

Am I awake! and is it no illuſion
That heaven thus deigns to look with mercy on me?
Thus, by his miniſters, to chear my heart,
And warm it into hope? But lo! he comes,
Whom angels deign to viſit and inſpire,
The holy ſage, deſcending from his cell
In yon hill's cavern'd ſide: ſweet ſylvan ſcene
Where ſhade and ſilence dwell!

SCENE VII.

ALFRED, HERMIT.

ALFRED.

Thrice happy HERMIT!
Whom thus the heavenly habitants attend,
Bleſſing thy calm retreat; while ruthleſs war
Fills the polluted land with blood and crimes.

In this extremity of *England*'s fate,
Led by thy ſacred character, I come
For comfort and advice. Say what remains,
What yet remains to ſave our proſtrate country?
Nor ſcorn this anxious queſtion even from me,
A nameleſs ſtranger.

HERMIT.

ALFRED, *England*'s king,
All hail, and welcome to this humble cell.

ALFRED.

Amazement!—by theſe humble weeds obſcur'd,
I deem'd my ſtate beyond diſcovery's reach:
How is it then to thee alone reveal'd?

HERMIT.

Laſt night, when with a draught from that cool fountain
I had my wholeſome ſober ſupper crown'd;
As is my ſtated cuſtom, forth I walk'd
Beneath the ſolemn gloom and glittering sky,
To feed my ſoul with prayer and meditation.
And thus to inward harmony compos'd,
That ſweeteſt muſic of the grateful heart,
Whoſe each emotion is a ſilent hymn,
I to my couch retir'd. Strait on mine eyes
A pleaſing ſlumber fell, whoſe myſtic power
Seal'd up my ſenſes, but enlarg'd my ſoul.
Led by thoſe ſpirits, who diſcloſe futurity,
I liv'd thro diſtant ages; felt the virtue,
The great, the glorious paſſions that will fire
Remote poſterity; when guardian laws
Are by the patriot, in the glowing ſenate,

Won from corruption; when th' impatient arm
Of liberty, invincible, ſhall ſcourge
The tyrants of mankind—and when the deep,
Thro all her ſwelling waves, from pole to pole
Shall ſpread the boundleſs empire of thy ſons.
I ſaw thee, ALFRED, too—But o'er thy fortunes
Lay clouds impenetrable.

ALFRED.

To heaven's will,
In either fortune, mine ſhall ever bend
With humbleſt reſignation—Yet, O ſay,
Does that unerring Providence, whoſe juſtice
Has bow'd me to the duſt; whoſe miniſters,
Sword, fire and famine, ſcourge this ſinful land,
This tomb of it's inhabitants—does he
Reſerve me in his hand, the glorious inſtrument
From fierce oppreſſion to redeem my country?

HERMIT.

What mortal eye, by his immediate beam
Not yet enlighten'd, dare preſume to look
Thro time's abyſs? But ſhould the flatterer, hope,
Anticipating ſee that happy time,
Thoſe whiter moments—Prince, remember, then,
The noble leſſons by affliction taught:
Preſerve the quick humanity it gives,
The pitying ſocial ſenſe of human weakneſs;
Yet keep thy generous fortitude entire,
The manly heart, that to another's woe
Is tender, as ſuperiour to it's own.

Learn to ſubmit: yet learn to conquer fortune.
Attach thee firmly to the virtuous deeds
And offices of life: to life itſelf,
With all it's vain and tranſient joys, ſit looſe.
Chief, let devotion to the ſovereign Mind,
A ſteady, chearful, abſolute dependance
On his beſt wiſeſt government, poſſeſs thee.

ALFRED.

I thank thee, father: and O witneſs, heaven,
Whoſe eye the heart's profoundeſt depth explores!
That if not to perform my regal taſk;
To be the common father of my people,
Patron of honor, virtue and religion;
If not to ſhelter uſeful worth, to guard
His well-earn'd portion from the ſons of rapine,
And deal out juſtice with impartial hand;
If not to ſpread, on all good men, thy bounty,
The treaſures truſted to me, not my own;
If not to raiſe anew our *Engliſh* name,
By peaceful arts that grace the land they bleſs,
And generous war to humble proud oppreſſors;
Yet more; if not to build the public weal,
On that firm baſe which can alone reſiſt
Both time and chance, on liberty and law;
If I for theſe great ends am not ordain'd—
May I ne'er poorly fill the throne of *England*!

HERMIT.

HERMIT.

Still may thy breaſt theſe ſentiments retain,
In proſperous life.

ALFRED.

Could it deſtroy or change
Such thoughts as theſe, proſperity were ruin.

Two SPIRITS *sing the following hymn.*

FIRST.

O joy of joys, to lighten woe!
Best pleasure, pleasure to bestow!
What raptures then his *heart expand,*
Who lives to bless a grateful land.

Second SPIRIT.

For him, ten thousand bosoms beat;
His name consenting crouds repeat:
From soul to soul the passion runs,
And subjects kindle into sons.

HERMIT.

HERMIT.

ALFRED, once more—since favour'd thus of heaven,
Since thus to cheer thee and confirm thy virtue
He sends his angels forth—remember well,
Should better days restore thy prosperous fortunes,
The vows these awful beings hear thee make:
Remember and fulfil them.

ALFRED.

O no more—
When those whom heaven distinguishes o'er millions,
And showers profusely power and splendor on them,
Whate'er th' expanded heart can wish; when they,
Accepting the reward, neglect the duty,
Or worse, pervert those gifts to deeds of ruin,
Is there a wretch they rule so base as they?
Guilty, at once, of sacrilege to heaven!
And of perfidious robbery to man!

HERMIT.

Such thoughts become a monarch—but behold,
The glimmering dusk, involving air and sky,
Creeps slow and solemn on. Devotion now,
With eye enraptur'd, as the kindling stars
Light, one by one, all heaven into a glow
Of living fire, adores the Hand divine,
Who form'd their orbs and pour'd forth glory on them.

ALFRED.

Then, this good moment, ſnatch'd from earth's affairs,
Let us employ aright: and, in yon cell,
To Him, with heart ſincere, our homage pay,
Who glorious ſpreads and gracious ſhuts the day.

End of the Firſt Act.

ACT

ACT II. SCENE I.

EMMA, *and other Peaſants.*

WISH'D evening now is come: but her ſoft hour,
Cloſe of our daily toil, that wont to ſound
Sweet with the ſhepherd's pipe and virgin's voice,
Is chearleſs all and mute.

Second SHEPHERDESS.

Heaven's will be ours.
And ſince no grief can yeſterday recall,
Nor change tomorrow's face; now let us ſoothe
The preſent as we may with dance and ſong,
To lighten ſad remembrance.

First SHEPHERDESS *sings.*

I.

The shepherd's plain life,
Without guilt, without strife,
Can only true blessings impart.
As nature directs,
That bliss he expects
From health and from quiet of heart.

II.

Vain grandeur and power,
Those toys of an hour,
Tho mortals are toiling to find;
Can titles or show
Contentment bestow?
All happiness dwells in the mind.

III.

Behold the gay rose,
How lovely it grows,
Secure in the depth of the vale.
Yon oak, that on high
Aspires to the sky,
Both lightning and tempest assail.

IV. *Then*

IV.

Then let us the ſnare
Of Ambition beware,
That ſource of vexation and ſmart:
And ſport on the glade,
Or repoſe in the ſhade,
With health and with quiet of heart.

Here a paſtoral dance.

SCENE II.

CORIN, EMMA, PEASANTS.

CORIN.

O happy hour! wife, neighbours—ſuch, ſuch news!
I ſhall run wild with joy!

EMMA.

Speak, ſhepherd; ſay,
What moves thee thus?

CORIN.

The king is in our iſle!

EMMA.

Can it be poſſible?

PEASANT.

What do I hear?

CORIN.

As now I paſs'd beneath the hermit's cell,
I heard that wonderous man pronounce his name.
O EMMA, the poor ſtranger whom we ſerv'd
And honour'd, all-unknowing of his ſtate,
Is he! our great and gracious ALFRED!

ALL.

Heaven!

Then are we bleſt indeed!

CORIN.

My humble cottage,
Long ages hence, when we are duſt, my friends,
In holy pilgrimage oft viſited,
Will draw true *Engliſh* knees to worſhip there,
As at the ſhrine of ſome propitious ſaint,
Or angel friendly to mankind—The thought
Brings tears into mine eyes.—

EMMA.

Does joy deceive
My ſenſe? or did I hear a diſtant voice
Sigh thro the vale and wake the mournful echo?

The following ſong
is ſung by a perſon unſeen.

I.

Ye woods and ye mountains unknown,
Beneath whose pale shadows I stray,
To the breast of my charmer alone
These sighs bid sweet echo convey.
Wherever he pensively leans,
By fountain, on hill, or in grove,
His heart will explain what she means,
Who sings both from sorrow and love.

CORIN.

The evening wood-lark warbles in her voice.
Who can this be?

EMMA.

Peace, peace: she sings again.

II.

More soft than the nightingale's song,
O waft the sad sound to his ear:
And say, tho divided so long,
The friend of his bosom is near.
Then tell him what years of delight,
Then tell him what ages of pain,
I felt while I liv'd in his sight!
I feel till I see him again!

CORIN.

CORIN.

What think ye, friends? Such moving, melting ſoftneſs
Breathes in theſe ſweet complainings, as till now
Mine ear was never bleſt with. Let us go
And find out this new wonder.

Second SHEPHERDESS.

Look, the king!

EMMA.

Now, by my holidame, a goodly perſon,
And of moſt noble mein.

CORIN.

Diſturb him not.

SCENE III.

ALFRED, HERMIT.

HERMIT.

Your enterpriſe is bold—and may be fatal:
Yet I condemn it not. All is not raſhneſs,
That valor of more common ſize might think,
And caution term ſo. Souls of nobler ſcope,
Whoſe comprehenſive ſight beholds at once
And weighs the ſum of things, are their own rule,
And to be judg'd but by themſelves alone.

ALFRED.

Then, in the name of that inſpiring Power,
Whoſe deputy I am, who ſends me forth
His miniſter of vengeance, on I go
To victory, or death.

[*As he is going out, he ſtops ſhort.*

What do I feel?
Save me! a holy horror ſtirs my frame,
And ſhivers thro each vein—What ſhapes are theſe,
Athwart the gloom, that ſtrike my dazled ſenſe?
Betwixt and where yon miſt along the marſh
Rowls blue it's vapoury wave, ſome unſeen hand
Pourtrays in air the viſionary ſcene
Diſtinct and full, in brighter colors drawn
Than ſummer ſuns reflect on evening cloud,
When all it's fluid boſom glows with gold—
And now, it reddens into blood!

HERMIT, *who had obſerved him fixedly, half-aſide.*

Ere night
Withdraws her ſhade, new accidents and ſtrange
Will ſhake this iſland's peace.

[*To him.*

Now, ALFRED, now,
Be all the hero ſhewn.

ALFRED.

What may this mean?

SCENE

SCENE IV.

ALFRED, CORIN.

CORIN, *kneeling.*

My honor'd ſovereign—

ALFRED.

How is this! ha! what!
Diſcover'd by this peaſant—Be it ſo:
The plain man is moſt loyal.

CORIN.

England's wealth,
The pearly ſtores her circling ſeas contain,
Should never ſhake your CORIN's faith—

ALFRED.

But what
Alarms thee thus?

CORIN.

My fears are for my king.
Some ſtrangers, Sir—their habits ſpeak them *Danes*—
Have found our iſle. Look this way.

ALFRED.

ALFRED.

Be of courage.
Now, I perceive them. Thro the evening ſhade
Their armor gleams a faint and moving light.
Weſtward they turn, and ſtrike into the path
That opens on this plain. Retire we, ſhepherd,
Behind yon duſky elm; from whence, unſeen,
We may diſcern their numbers and their purpoſe.

SCENE V.

DANES *paſſing along.*

Firſt DANE.

No more. 'Twas ſhe: I could not be deceiv'd.
A lover's eye is as the eagle's ſharp,
And kens his prey from far—But liſt a while,
If ſound of human voice, or bleat of flocks
May guide our loſt enquiry thro this wild.

Second DANE.

No: all is lonelineſs around, and huſh'd
As our dead northern waſtes at midnight hour.
Our gods protect us! Prince, it was moſt raſh,
So few our numbers, at this cloſe of day
Headlong to plunge amid theſe horrid ſhades,
Where danger lurks unſeen.

Firſt

First DANE.

How! know'st thou not
That *England* is no more? Her sons of war,
To dens and caverns fled, like fearful hares
Sit trembling at each blast the chill wind blows.
Her king himself or sleeps in dust, or roams
Wild on the pathless mountain. As for me;
Our country gods, those spirits that possess
The boundless wilderness, that love to dwell
With dreary solitude and night profound,
Will guard the son of IVAR, to whose house
Their vassalage is bound by magic spell.
Come on. She must be found, this unknown fair
Who fir'd me at first view; and rages still
A fever in my youthful blood. Away.

SCENE VI.

ALFRED, CORIN, *advancing.*

CORIN.

They are but three.

ALFRED.

And were that number trebled,
This island is their grave; this sacred spot,

Fair freedom's laſt retreat. We muſt, we will
Preſerve it, all-inviolate and holy,
From impious infidels: or, with our blood,
If now we periſh, ſanctify it's earth
For after-times to viſit and revere.

CORIN.

Liſt, liſt, my lord—

ALFRED.

What noiſe was that?—By heaven,
The ſhrieks of women! Now, ſtern vengeance guide
The ſword we draw.

SCENE VII.

EMMA, *and other peaſants.*

EMMA.

Ah, whither ſhall we fly?
Immortal virgin! queen of mercy! ſave us—
See, ſee, my friends, they ſeize the lovely ſtranger—
They bear her off—Behold the king appears—
My huſband too—Now, heaven, defend alike
The mighty and the mean, the prince and peaſant!
Two of them fall beneath our monarch's arm—
The third, my CORIN—O I dare no more
Look that way—Yet I muſt—The third is ſlain!
O gallant ſhepherd! O moſt happy hour!

SCENE

SCENE VIII.

ALFRED, CORIN,
supporting the lady.

ALFRED.

This way, brave ſhepherd, from theſe cloſer ſhades—
Here the free air and breezy glade will rouſe
Her fainting ſpirits—So—Who may ſhe be?
Perhaps, ſome worthy heart at this ſad moment
Akes for her ſafety.

ELTRUDA.

Save me, ſave me, heaven!

ALFRED.

Ye powers! what do I hear?—Yes—yes—'tis ſhe!
My wife, my queen! the treaſure of my ſoul!

ELTRUDA.

My ALFRED!

ALFRED.

My ELTRUDA!

ELTRUDA.

Can it be?
Or is it all th' illuſion of my fear?
O no: 'tis he—my lord! my life! my huſband!
My guardian angel ALFRED.

ALFRED.

My ELTRUDA!

Black horror chills me while I view the brink,
The dreadful precipice, on which we ſtood—
And was it thee I reſcu'd from theſe ruffians—
O Providence amazing!—thee, ELTRUDA!

ELTRUDA.

I tremble ſtill!—from worſe than death deliver'd!
And am I then ſecure in ALFRED's arms?

ALFRED.

There let me hold thee; lull thy fears to reſt:
There huſh thy ſoul with everlaſting fondneſs.
The panting bird ſo flutters, juſt eſcap'd
The fowler's ſnare.

ELTRUDA.

My heart, my heart is full—
And muſt o'erflow in tears. A thouſand thoughts
Are buſy here—That ever we ſhould meet
In ſuch a dire extremity!—Ah me!
That ever ALFRED's family and children
Should need the ſhelter of his ſingle arm!

ALFRED.

My children!—where, where are they?

ELTRUDA.

Turn thine eyes
To yonder cottage: there conceal'd—

ALFRED.

My CORIN,
Fly, bring them to my arms. But ſay, my love,
Why didſt thou leave the convent, where I plac'd thee?

Why,

Why, unprotected, truſt thee to a land,
A barbarous land, where violence inhabits?
Our hoſpitable *England* is no more.

ELTRUDA.

Alas! my ALFRED, even the peaceful cells,
Where ſafe beneath religion's holy veil
Her cloiſter'd votaries dwelt, from impious *Danes*
No reverence claim. The villages around,
Diſpers'd and flying wild before their arms,
Inform'd us, a near party, on whoſe courſe
Deſtruction waits, were marching full to us.
Inſtant I fled. Two faithful ſervants bore
Our children off: and heaven has ſav'd us all!

ALFRED.

O welcome to my ſoul!—O happy ALFRED!
Thus to have reſcu'd what the feeling heart
Moſt dear and precious holds, from men who war
With earth and heaven.

ELTRUDA.

Tho terrible at firſt,
Bleſt be the tempeſt that has driven me hither,
Into this ſafe, this ſacred harbor!

ALFRED.

Come,
O come, and here repoſe thee from the ſtorm,
Within theſe ſheltering arms.

ELTRUDA, *holding him off.*

Yet—let me view thee—
My king and huſband—do I find thee thus?
[*falling into his arms.*

Unknown!

Unknown! unſerv'd! unhonor'd! none to tend thee!
To ſoothe thy woes, to watch thy broken ſlumbers,
With every fonder ſervice, pious love
Beſt knows to pay!—There is in love a power,
There is a ſoft divinity that draws,
Even from diſtreſs, thoſe tranſports that delight
The breaſt they pain, and it's beſt powers exalt
Above all taſte of joys from vulgar life!

ALFRED.

O 'tis too much—thou all that makes life glorious!
Nay look not on me with this ſweet dejection;
Thro tears that pierce the ſoul—

My children too!

My little ones! Come to your ſire's embrace:
'Tis all he can beſtow—In them behold
What human grandeur is—The peaſant's offspring
Have ſome retreat, ſome ſafe, tho lowly home:
But you, my babes, you have no habitation!
With pain and peril wandering thro a land,
A ruin'd country you were born to rule!
The thought unmans my reaſon.

SCENE IX.

ALFRED, ELTRUDA, HERMIT.

HERMIT.

I have heard
Thy fond complainings, ALFRED.

ALFRED.

You have then,
Good father, heard the cause that wrings them from me.

HERMIT.

The human race are sons of sorrow born:
And each must have his portion. Vulgar minds
Refuse, or crouch beneath their load: the brave
Bear theirs without repining.

ALFRED.

Who can bear
The shaft that wounds him thro an infant's side?
When whom we love, to whom we owe protection,
Implore the hand we cannot reach to save them.

HERMIT.

Weep not, ELTRUDA.—Yet, thou art a king;
All private passions fall before that name.
Thy subjects claim thee whole.

ALFRED.

Can public truſt,
O reverend ſage! deſtroy the ſofter ties
That twine around the parent's yearning heart?
This holy paſſion heaven itſelf infus'd,
And blended with the ſtream that feeds our life.
All nature feels it intimate and deep,
And all her ſons of inſtinct and of reaſon.

HERMIT.

Then ſhew that paſſion in it's nobleſt form.
Think what a taſk it is, to rear thoſe minds,
On whom the fate of millions, general bliſs,
Or univerſal miſery, depends.

ALFRED.

That taſk then, difficult alike and noble,
Be thine, O ſacred ſage; to whoſe try'd wiſdom
I, henceforth, ſolely truſt their tender years.
Let truth and virtue be their earlieſt teachers.
Keep from their ear the ſyren-voice of flattery;
Keep from their eye the harlot-form of vice,
Who ſpread, in every court, their ſilken ſnares,
And charm but to betray. Betimes inſtruct them,
Superior rank demands ſuperior worth;
Pre-eminence of valor, juſtice, mercy:
But chief, that tho exalted o'er mankind,
They are themſelves but men—frail ſuffering duſt;
From no one injury of human lot
Exempt: but fever'd by the ſame heat, chill'd
By the ſame cold, torn by the ſame diſeaſe,
That ſcorches, freezes, racks, and kills the beggar.

Should

Should fairer days, returning, ſmile again
On *England* and on me—
Ha! EDWIN here?
This way, my friend—ſpeak ſoftly—

EDWIN *whiſpers the king aſide.*

How!—'tis well!—
Back to thy poſt: I follow on the inſtant—
Yet ſtay—Behold my queen, and infant-ſons!
EDWIN—thy king's whole wealth is there ſumm'd up!
Nay, wipe thine eyes: and tell my gallant friends
What thou haſt ſeen. The tale will lend new force
To each man's arm, and with redoubled weight
Urge every well-aim'd blow. Hence! ſpeed thee well.
ELTRUDA—we muſt part—

ELTRUDA.

What do I hear?
My life, my love—

ALFRED.

Part for a few ſad moments,
That our next meeting may be long and happy.

ELTRUDA.

What leave me now? O my preſaging heart!
Already leave me! 'Tis the dreadful call
Of glory, ſomewhat perilouſly great,
And big with urgent haſte, that tears thee from me.
Oh ALFRED—

ALFRED.

No fond weakneſs now be ſhewn,
ELTRUDA, no diſtruſt of virtue's fate.
Thou and thy children are, at preſent, ſafe

In this wiſe Hermit's care. For what remains;
My cauſe is juſt, my fortune in His hand
Who reigns ſupreme, almighty and all-good.
* That Power who ſtills the raging of the main,
The rage of all our foes can render vain.
To his unerring will reſign'd ſincere,
I fear that God, and know no other fear!

End of the Second Act.

* Tranſlated from RACINE's ATHALIE.

Celui, qui met un frein à la fureur des flots,
Sçait auſſi des méchans arreſter les complots.
Soûmis avec reſpect à ſa volonté ſainte,
Je crains Dieu, cher Abner, & n'ay point d'autre crainte.

ACT

ACT III. SCENE I.

EMMA, *and other shepherdesses.*

EMMA.

YES, EDITH, we will watch, till morning shines,
Around this cottage, now made rich and glorious—
Who durst have thought such wonders?—by a queen,
And her bright offspring! Thou, mean while, invoke,
With sounds of soothing strain, the gentle sleep
To pour his timely vapours on their eye-lids.

EDITH *ſings.*

I.

In cooling ſtream, O ſweet repoſe,
Thoſe balmy dews diſtill,
That ſteal the mourner from his woes,
And bid deſpair be ſtill.

II.

Prolong the ſmiling infant's reſt,
Who yet no ſorrow knows:
But O the mother's bleeding breaſt
To ſofteſt peace compoſe!

III.

For her the faireſt dreams adorn,
That wave on fancy's wing;
The purple of aſcending morn,
The bloom of opening ſpring.

IV.

Let all, that ſoothes the ſoul or charms,
Her midnight hour employ;
Till bleſt again in ALFRED'*s arms,*
She wakes to real joy.

EMMA.

EMMA.

Alas! ſhe comes. Let us withdraw, my friends:
Her ſorrows claim all reverence: and 'tis meet
We leave her to herſelf.

SCENE II.

ELTRUDA.

Amid the depth of this ſurrounding gloom,
While nature all is huſh'd, ELTRUDA wakes
To think—and to be wretched. Oh my love!
My heart's ſole reſt and refuge! Where is he!
Victor or vanquiſh'd—what is now his fate?
Moments of terror—Ha! what noiſe was that?
Each ſound appalls me, and each thought is death!
'Twas more than fancy ſure: it ſeem'd the groan
Of bleeding men—O every guardian wing
Of ſaints and angels ſhield him! from his breaſt
Turn wide the flying ſhaft, the lifted ſteel,
And, ſheltering him, a ruin'd nation ſave.
Who comes? Speak, quickly ſpeak.

SCENE III.

ERTRUDA, *an* ATTENDANT.

ATTENDANT.

My gracious miſtreſs,
Why to the breath of this untimely ſky
Expoſe your health?

ERTRUDA.

Away—the health, the life
Of *England* is at ſtake: my ALFRED fights—
Perhaps he bleeds: and I am loſt for ever!
But is there none, no meſſenger return'd
From that dark ſcene of death?

ATTENDANT.

No, madam, none.

ELTRUDA.

O my torn, tortur'd heart! What is the hour?

ATTENDANT.

By yon faint light, that glimmering ſteals along
From eaſt to north, I gueſs the morning near.

ELTRUDA.

Then all my hopes and fears ſuſpended hang
On this dread moment's wing—Ah! hear'ſt thou not
The trumpet's diſtant voice?

ATTENDANT.

It ſpeaks aloud,
And ſhakes the echoing woods.

SCENE IV.

ELTRUDA, ATTENDANT, EMMA, *and others.*

EMMA.

O mighty queen,
They come, the murderers come. Protect us, heaven, [*kneeling.*
Our huſbands, and our infants, from their rage.
Without thine aid we periſh.

ELTRUDA.

O my ſoul!
Why what a ſight is this? A tyrant's eye
Might melt with pity o'er it. Thou ſupreme, [*kneeling.*
All-ruling arbiter of human fate!
Whoſe univerſal family is nature,

On Alfred, on his children, on his people,
Look down with mercy—for their cauſe is thine,
And now, even now, deciding!

SCENE V.

Hermit, Eltruda, *and others.*

Hermit.

Glorious princeſs!
This is indeed to reign. Comfort, great queen:
It comes, it comes! the promis'd ſcene diſcloſes!
I ſee the *Daniſh* raven droop his wing!
See *England*'s genius ſoar again to heaven,
And better days in white ſucceſſion roll,
Without a cloud between!

The clouds break away; and on the edge of a rock, in full view, a ſpirit is ſeen amidſt a blaze of light, who ſings the following

ODE.

ODE.

From those eternal regions bright,
Where suns that never set in night,
Diffuse the golden day;
Where spring, unfading, pours around,
O'er all the dew-impearled ground,
Her thousand colors gay;
The messenger of heaven's high King,
I come; and happy tidings bring,
To chear this drooping isle:
Behold her cruel foes are fled!
Behold fair freedom lifts the head,
And all his children smile!
The dawn, that now unveils her skies,
See England's *future glory rise:*
A better age is born!
Then, let each voice of sprightly strain,
Around from warbling hill and plain,
Hail this triumphant morn!

Grand Chorus.

Then let each voice of sprightly strain,
Around from warbling hill and plain,
Hail this triumphant morn!

SCENE VI.

ELTRUDA, HERMIT, *Earl of* DEVON.

DEVON, *kneeling.*

Succefs is ours—

ELTRUDA.

The king, my lord—

DEVON.

Returns,
Victorious and unhurt.

ELTRUDA.

Then, firft, to heaven,
For this beft news I humbly bend the knee
In grateful adoration.—Now proceed,
My lord; and leave no circumftance untold
Of this amazing night.

DEVON.

Her mifty fhade
Had now enclos'd us round; when, led fecure
By EDWIN's eye, the darkeft depth I reach'd
Of *Kinwith-wood.* We parted.—He, in hafte,
Back to his charge. I thro the cavern'd path,
Whofe inlet there is found, defcending dark,
Long, under ground, it's folitary maze

Purfu'd

Purſu'd as beſt I could; and roſe at length
Safe in the fort our foes had cloſe begirt.
'Twas joy, 'twas rapture there, among the few
Who wiſh'd, not hop'd, my unforeſeen return.

ELTRUDA.

What follow'd this, my lord?

DEVON.

Prepare, I cry'd,
To live or die like men. Our king ſurvives;
And, now in arms, expects your inſtant aid.
To him then let us cut our glorious way
Thro yonder camp: or, if we nobly fall,
There offer to the genius of our country
Whole hecatombs of *Danes*.—As if one ſoul
Had mov'd them all, around their heads they whirl'd
Their ſounding faulchions—" Lead us to thoſe *Danes*:
Revenge and *England*"—was the general cry.

ELTRUDA.

I feel it here: my heart applauds their virtue.
How was this follow'd on?

DEVON.

To ſouls reſolv'd
Small preparation needs—The clock ſtruck three—
At once our gates flew wide: at once we ruſh'd
Prone on the *Daniſh* trenches—While behind,
Juſt to the fatal inſtant, ALFRED roſe
In all his terrors; o'er the mounded camp
Tempeſtuous drove; from ſpace to ſpace along
Spred ſlaughter and diſmay. Nor reſt, nor pauſe:
Back'd by his ardent band, right on he bore
Even to the tent, where ſunk in ſleep profound

The *Danish* monarch lay. His guards, a few
Whom honor prompted to defend their prince,
Fell round him. He yet lives: but, O dire chance
Of cruel war!—a prisoner and in chains.

ELTRUDA.

A fall how terrible! My breast is thrill'd,
And in the fierce barbarian mourns the captive.

HERMIT.

Such fortune ever wait on wild ambition!
On war unjust that desolates whole nations,
And leaves a world in tears for one man's guilt!
But yet—fallen as he is—he knows not yet
What new distress, what keener pangs attend
To wound his inmost heart—That trumpet speaks
The king's approach—Ye ministers unseen!

Spirits, whom the King of kings
Gives to watch o'er human things,
Hither, from each blest abode:
From the morning's purple road;
From the solar world of light;
From the planet of the night;
From the rainbow's evening-round;
From the blue horizon's bound;
Hither, borne thro seas of air,
Sons of life and love repair!
And now, with all that charms the eye,
This monarch's triumph dignify.

SCENE

SCENE VII.

To a grand flourish of instruments the scene, gradually opening, discovers several triumphal arches, adorned with trophies and garlands, and from space to space beautifully illuminated. The procession is led by shepherdesses, strewing flowers.

First SHEPHERDESS.

Arise, sweet messenger of morn,
With thy mild beam our skies adorn:
For long as shepherds pipe and play,
This, this shall be a holy-day.

Second SHEPHERDESS.

See, morn appears; a rosy hue
Steals soft o'er yonder orient blue:
Soon let us meet in trim array,
And frolic out this holy-day!

These are followed by soldiers with palm branches in their hands. An officer behind bears the Danish *standard. Flourish of instruments.*

First Voice.

Swell the trumpet's boldest note!

Second Voice.

Let the drum it's thunders roll!

Both.

And, as on aery wings they float,
Spread Alfred*'s name from pole to pole!*

Chorus.

Our sons unborn,
Still on this morn
With annual joy shall tell;
How by his might,
In daring fight,
The foes of England *fell.*

Air.

AIR.

Prince, of every fame possest!
Prince and patriot both confest!
Thy grateful Albion *shall to latest days*
Roll down thy glories in a tide of praise!

CHORUS.

Thy grateful Albion *shall to latest days*
Roll down thy glories in a tide of praise!

ELTRUDA.

Yon pictur'd raven—tell me is it not
Their wonderous magic ſtandard!

DEVON.

'Tis the ſame:
Wrought by the ſiſters of the *Daniſh* king,
At midnight's blackeſt hour; when the ſick moon,
Wrapt in eclipſe by their enchanting ſong,
Down thro the turbid clouds her influence ſhed
Of baleful power. The ſiſters ever ſung—
" Shake, ſtandard, ſhake deſtruction on our foes."

SCENE VIII.

ELTRUDA, HERMIT, *and the others.*

ALFRED *paſſing under the triumphal arches: The ſun, at the ſame time, riſing above the horizon.*

ELTRUDA.

He comes! the conqueror comes—

ALFRED.

In theſe lov'd arms
To loſe all ſorrow, and all bliſs to find!

ELTRUDA.

ELTRUDA.

O from what fears deliver'd for thy life,
And in that life for a whole people's being,
I thus receive thee back! thus fold thee ſafe!
Love only, love like mine, can feel, not utter!

ALFRED.

To Him aſcend all praiſe! whoſe will inſpir'd,
Whoſe arm ſuſtain'd this action, that reſtores
My better name—and, O more glorious ſtill,
Of nobler, dearer conſequence!—reſtores
Loſt *England* to her vigor, fame and freedom.

HERMIT.

For her, O ALFRED, your more arduous task
But now begins: this conqueſt to ſecure;
To ſpread it's influence wide, and, well improv'd
By unremitting vigilance and valor,
Make this one blow deciſive of her fate.
But now behold, to animate thy hope,
In myſtic ſhew expreſs'd what late thy fortune
Seem'd to portend; and what the brightening ſcene
With fairer promiſe opens.

Four Furies arise, to the sound of instruments in discord, at four different openings from under ground, with torches in their left hands, and bloody swords in their right. They form a confused Pyrrhic *dance, shaking and pointing their swords and torches round the king in their centre: till, upon a change of the music into regular harmony, descends the Genius of* England, *with a crowned sword in one hand, and a lawrel wreathe in the other. On sight of whom the four Furies sink thro the openings they arose from. He presents the crowned sword and lawrel-branch at the feet of the king, and reascends, while the following song is sung.*

At last, at last,
Our night is past,
The gloomy night of fear:
And o'er our skies
Fair beams arise
Of peace and joy sincere.
Then let triumph abound!
Let ecstacy reign!
Till these hills all around,—around
Improving each strain,
Our transports resound;—resound
The heart-felt transport that succeeds to pain!

ALFRED.

ALFRED.

I hail th' auſpicious omen—but ah me!
ELTRUDA, ſee, where comes th' unhappy king!

ELTRUDA.

Oh ſight of woe!

ALFRED.

Retire, my gentle love:
An interview like this were too ſevere
For thy ſoft nature.

SCENE IX.

ALFRED, HERMIT, DANISH KING.

ALFRED, *after a pauſe.*

See, at laſt, O king,
In thy ſad fate, which even a foe laments,
See and acknowledge heaven's impartial hand.
For violated oaths and plunder'd realms,
For the heap'd guilt of baſe perfidious war,
This retribution is moſt juſt.

DANE.

Away—
I own no guilt: or kings of every age
Are criminal, thy anceſtors and mine.
What is all war, but more diffuſive robbery
Made ſacred by ſucceſs? What object ſwells
A monarch's higheſt aim?—increaſe of power
And univerſal ſway. This glorious end
All means muſt ſanctify, that can ſecure.
For what remains—Of bondage, or of death,
The leſſer ill, I reck not. But, by THOR,
The gloomy thunderer! one diſtracting thought
Bends my ſoul's ſtrongeſt temper; ſinks me down
Beneath my own contempt.

ALFRED.

Such fears diſmiſs
As muſt diſhonor both. The truly brave
His foe in equal arms will dare to meet:
Vanquiſh'd, he dares not injure, nor inſult him.

DANE.

Nor that, nor ought without myſelf could thus
Unman me. No: my hell is here, within—
How! like a wretch, a nameleſs ſlave who fights
But for vile hire—in my own tent ſurpris'd!
Aſleep! unarm'd!—theſe ſhameful chains thrown o'er me,
And not one blow exchang'd! O baſer far
Than that low herd, who fled without a wound
Before thy ſword.—They but deſerted him,
Who firſt himſelf abandon'd—But thy gods
Were vigilant for thee: while mine all ſlept.

ALFRED.

Your gods are idols: that ſole Power I ſerve,
Supreme and one, is univerſal Lord
O'er earth and heaven. Be it my daily taſk,
As 'tis my nobleſt theme, to own, by Him
Alone I conquer'd: as for him alone
I wiſh to reign—by making mankind bleſt!

DANE.

No more—Convey me to your baſeſt dungeon.
Let me explore it's darkeſt depth; ſhut out
The light of heaven; forget there is a ſun
Who ſhines on my diſhonor. Would I might
Exclude too my own thoughts—But yet, my ſon
Lives—and is free! lives to revenge my fall!
To waſh my ſtains in blood—Ha! where was he
This fatal night, when every god forſook me!
Where, where was IVAR then?

HERMIT.

Unhappy prince!
That ſon, alas!—

DANE.

Ha! what! why, who art thou?
What of my ſon?

HERMIT.

Thy truſt in him is vain.
To his own raſhneſs and intemperate luſt,
This very night, a victim, here, he fell—
Lo! where he lies.

DANE.

DANE.

My ſon—my ſon—Ha! dead—
My only child!—But no: I will not weep.
Is he not ſafe, beyond misfortune's hand?
Beyond all feeling of his father's ſhame?
Falſe hope, farewell!—Let madneſs, let deſpair
Surround me, ſeize me whole; till life's loath'd flame,
For ever quench'd in death, reſigns me o'er
To darkneſs and oblivion.

ALFRED.

Dire reverſe!
Dreadful impatience!—But theſe roving *Danes*
A ſtricter watch demand. Means more effectual
Muſt now be try'd, from our inſulted ſhores
To keep aloof this ſtill-deſcending war.
'Tis naval ſtrength, that muſt our peace aſſure.
Be this the firſt high object of my care,
To wall us round with well-appointed fleets.
In them our ſole dominion of the ſea,
Our wealth and grandeur, can alone be found,
The one great bulwark of our ſeparate world.

HERMIT.

ALFRED, go on; the noble taſk purſue,
Thy ſafety urges, and thy fame demands.
Yes, in her fleets, let *England* ever ſeek
Her ſure defence: by them, thro every age,
At home ſecure, renown'd and fear'd abroad,
Great arbitreſs of nations—Ha! the ſcene,
The radiant proſpect opens full before me!
Thro diſtant depths of time tranſported down,

The

I ſee whole moving foreſts, from her hills
Uprooted, bound triumphant o'er the main!
White tracks of glory brighten *Albion*'s ſkies,
As navies grow, as commerce ſwells her ſail
With every breeze that under heaven can blow,
From either pole; thro worlds yet unexplor'd,
In eaſt and weſt, that to thy ſons diſcloſe
Their golden ſtores, their wealth of various name,
And laviſh pour it on BRITANNIA's lap!

ALFRED.

Thy words new ſun-ſhine thro my breaſt diffuſe,
And ſmiling calm. But let us, HERMIT, try,
By juſtice, mercy, arms and arts improv'd,
By freedom fenc'd around with ſacred laws,
Our promis'd bliſs to merit and adorn.
Now, to my glorious taſk—

HERMIT.

Yet ere you go,
One moment, ALFRED, backward caſt your eyes
On this unfolding ſcene; where, pictur'd true,
As in a mirror, riſes fair to ſight
Our *England*'s genuine ſtrength and future fame.

Here is ſeen the ocean in proſpect, and ſhips ſailing along. Two boats land their crews. One ſailor ſings the following Ode: after which, the reſt join in a lively dance.

I. *When*

I.

When BRITAIN *first at heaven's command,*
Arose from out the azure main;
This was the charter of the land,
And guardian angels sung this strain:
Rule, BRITANNIA, *rule the waves:*
BRITONS *never will be slaves.*

II.

The nations, not so blest as thee,
Must in their turns to tyrants fall:
While thou shalt flourish great and free,
The dread and envy of them all.
Rule, BRITANNIA, *rule the waves:*
BRITONS *never will be slaves.*

III.

Should war, should faction shake thy isle,
And sink to poverty and shame;
Heaven still shall on BRITANNIA *smile,*
Restore her wealth, and raise her name.
Rule, BRITANNIA, *rule the waves:*
BRITONS *never will be slaves.*

IV.

As the loud blaſt, that tears thy ſkies,
Serves but to root thy native oak;
Still more majeſtic ſhalt thou riſe,
From foreign, from domeſtic ſtroke.
Rule, BRITANNIA, *rule the waves:*
BRITONS *never will be ſlaves.*

V.

How bleſt the prince, reſerv'd by fate,
In adverſe days to mount thy throne!
Renew thy once triumphant ſtate,
And on thy grandeur build his own!
Rule, BRITANNIA, *rule the waves:*
BRITONS *never will be ſlaves.*

VI.

His race ſhall long, in times to come,
So heaven ordains, thy ſceptre wield,
Rever'd abroad, belov'd at home,
And be, at once, thy ſword and ſhield.
Rule, BRITANNIA, *rule the waves:*
BRITONS *never will be ſlaves.*

The End of the Maſque.

EPILOGUE.

Spoken by Mrs. CLIVE.

WHile our grave Hermit, busy above stairs,
Employs his serious head on state affairs,
Gallants, look here—faith I have plaid the rogue,
And stole his wand—by way of epilogue.
You critics, there below, had best be civil:
For I, with this same rod, can play the devil;
Ty all your busy tongues up, one by one,
And turn what share of brains you have—to stone:
The beau's soft scull convert to solid rock—
What then?—the wig will always have it's block.
But for the men of sad and solemn face,
The deep dark sages in or out of place,
Who much in port and politics delight,
Small change, God knows, will make them statues quite.
The ladies too—but now these witlings sneer—
No, fair ones, you shall meet no insult here:
I only hint my power—that, if I list,
I yet can charm you two long hours from whist.
But, cards are ready, you are all bespoke—
To spoil a dozen drums, would be no joke.
Besides, 'twould be mere arbitrary sway:
Such as, of old, was us'd at Nero's *play,*

Who, when he sung and fiddled to the town,
Still, as his subjects yawn'd, would knock them down.
No, sirs; to gain a heart, we must not teize:
Who would engage it, first should aim to please.
This part be mine: and, if I now succeed
To my own wish, you will be pleas'd indeed.
Then—for a trial: thus, I wave my hand,
To prove the power of this inchanting wand.

On waving her wand,

The scene opens, and discovers a beautiful valley, bordered on each hand by forest trees, rising irregularly, and forming from space to space various groves. The prospect behind is a landschape of woodlands, and of mountains that ascend above one another, till the last seem to lose themselves in the sky. From the summit of the nearest hill a river pours down, by several falls, in a natural cascade. The warbling of birds is heard.

First Entry.

A husbandman, his wife, and family.

She.

How soft is the scene!
The woodlands how green!
What charms in the nightingale's lay!

He.

Fair peace, that now reigns
On our hills and our plains,
'Tis peace bids all nature be gay.

Chorus.

'Tis peace bids all nature be gay.

She.

The distaff,

He.

The plow,

Both.

Shall employ our hands now,
For ourselves and our children alone.

He.

Secure from the foe,
We shall reap what we sow:
And the year, the whole year is our own!

Chorus.

And the year, the whole year is our own.

She waves her wand. SECOND ENTRY.

A ſhepherd, and ſhepherdeſs.

They run into each others arms.

SHE.

If to meet is all this pleaſure,
Sure, to part was killing pain!

BOTH.

Yes, to part was killing pain!

HE.

If 'twas grief to loſe our treaſure,
How tranſporting to regain!

BOTH.

O 'tis tranſport to regain!

HE.

Thus poſſeſſing—

SHE.

every bleſſing
Crowns the maid—

HE.

And crowns her ſwain.

BOTH.

Crowns the happy maid and ſwain!

She waves her wand. THIRD ENTRY.

Soldiers deſcend the mountain by two different paths: at the bottom they lay down the ſpoils with which they are loaded; and then, advancing, two of them ſing the following ballad.

FIRST MAN.

We have fought; we have conquer'd: and England *once more*
Shall flouriſh in fame, as ſhe flouriſh'd before.
Our fears are all fled, with our enemies ſlain:
* *Could they riſe up anew—*

SECOND.

We would ſlay them again.
His monarch to ſerve, or to do himſelf right,
No Engliſhman *yet ever flinch'd from the fight.*
For why, neighbours all, we are free as the king:
* *'Tis this makes us brave—*

FIRST.

And 'tis this makes us ſing.
Our prince too, for this, will be thankful to fate—
It is, in our freedom, he finds himſelf great!
No force can be wanting, nor meaner court-arts:
* *He is maſter of all—*

SECOND.

Who will reign in our hearts!
Should rebels within, or ſhould foes from without,
Bring the crown on his head, or his honor, in doubt;

* The verſes marked with an
aſteriſk to be ſung a ſecond time by both.

We

We are ready—

FIRST.

Still ready—and boldly foretell,

** That conqueſt ſhall ever with liberty dwell!*

SECOND.

But now, bring us forth, as the crown of our labor,

Much wine and good chear—

FIRST.

With the pipe and the tabor.

Let our nymphs all be kind, and our ſhepherds be gay:

For England, *Old* England, *is happy to day.*

CHORUS.

Let our nymphs all be kind, and our ſhepherds be gay:

For England, *Old* England, *is happy to day!*

They all mix in a dance,
to the pipe and tabor.

The End.

Prologue to
BRITANNIA

Jas. Taylor del et sculp.

Mr. GARRICK in the Character of a DRUNKEN SAILOR,
Speaking the Prologue to Britannia a Masque.

Published by T. Lowndes, Jany. 20, 1778.

PROLOGUE:

ſpoken by Mr. GARRICK,*

in the character of a Sailor, fuddled and talking to himſelf.

He enters, ſinging,

How pleaſant a ſailor's life paſſes——

WELL, if thou art, my boy, a little mellow?
A ſailor, half ſeas o'er—'s a pretty fellow!
What chear ho? * *Do I carry too much ſail?*
* to the pit.
No—tight and trim—I ſcud before the gale *—
* he ſtaggers forward, then ſtops.
But ſoftly tho—the veſſel ſeems to heel:
Steddy! my boy—ſhe muſt not ſhew her keel.
And now, thus ballaſted—what courſe to ſteer?
Shall I again to ſea—and bang Mounſeer?
Or ſtay on ſhore, and toy with Sall *and* Sue—
Doſt love 'em, boy?—By this right hand, I do!
A well-rigg'd girl is ſurely moſt inviting:
There's nothing better, faith—ſave flip and fighting:

* Some of the lines too were written by him.

For

For shall we sons of beef and freedom stoop,
Or lower our flag to slavery and soop?
What! shall these Parly-vous make such a racket,
And we not lend a hand, to lace their jacket?
Still shall old England be your Frenchman's butt?
Whene'er he shuffles, we should always cut.
I'll to 'em, faith—Avast—before I go—
Have I not promis'd Sall to see the show?

Pulls out a play-bill.

From this same paper we shall understand
What work's to night—I read your printed hand!
But, first refresh a bit—for faith, I need it—
*I'll take one sugar-plumb *—and then I'll read it.*

* Takes some tobacco.

He reads the play-bill of Zara, which was acted that evening.

At the The-atre Royal—Drury-Lane—
will be presen-ta-ted a Tragedy called—

SARAH.

I'm glad 'tis Sarah—Then our Sall may see
Her namesake's Tragedy: and as for me,
I'll sleep as sound, as if I were at sea.

To which will be added,
a new Masque.

Zounds!

Zounds! why a **Masque?** *We sailors hate grimaces:*
Above board all, we scorn to hide our faces.
But what is here, so very large and plain?
Bri-ta-nia—*oh* Britania!—*good again*—
Huzza, boys! by the Royal George *I swear,*
Tom *coxen, and the crew, shall strait be there.*
All free-born souls must take Bri-ta-nia's part,
And give her three round cheers, with hand and heart!

going off, he stops.

I wish you landmen tho, would leave your tricks,
Your factions, parties, and damn'd politics:
And like us, honest tars, drink, fight, and sing!
True to yourselves, your Country, and your King!

BRITANNIA

BRITANNIA:

A

MASQUE.

[Price Sixpence.]

BRITANNIA:

A

MASQUE.

ACTED at the

THEATRE-ROYAL

IN

DRURY-LANE.

LONDON:

Printed for A. MILLAR.

MDCCLV.

The PERSONS.

BRITANNIA,	Mrs. JAFFERSON.
GENIUS,	Miſs ISABELLA YOUNG.
MARS,	Mr. BEARD.
SERJEANT,	Mr. CHAMPNESS.
TRITON,	Mr. VERNON.
NEPTUNE,	Mr. CHAMPNESS.
BOATSWAIN,	Mr. BEARD.
NANCEY,	Miſs THOMAS.

SOLDIERS, SAILORS, *&c.*

The MUSIC compoſed by Mr. *ARNE*.

BRITANNIA:

A

MASQUE.

The SCENE,

On one hand a rocky coaſt; woods and fields on the other: the whole terminated by a view of the ocean.

Britannia *is ſeen reclining againſt a cliff, in a penſive poſture: her helmet, ſhield and ſpear ſtrewed negligently on the ground. The face of the landſchape around cloudy and lowering. Soft and plaintive muſic.*

The general gloom is gradually diſperſed by a riſing light that ſpreads over and enlivens the whole ſcene.

Amidſt this blaze of glory, and while the muſic changes into gay and animating airs, appears the Genius *of* Britain.

GENIUS.

Recitativo.

Britannia! ſovereign queen of Iſles!
Where freedom reigns, where plenty ſmiles;
Whence commerce ſpreads, with every gale,
For every ſhore, her boundleſs ſail——

SONG.

Awake! arise! nor longer wear
This downcast look, this doubtful air,
That cloud thy native charms.
Resume the trident of the main;
Or, gaily-dreadful on the plain,
Shine out again in arms!

RECITATIVO.

Those arms BRITANNIA best can wield,
When, foremost in the sanguine field,
She bids the storm of battle glow,
And pours it's thunder on her foe!

SONG.

Let not Punic arts amuse thee;
Let not Punic oaths abuse thee:
Grasp thy shield, and shake thy spear!
Should a faithless friend invade thee,
All—yes, all thy sons shall aid thee:
What has BRITAIN *then to fear?*
What has BRITAIN *then to fear?*

BRITANNIA, [*rising.*]

Oh would my jarring sons unite,
To do their sacred country right!

And in one filial league combine,
All intereſts to diſclaim but mine!

GENIUS.

RECITATIVO.

If ſenſe, if ſpirit are not flown,
They muſt in thy defence be ſhown.
Wherever courage dwells, or worth,
Occaſion now will call them forth.

BRITANNIA.

O come, and on thy ſpeeding wing,
Fair hour! thoſe happy moments bring.

SONG.

Th' inſpiring hope my boſom warms:
What can a world, a world in arms,
At ſea, on land, to me oppoſe,
When Britiſh boſoms, Britiſh hearts incloſe?

GENIUS.

RECITATIVO.

Lo! where, deſcending from on high,
The radiant God of War draws nigh.

SCENE II.

BRITANNIA, GENIUS, MARS.

MARS appears in air, in complete armor, and diſtinguiſhed by the red ſtar on his helmet. As his car approaches the ground, a full ſymphony of warlike muſic is heard.

MARS.

RECITATIVO.

From yonder ſun-pav'd fields above,
Commiſſion'd by the nod of JOVE,
Behold me, ſea-girt nymph, appear,
Thy hope to raiſe, thy heart to chear!

RECITATIVO.

The righteous ſword when Juſtice draws,
When Honor ſanctifies the cauſe,
Let BRITAIN then provoke the fight:
Heaven, that approves, will aid her right!

SONG.

SONG.

Let each ſofter note be dumb——
Let deep ſilence reign around——
[A full pauſe of all the inſtruments.
Then loudly wake the thundering drum!
Then ſwell the trumpet's nobleſt ſound!
Prolong, prolong
The magic ſong!
Raiſe high to heaven it's potent ſtrain!
Till martial heat
Conſenting beat
In every BRITON'*s every vein!*

SCENE III.

As the drum beats, ſoldiers approach from different parts of the ſcene, and range themſelves: A recruiting ſerjeant at their head.

He ſings.

Adieu for a while to the town and its trade;
Adieu to the meadow and rake:
Our country, my boys, calls aloud for our aid;
And ſhall we that country forſake?

II.

II.

It never was known, that true hearts like our own
From hardſhips or hazards would flinch:
Let our foes then unite; we will ſhew them in fight,
What BRITONS *can do at a pinch.*

III.

A ſlave may he be, who will not agree
To join with his neighbours and ſing,.
" *That the Brave and the Free—ſuch,* BRITONS, *are we*--
" *Live but for their Country and King!*"

BRITANNIA.

I with a parent's fondneſs view
My bold rough ſons revive in you.
To ſuch I dare my cauſe commend,
Born to revenge me, or defend.
Yes, each will act a BRITON's part:
The plaineſt is the trueſt heart.

SCENE

SCENE IV.

As this speech ends, a TRITON *rises above the waves, and sounds his shell.*

TRITON.

RECITATIVO.

Behold! the sovereign of the sea,
BRITANNIA's patron-deity,
Now rising awful from the deep,
With her this festival to keep!
He leaves the pearly dome, the coral-shade,
To rouse her spirit, and her arms to aid!

SONG.

Wide o'er this bright aëreal scene,
Let only Zephir wave the wing:
And let all ocean be serene,
To honor her ascending King.

SCENE

SCENE V.

During this ſong, NEPTUNE's *car, faſhioned like a ſhip, with the* BRITISH *lion in it's prow, and turned ſhore-ward, ariſes ſlowly to view, attended by a train of Sea-Nymphs and Tritons.*

NEPTUNE.

RECITATIVO.

Hail! faireſt daughter of the ſea;
Imperial ſeat of liberty;
Indulgent nurſe of arms and arts,
Of cooleſt heads and warmeſt hearts;
Thy ſons for every worth renown'd,
With every charm thy daughters crown'd;
The land's great umpire, ocean's queen—
All this has fam'd BRITANNIA been:
And to this envy'd height, the Gods once more,
Leagu'd in her cauſe, their favorite would reſtore.

SONG.

SONG.

Inspire the vocal shell!
Let harmony explore
Her sacred store,
Through all its moving, mazy swell:
For sounds that warm
Exalt and charm
The soul untouch'd before!
Then roll their rising flow from eccho ing shore to shore!

BRITANNIA.

Chief let their mighty power be shown
On those I gladly call my own:

GENIUS.

SONG.

Those best sons of BRITAIN, *bold, open, and brave,*
Who dare the loud tempest, and stem the rough wave.
Theirs is the sound bottom, on which to rely;
And theirs the firm heart, that will conquer or dy!

SCENE VI.

At the ſound of a boatſwain's whiſtle, blown by one of the Tritons, a croud of ſailors ruſh in; a boatſwain at their head, ſinging.

Yes—ours is the bottom, on which to rely;
And ours the ſound heart, that will conquer or dy.

[These verſes are repeated by all the reſt in chorus.

BOATSWAIN ſings.

'Tis our country that calls us: her voice we obey.
When ſhe wants our aid; ſhall a ſailor ſay nay?
With the foes of old ENGLAND *our Rulers may cope,*
While a ſword we can brandiſh, or handle a rope:
For BRITAIN *ſhall find us, both body and ſoul,*
As true to her cauſe, as our ſteel to it's pole.

CHORUS.

*Yes—*BRITAIN *ſhall find us, both body and ſoul,*
As true to her cauſe, as our ſteel to it's pole.

SECOND SAILOR.

Dares the coxcomb in heart, dares the capering ſlave
Deſpiſe us plain fellows, whom freedom makes brave?
Huzza! gallant hearts: let the Triflers behold
Such ENGLISHMEN *now, as they fled from of old.*

CHORUS.

Huzza! gallant hearts: let the Triflers behold
Such ENGLISHMEN *now, as they ran from of old.*

THIRD SAILOR.

From the miſtreſs we love, from the monarch we ſerve,
No diſtance, no danger ſhall e'er make us ſwerve.
Let landmen delight in deceit and grimace,
Attempt at your throat, while they laugh in your face;
Too honeſt for art, and too gallant for guile,
We frown where we hate, as we love where we ſmile.

CHORUS.

Then—ours is the bottom, on which to rely;
And ours the ſound heart, that will conquer or dy!

SCENE VII.

The ſound of a tabor and pipe is heard at a diſtance: NANCEY *and* SUKEY *come forward.*

BOATSWAIN.

RECITATIVO.

See where young NAN and SUE appear:
Away—or you are wind-bound here.
Ah let them not, my lads, come nigh:
Each carries witchcraft in her eye.

NANCEY ſings.

Hear me, gallant ſailor, hear me!
While your country has a foe,
He is mine too—Never fear me;
I may weep: but you ſhall go.

SUKEY ſings.

Tho this flowery ſeaſon wooes ye
To the gentler ſports of May,
And love ſighs, ſo long to loſe ye—
Honor calls: let Love obey.

FIRST

FIRST SAILOR sings.

Can the Sons of BRITAIN *fail her,*
While her Daughters are so true?
Your soft courage must avail her:
We love glory—loving you.

SECOND SAILOR sings.

War and danger now invite us:
Blow, ye winds; for BRITAIN *blow!*
Every gale will most delight us,
That wafts us soonest to the foe!

GENIUS.

Then, away from idle pleasures:
You are bent on nobler measures,
And must now your worth approve.
Teach these peaceful shores to wonder,
At the cannon's mortal thunder:
'Tis the music BRITONS *love.*

CHORUS.

Soon these peaceful shores shall wonder,
At the cannon's mortal thunder:
'Tis the music BRITONS *love.*

SONG.

Teach these hills to resound, and these vallies to ring,
Success to our country, renown to our king!

ALL.

These hills shall resound, and these vallies shall ring,
Success to our country, renown to our king!

Here a dance:
Which ended, BRITANNIA *speaks.*

Go then: the call of glory each attend:
At home, abroad, your country's rights defend.
While this great aim, united, you pursue,
And BRITAIN is, to BRITAIN, nobly true,
Bear high your hopes to conquest and renown:
The cause, that heaven inspires, success shall crown!

THE END.

ELVIRA

ELVIRA:

A

TRAGEDY.

ACTED at the

THEATRE ROYAL

IN

DRURY-LANE.

LONDON:

Printed for A. MILLAR, in the Strand.

MDCCLXIII.

TO THE

RIGHT HONORABLE

THE

EARL of *BUTE.*

MY LORD,

AS the performance I here offer to the public, under the ſanction of your name, bears no immediate relation to public affairs; this addreſs is more properly to the private Nobleman than to the Miniſter of ſtate. To One, who in the former character, has diſtinguiſhed himſelf, thro' the whole courſe of an unblameable life, as a friend to all the liberal arts: and whoſe love of them has ariſen from his being able to taſte their genuine beauties, and to diſcern their real utility. The more uſeful have been the employment of his ſerious hours; the more ornamental, the amuſement of his leiſure: and thoſe, who cultivated either with any degree of ſufficiency, have ever found in him a Patron as well as a Judge. I wiſh, for the honor of my country, that this praiſe were not, almoſt excluſively, his own.

But, while I do this ſcanty juſtice to the Man, I muſt appear inſenſible to the welfare of Britain, I had almoſt ſaid to the general intereſts of humanity, if I omitted all mention of the Miniſter for ſervices of another importance; and which have the happineſs of a whole people for their aim.

The beſt and moſt amiable of Princes has ardently deſired that this long and conſuming tho' ſucceſsful war might be terminated by ſuch a peace, as ſhould leave his dominions ſecure and great and flouriſhing: and to render this his paternal care of us effectual, has been the firſt object of your Lordſhip's miniſtry. Yet, in a government conſtituted as ours is, where every member of the community may freely diſcover his ſentiments, and where a diverſity of intereſts will ſet the ſame object in different, perhaps in contrary lights; an oppoſition both to miniſters and meaſures may be the immediate conſequence. Indeed, a diſlike, real or pretended, of the former has ever, in the common courſe of things, produced oppoſition to the latter. But the good ſenſe of the nation in general, aſſiſted by the moderation of ſuch individuals as think largely, and embrace in one comprehenſive view the preſent and future intereſts of their country, muſt gradually allay the heats, that never fail to ariſe on ſuch occaſions: And our poſterity will look back, with admiration and gratitude, to the year ſeventeen hundred and ſixty two, as to the brighteſt period of Britiſh glory! In the mean while, my Lord, the *mens ſibi conſcia recti* will be your preſent reward: and to certain men, for they appear among us but ſeldom, it is the nobleſt and moſt valuable. To ſuch men, there is ſomething beyond wealth and titles and power; which no popularity can give, no temporary want of it can deſtroy. I am, my Lord, with the higheſt regard,

Your Lordſhip's

moſt faithful

humble Servant,

D. MALLET.

PROLOGUE.

WAR is no more: those thunders cease to rowl,
That lately shook the globe from pole to pole;
When Britain *sought and triumph'd o'er her foe,*
Wherever winds can waft or waters flow.
She, *and she only could, bade discord cease,*
And, having humbled, gave the nations peace.
May its wish'd influence, thro' this favor'd Isle,
On every brow, in every bosom, smile!
'Twas union made her Queen of land and main:
'Tis that alone her triumphs can maintain;
Improve those blessings, arts will now adorn,
And send them safe to Britons *yet unborn.*

O might no other strife your hearts divide,
Than how a culprit-author should be try'd;
Ours, whom no mean, no partial interest moves,
Would be the victim of that peace he loves.
Yet, why this fear? Good nature is your boast:
And, who most want it, ever feel it most.
Abroad, you knew to conquer and to spare:
And, as your cause, your conduct too was fair.
Then, what you gave so nobly to the foe,
At home, and to a friend, you sure will show.

His scenes, to night, no feign'd adventure bring:
If tears shall flow, from real ills they spring.

What

PROLOGUE.

What Liſbon *trembling ſaw and truly mourn'd;*
What her firſt Muſe *in epic ſtrains adorn'd;*
What Paris next bedew'd with copious tears,
Now, to the Sons of Britain, *late appears.*
To you, wherever Truth and nature reign,
And Terror ſhakes, and Pity melts the ſtrain;
Wherever theſe declare the genuine bard,
Your warm applauſes are his ſure reward:
Then, while ſuch Judges ſtrike our author's view,
His fears are from himſelf, and not from you.

The

The PERSONS.

Don ALONZO IV. King of PORTUGAL,	Mr. *Garrick.*
Don PEDRO, his Son,	Mr. *Holland.*
The QUEEN,	Mrs. *Pritchard.*
ALMEYDA, her Daughter, promiſed to Don PEDRO,	Miſs *Bride.*
ELVIRA, Maid of honor to the Queen,	Mrs. *Cibber.*
Don RODRIGO, a Prince of the Blood,	Mr. *Packer.*
Don ALVAREZ, a Grandee of PORTUGAL.	Mr. *Love.*
MENDOZO,	Mr. *Caſtle.*
RAMIREZ,	Mr. *Ackman.*

An AMBASSADOR from the King of CASTILE.

COURTIERS, GUARDS, ATTENDANTS.

SCENE, the Palace of ALONZO.

ELVIRA:

A TRAGEDY.

ACT I. SCENE I.

RODRIGO, ALVAREZ.

ALVAREZ.

HEALTH to your highneſs!

RODRIGO.

Brave Alvarez, welcome.
This long-expected, this auſpicious morn
Will ſee confirm'd the league of amity
Betwixt Caſtile and Portugal. You time
Your wiſh'd arrival well; to be at once
The witneſs and partaker of our joy.

ALVAREZ.

My abſence, and th' unceaſing cares of war
On Afric's plains, againſt her ſwarthy ſons,
Where, till Don Pedro, our brave prince, return'd,

The chief command was mine; that tedious abſence
Has left me ignorant, or ill-inform'd,
Of moſt particulars.

RODRIGO.

Then know, my Lord,
Our preſent queen, the mother of Almeyda,
Brought with her from Caſtile that blooming princeſs,
The wiſh of all beholders! And, no doubt,
You muſt have often heard her lover's voice
Moſt laviſh in the praiſes of the fair one,
Whom he this day eſpouſes, and in her
Whate'er is excellent or lovely.

ALVAREZ.

Never!
Don Pedro, with that chaſte reſerve and caution
Which would become the coldeſt virgin's fear,
Even on a theme ſo pleaſing ſtill was ſilent;
Or only, when alone, indulg'd his rapture.

RODRIGO.

So cold a lover, and ſo warm a hero,
Are contraries that ſeldom blend in youth.
'Tis moſt ſurprizing! for, as we have heard,
His heat of valor is a rapid flame,
Encreaſing as it ſpreads——

ALVAREZ.

And yet his prudence,
Serenely cool, keeps meaſure with his fire.
Had you, in this laſt battle with the Moors,
Had you beheld the mutual poize of each,
As either was call'd forth by fair occaſion,
Your praiſes would be tranſport!—but proceed.

RODRIGO.

The ſum of all is this. To-day he weds
The bright Caſtilian princeſs; and this hour

Her

Her brother Ferdinand's ambaſſador
Has audience of our King—— [*Trumpet ſounds.*

ALVAREZ.

That trumpet ſpeaks
The happy moment come. May peace, my lord,
A long, a glorious peace be the fair iſſue!

SCENE II.

Trumpets ſound again.

ALONZO, *the* QUEEN, ELVIRA
RODRIGO, ALVAREZ, *Courtiers.*

ALONZO.

The heavens, my Queen, look ſmilingly upon us,
As pleas'd to ſee, thus ſolemnly ſecur'd,
The league that joins your Ferdinand to me
In one true bond of love——Where is my ſon?
Not follow us?

RODRIGO.

His modeſt fear avoids
To be the hearer of his own juſt praiſe.

ALONZO.

Such fear, attendant on ſucceſsful arms,
Becomes the brave, and moſt of all in youth:
'Tis then the nobler conqueſt. Gentle couſin,
The ties of blood have made his glory yours:
I know they have, Rodrigo. You, Alvarez,
Were partner of his day; you nobly fought
And conquer'd with him. Both of you muſt ſhare
The joy ſincere that ſwells a father's boſom,
Made young again and blooming in a ſon.

SCENE III.

ALONZO, *the* QUEEN, ELVIRA, RODRIGO, ALVAREZ, *Courtier, &c.*

COURTIER.

The ambaſſador of Spain, my lord——

ALONZO.

'Tis well.
Conduct him hither.

SCENE IV.

ALONZO, *the* QUEEN, ELVIRA, RODRIGO, ALVAREZ.

[*The King aſcends his throne, placing the Queen on his left, the Ambaſſador and his train range themſelves.*]

AMBASSADOR.

Sir, my royal maſter,
Don Ferdinand, by his ambaſſador
Thus ſpeaks the true fraternal part he takes
In your full joy. He holds himſelf moſt happy,
That his lov'd parent ſhares a throne with you;
And that his ſiſter, his Almeyda, weds
So great a monarch's heir, and who renews
The virtues of his race. Don Pedro's fame
Spreads not o'er Portugal more welcome beams
Than o'er our friendly Spain. And you enjoy
The bliſs ſupreme, that nobleſt minds taſte deepeſt,
A ſon that loves the ſire he emulates!
Yes, you have ſeen him, from his earlieſt youth,
Purſue the path your valour trod before
To conqueſt and renown. Your arm, by him,
Has oft been felt in Afric; oft has ſhook
Her ſtrongeſt forts, her deepeſt ſquadrons pierc'd;
And now, even now, of laurels fairly won

2 A mighty

A mighty harveſt reap'd. Your intereſts, Sir,
Are link'd with ours by bonds of mutual friendſhip:
And where allies are mutual in their love,
The happineſs is common. Our Caſtile,
Itſelf triumphant, triumphs too with you!

ALONZO.

Your ſovereign is the partner of my heart.
His mother, now my queen, and who adorns
The ſeat ſhe fills, has made our nations one:
And that ſame treaty, which declar'd her mine,
Aſſures Don Pedro to her daughter's arms;
Aſſures my kingdom's ſafety: for theſe nuptials,
Tho by the guilt of intervening war
Too long delay'd, ſhall be accompliſh'd now;
While, to the holy temple, Peace and Leiſure,
His beſt attendants, wait in Hymen's train.
Go, bear this meſſage to my brother back;
That all Caſtile may ſhare the joy it gives.

SCENE V.

ALONZO, *the* QUEEN, ELVIRA.

ALONZO.

Yes, madam, your lov'd daughter ſoon ſhall ſee
This happy union fix her future fate.

QUEEN.

I could have wiſh'd the ſame propitious morn,
That join'd our hands, had ſeen compleated too
Their plighted vows.

ALONZO.

It was my fondeſt aim.
But could a father's love to ſuch a ſon
Deny what his impatient courage urg'd?
Some ſhort delay, ſome reſpite, till his arm

By deeds of noble daring ſhould have earn'd
The bleſſing he aſpir'd to.

QUEEN.

Yet, my lord———

ALONZO.

I plac'd myſelf the ſword within his hand,
And whetted his young ſpirit. Fortune oft
Companions youth moſt willingly, and leads
The neareſt road to fame. I then foreſaw,
He would be all that I had been before.
I thenceforth ceas'd to conquer, but by him:
And, thanks to heaven! his actions have outgone
A parent's warmeſt hope.

QUEEN.

To this my heart
Gives unreſtrain'd aſſent.

ALONZO.

The Moors, you ſee,
Reduc'd to ſue for mercy. Part, in chains,
His conquering arm confeſs, and grace his triumph:
The reſt, ſubdu'd by his victorious name,
Lie trembling in the depth of diſtant deſarts.
To him what glory! what true joy to me!
I now dare hope, he may deſerve to wed
The beauty he deſires.

QUEEN.

Forgive me, Sir——
Have you no doubt, no foreſight of reſiſtance,
Nay of refuſal, on the prince's part?
For me, in ſpite of all my partial hopes,
I dread ſome bar, ſome obſtacle unknown
Betwixt us and our wiſhes.

ALONZO.

Whence can riſe
Suſpicions ſo unlikely?

QUEEN.

I have mark'd,
With all a mother's watchfulneſs of fear,
His ſtrange demeanor. Gloomy, loſt in thought
He ſees his bride, as if he ſaw her not.
No beam of kindneſs brightens in his eye;
No word of tenderneſs melts from his lip;
As if nor bloom, nor grace, nor gentle ſpirit
Grew with her opening years.

ALONZO.

Th' alarm is vain.
Grant ſome indulgence to the pride of youth,
An early hero's ardor, with the blaze
Of his firſt conqueſt dazzled and engag'd.
A ſofter paſſion, doubt it not, will ſoon
Diſpel that gaudy dream, and leave his breaſt
All-open to the better bliſs that waits him.

QUEEN.

And yet, my buſy fears ſtill whiſper to me,
Why was he abſent this diſtinguiſh'd day?
Why, with his preſence, deign'd he not to grace
My Ferdinand, your brother and ally,
Here in the perſon of his miniſter?
Should he reſiſt, my Lord?

ALONZO.

Reſiſt? Juſt heaven!
I ſhudder at the thought. In ſuch reſiſtance
The rebel would at once efface the ſon.
Ha! ſhould he puſh his pride to that extreme,
More guilty as the more with glory bright,

He then ſhould find, that conqueſt and renown,
That even the bonds of nature, cannot free
A ſubject from the laws; that all are light
As the blown bubble, weigh'd with a king's honor

QUEEN.

Sir, I would yet adviſe———

ALONZO.

No: a firſt ſubject,
From whoſe example each deſcending rank
Should learn obedience, is himſelf moſt bound.
In him reſiſtance would be deepeſt treaſon.
It cannot be, my queen: turn we our thoughts
From ſuch forebodings of imagin'd guilt.
I will, this coming moment, to the princeſs
Diſcloſe what I have fix'd. That done, the prince
Shall know my laſt reſolve.

QUEEN.

Ah! in what words?
How will a father ſpeak it?

ALONZO.

As his king!

SCENE VI.

The QUEEN, ELVIRA.

QUEEN.

Elvira—You have heard your queen's complaints;
Have heard too what Alonzo, fix'd as fate
And reſolutely juſt, has now determin'd.
The fatal ſecret that alarms us both,
I think, is in your keeping.

ELVIRA.

Heaven! in mine?

QUEEN.

QUEEN.

In yours. Whene'er the prince vouchsafes a visit
To my poor court, his eyes are ever turn'd,
Are ever fix'd on you——What should that mean?

ELVIRA.

Your words amaze me!———

QUEEN.

Are Almeyda's charms,
Whatever Nature's kindest hand can lavish
On favor'd youth, to justify at full
A mother's fondness—tell me, are those charms
Hid but from him? while all beholders else
Divide, with mine, the transports they confess.
They see in her combin'd each brighter grace
Of look and air, see virtue's fairest stamp
Upon her brow imprest, and over all
And all exalting, modest ignorance
Of her own worth: And have I yet to fear,
For such a daughter, coldness or disdain?

ELVIRA.

How can you deem the prince so stern of nature,
That beauty has no power upon his heart?
No, Madam, he has felt it, and admires
Its awful influence in Almeyda's eyes!

QUEEN.

You know it then?

ELVIRA.

It is not mine to read
The secret of his bosom; but he oft,
With me confessing her superior charms,
And that true virtue, lovely as unfeign'd,
The beam that lights those beauties into blaze,
Has oft proclaim'd her all your fondness thinks.

QUEEN.

QUEEN.

And ſought out you, and only you, to pour
His amorous rapture in your willing ear?
Indeed!—Elvira—tremble! You but pull
Deſtruction on your head—yes, ſure deſtruction,
By daring to deceive me! No: not her,
When you are by, his theme is not Almeyda.
Of you he talks!

ELVIRA.

Of me!

QUEEN.

Of you alone!
You either dare to love—or, calm my fears,
And point me to the boſom I ſhould pierce!
For here—I here diſcloſe my inmoſt ſoul——
She, the raſh fair one, who ſhould lift her eyes
To that forbidden height; ſhould wound my breaſt,
A parent's breaſt, in its moſt tender ſenſe,
She, the devoted victim of my rage,
The wretch, the vain preſumer, then ſhould feel
How far a mother and a queen can puniſh!

ELVIRA.

Ye ſaints and angels!—Madam, let calm reaſon——

QUEEN.

My daughter is to me health, pleaſure, fame!
My ſum of good or ill is wrapt in her!
Mine her affront, her rival too is mine!
And to revenge her, earth and heaven in vain
Would bar my way. I am on fire to know
Where I ſhould ſtrike. Then—mark me—find her out,
This guilty head—or ruin hangs o'er thine!

SCENE

SCENE VII.

ELVIRA.

What have I heard! If my ſtun'd ear may credit
Her direful threats, the tempeſt is at hand
That muſt o'erwhelm us both! And yet how firm,
Amid theſe horrors, would my heart be found,
If only I ſtood obvious to the bolt!
If all my fears were for myſelf alone!

SCENE VIII.

ELVIRA, DON PEDRO, RAMIREZ.

DON PEDRO.

Elvira! my ſoul's happineſs——

ELVIRA.

Ah! Prince!
I have to tell—O heaven!—But look that none,
No eye may here ſurprize us.

DON PEDRO.

You, Ramirez,
Will watch without. Now, in the name of love,
What mean theſe ſtreaming eyes? this face o'ercaſt
With dark deſpair? Speak, ſave me from my fears.
Suſpence is torture!

ELVIRA.

And diſcovery, death!
My Lord! my huſband! now the hour is come,
The fatal moment my ſad thought preſag'd!
Even at the ſacred altar, when our hearts
Were wedded with our hands, even then I fear'd it—
O were the threaten'd ruin all my own!

DON

DON PEDRO.

Our fate is one; our happineſs or woe
Inſeparably link'd——But whence, my love,
This deep alarm?

ELVIRA.

Your marriage with the Princeſs——
O thence it ſprings! Alonzo too has nam'd
Th' approaching hour to tell you, it is fix'd!
Yet more, th' offended Queen ſuſpects our loves!
Had you beheld the rage to which her ſoul
Abandons all its faculties!——And now,
Made furious by deſpair, to what a height
Will jealouſy tranſport her, when its eye,
In this ſuſpected miſtreſs, finds a wife!

DON PEDRO.

Yet, calm thy fears. Since on Don Pedro's faith
Depends the ſacred charge of ſaving thee,
His ſum of bliſs! what anger, whoſe revenge
Should wake ſuch tempeſt in Elvira's boſom?

ELVIRA.

Prince, judge more nobly of me. This alarm
Is all for him, whoſe every pain is mine.
My dangers touch me, but as your diſtreſs;
As they muſt wound—for Oh too ſure they will!
Thy generous breaſt. And it will witneſs for me,
The ſplendor of a crown, that worſhip'd ſun
Of vulgar eyes, could never dazzle mine:
For when I dar'd, in giving you my hand,
To violate the law, the rigid law,
That makes a marriage, ſuch as mine, rebellion;
I came the willing victim of your love,
Reſign'd, devoted to whatever fate
Heaven may reſerve for either!

DON

DON PEDRO.

Yes, Elvira,
Thy generous virtue was the charm ſupreme
That made me firſt, and binds me thine, for ever!

ELVIRA.

Nor do I now repent me. No, my Lord:
Even on the ſcaffold, at the lifted ax
My heart could ſmile; remembring it had once,
By being yours, brought happineſs to both.

DON PEDRO.

The ſame bright flame, which angels might avow,
Inſpires thy lover's breaſt—for ſuch I am,
Such will to death be found. The name of wife,
While it refines this paſſion, makes it duty:
And if I needs muſt tremble for thy days,
All other names, however holy deem'd,
Son, ſubject, father, king, are light as air,
When in the ballance laid to counterpoiſe
Thoſe, ſtill more ſacred, that connubial love
Has rais'd, has ſanctify'd——

ELVIRA.

My ſoul ſhrinks back
With horror from theſe tranſports. O remember,
When Hymen's ſecret rite firſt join'd our hands,
Remember what my tenderneſs exacted,
And what your vows aſſur'd me—ſtill to hold
Elvira dear; but ſtill, as death, to ſhun
The crime of civil war! and O what doom,
What fate ſoever heaven may have in ſtore
For her you honor'd, never to forget,
Your father is your ſovereign!

DON

DON PEDRO.

By the Power,
Whoſe primal law has made our being one!
No promiſes ſhall ſtay a huſband's arm
From ſheltering thee. There is on earth no claim,
No tie of duty ſtrong enough to hold
My fierce impatience. Thou to me art all,
Faith, virtue, honor: or theſe ſhadowy names
All vaniſh at the brightneſs of thine eye!

ELVIRA.

My Lord, I muſt not hear you——

DON PEDRO.

Then——retire:
Fly, if it muſt be, this tumultuous court,
This ſcene of ſtorm and danger. To the ſhade,
To that ſweet ſolitude where firſt our loves
Were ratify'd and bleſt, where calm Content
And true Repoſe have fix'd their ſoft abode,
Return, Elvira: ſafety there awaits thee.

ELVIRA.

O dear remember'd ſcene! O hours of peace
That are no more! Beneath its penſive pines,
And by the murmurs of its mazy ſtream
That breath'd out freſhneſs on our ſecret walk,
The morn aroſe, the peaceful evening clos'd
On our united hearts! All fear was far,
All jealouſy of courts; for Love himſelf
Stood guardian of the ſhade!

DON PEDRO.

No more, no more:
Theſe thoughts but ſoothe, but ſoften both to weakneſs.
For me, no color of delay remains.
I know Alonzo well; his eye ſevere,

His breaſt inflexible: and I this hour
Muſt meet their utmoſt terror. Then the Queen——
Should her unſleeping jealouſy at laſt
Surprize the dangerous ſecret of our loves,
The King, moſt ſure, to her inſulted pride,
And to the voice of Juſtice, would give up
Elvira's head---O fly, and guard my ſoul
From this diſtracting fear!

ELVIRA.

It muſt not be.
For me to fly at preſent would be fatal:
At once diſcloſing what with all our care
We ſhould conceal. 'Tis ſafer to remain;
To guide our ſteps with prudence, and our breaſts
With firmneſs arm. From this alarming hour,
We meet no more---and is it I, O heaven!
Who give the hard advice?---no more exchange
A look, a ſmile, where other eyes are preſent;
For all around are hoſtile!

DON PEDRO.

Be it ſo.
I go reſolv'd---But, O my ſoul's beſt treaſure!
O'er every motion, every look and word,
Let cloſe-ey'd Caution watch.

ELVIRA.

Alas, my Lord!
All that a woman's feeble reaſon can,
Elvira will attempt. Ye pitying powers,
Who ſee with what reluctance from his ſight
I turn my parting ſteps, around his head
Spread your protecting wings! for oh! who knows
What can aſſure us, but we both receive,
And both an everlaſting farewel give!

End of the firſt ACT.

ACT II. SCENE I.

ALONZO, ALMEYDA.

ALONZO.

NO more, Almeyda.

ALMEYDA.

Then, I hop'd in vain
To touch a King, in whom my heart reveres
A ſecond father? Yet, a while delay
This promis'd union of your ſon and me,
Till he himſelf with fond impatience chides
The tardy hours, and preſſes to be mine.
It moſt becomes us both.

ALONZO.

It ſuits at leaſt
The conſcious pride that dignifies your ſex,
More nicely fram'd, more delicately coy,
Than groſſer man, ſuch chaſte reſerve, that ſpreads
New brightneſs o'er your charms, exalts them too.
Complaint, on ſuch a theme, would ill beſeem
A virgin's mouth. I know it: and the leſs
You urge my promiſe, a King's honor given
Exacts, with ſtricter care, its full performance.
My orders are already ſent.

ALMEYDA.

O Sir,
If my true cares, by all a daughter's duty,

To

To merit your esteem, can have inspir'd
Alonzo's least regard; and if amidst
A kingdom's high concerns, you deign a thought
On what may stain Almeyda's life with shame,
Or make it bright and happy! yet recall
Those orders: yet suspend——

ALONZO.

Your words amaze me!
I, in my turn, am left in equal doubt;
Nor know I what this strange reluctance means.
My son! Don Pedro!——is he to your thoughts
An object of such horror? Why this dread
Of calling me your father? Must I think
Contempt of him——

ALMEYDA.

Contempt? Alas, my Lord!
Could he deserve it, did my reason judge him
Less worthy of the blood from whence he springs;
I then—O Sir!—I then might wait his pleasure,
With less emotion trembling at this heart.
To you I dare disclose its inmost weakness,
Tho shame arises blushing to forbid me——
Then know—because I love—I dread his answer!
Yes, from the moment I beheld him first,
A sudden softness, to myself unknown,
Sprung in my bosom; charm'd at once and pain'd me
With all the mingled war of love and doubt:
And gave me soon——alas! too soon to know,
Almeyda's future fate was in his power!
And——if I miss'd his heart——

ALONZO.

Proceed, fair Princeſs.
The bluſh that reddens there is Virtue's color:
Her chaſte hand ſpreads it. But proceed unmov'd:
And be aſſur'd a parent's kindeſt ear
Is open to your tale.

ALMEYDA.

I need not ſay
How, with his riſing fame, my paſſion grew.
'Twas glory fed it: and each added conqueſt,
Like heaven's kind dew upon th' unfolding roſe,
Nurs'd the new bloſſom into ſtrength and beauty.
But, more unhappy as more fondly his,
The cold that hangs on his conſtrain'd addreſs
Is winter here, and withers all my hopes!
Hence grows, my Lord, the backwardneſs you blame:
Permit it to my ſex, till ripening time
Shall warm his boſom into mutual ſoftneſs.

ALONZO.

Daughter!——for that dear name is juſtly due
To ſuch exalted openneſs of heart,
True Honor's fair companion——truſt to me;
Rely on all a father's love. I feel,
Yes, feel already every ſoft emotion
Theſe tender names convey. Let not a dream,
A diſtant doubt of ills impoſſible
Alarm that gentle boſom. No, Almeyda!
When you ſhall learn, as inſtantly you may,
Not his obedience only, but his love,
Your fears will fly before them.

SCENE

SCENE II.

ALONZO, ALMEYDA.

GUARD.

Sir, the Prince
Attends your pleaſure.

ALMEYDA.

Ah! I muſt be gone:
But if my tears have influence——

ALONZO.

Go, my daughter,
And on my love repoſe your every care.

SCENE III.

ALONZO, DON PEDRO.

ALONZO *ſits.*

My ſubjects, Prince, the triumphs of your ſword
Have oft beheld, oft hail'd with loud applauſe:
Alonzo too has felt a parent's ſhare
Of joy in theirs. The time is come at laſt
For other feſtivals, the gentler triumphs
That wait on love and hymeneal rites.
Theſe are the honors that can beſt reward
The warrior's glorious toils: and much it moves
My wonder, Prince, that I, who ought to find
In your impatience all a lover's ardor,
Muſt here adviſe, nay muſt impoſe, obedience!

DON PEDRO.

Sir, from a father's kindneſs I had hop'd
Commands leſs rigid, leſs ſeverely urg'd:
And that his love would in my ſilence read,
What filial reverence ſtifles on my tongue.
Ah, Sir! recall this harſh command.

ALONZO.

Recall it!
By heaven! this rude demeanour, ſhould I give
The rein to my juſt wrath, might coſt thee dear——
Nor think thy blindneſs to Almeyda's worth,
This ſavageneſs of ſoul by love unſoften'd,
Thy ſole offence.

DON PEDRO.

Alas! what elſe can ſtir
My ſovereign's anger?

ALONZO.

A King's word is paſt!
Alonzo's word and oath! the league too ſeal'd
And ratify'd, on this expreſs condition!

DON PEDRO.

And yet, Don Pedro's heart——

ALONZO.

Ha! canſt thou dream,
The nuptials of a Prince, thoſe general ties
On which depend the peace and bliſs of millions,
Are bound with flowery bands, which Fancy twiſts
With idle fingers? twiſts for thoſe alone,
Th' inferior herd, who live but for themſelves?
Far other maxims guide the royal choice,
More noble, more exalted. Not enſlav'd
By vulgar forms, the common good decides
A prince's fate: and, where his people's welfare
Directs his judgment, there he gives his hand.

DON PEDRO.

Then—in the dearest interest of our heart,
Its truest bliss or its severest woe,
The heart itself has no election left!
This would be binding hard, nay rivetting,
Those artificial chains, which Craft of state
First forg'd, and Vanity still deigns to wear.
Yet Nature has her claims, her elder rights,
More holy, more inviolably binding.
Are these extinguish'd only to the wretch,
Who, nearest to a throne, is most a slave?
The lowest slave———

ALONZO.

What mean'st thou? Whither tends
This raving talk?

DON PEDRO.

Yes, here the cottage-hind,
Burnt by the beam or shivering in the shade,
Smote by the sore vicissitude thro life
Of cold, heat, hunger, is a king to him.
He, with his heart, can freely give his hand:
Can chuse—Ah, Sir, you tremble with your anger—
But, at your knees, behold a son with pity!
O with a father's gracious ear receive
What now he must unfold!

ALONZO.

Thou shalt be heard.
That justice bids; by whose eternal rule
All kings should reign. Arise.

DON PEDRO.

When first the Mother
Of Ferdinand became your Queen, alas!
You deign'd not, Sir, to read my heart, or know

The ſprings that move it; but engag'd your faith,
And promis'd me at once to his fair Siſter.

ALONZO.

True: and that promiſe is inviolable.
What would a king be, where the reverent awe
That makes his perſon ſacred, ſhould mankind
Not dare to reſt their faith upon his honor?
Aſk thy own boſom.

DON PEDRO.

O! I well believe,
The youth, the beauty of that charming maid
Left you no doubt of their full influence
On my touch'd heart: you could not then foreſee
The bar invincible it ſtill oppoſes——
I ſpeak it with regret—to this wiſh'd union.

ALONZO, *riſing*.

Am I awake?

DON PEDRO.

I feel, ſeverely feel,
Fair as ſhe is, ſhe never can be mine.
Tho Beauty form'd her in the trueſt mold,
Tho Love has added to her flowering youth
Each winning grace, each air of ſweet attraction;
By all unmov'd, how can I bear the thought
Of wedding her my heart can never own?
O! if my ſoul is precious in your ſight,
If virtuous deeds, inſpir'd by your example,
Have made me not unworthy to be call'd
The ſon of him who moſt adorns a throne;
To Nature's nobler law let thoſe of ſtate
For once give place! and ſave a breaking heart,
That cannot to itſelf be falſe or baſe,
My ſire and ſovereign! ſave it from the crime
Of diſobedience!

ALON-

ALONZO.

Thou haſt ſaid: and ſtill
A parent's fondneſs here is ſtrongly pleading
The cauſe of Mercy for thee. Yet, be warn'd;
That parent is thy king! and all his love
Will plead in vain againſt the voice of duty.
The ſanctity of thrones ſhould be preſerv'd,
Like that of altars, pure; the faith of leagues,
Inviolate, as Heaven's own law ſupreme.
And wouldſt thou, by the breach of ties like ours,
Wouldſt thou afford to Ferdinand pretence
For kindling up, as then he fairly might,
The flames of cruel and conſuming war,
And leave to us the deep, the long remorſe
Of ſhedding in a cauſe, unjuſt and baſe,
The blood of thouſands?

DON PEDRO.

Can Alonzo fear
To light a fire of ſtubble, which his nod
Extinguiſhes at once? Secure to conquer,
Why ſhun to fight? The laurel in our reach,
Why pauſe to make it ours? No: rather urge,
Invite a foe, your power is ſure to cruſh;
And, from the wiſh'd occaſion, add Caſtile
To thoſe late conqueſts that renown your arms.
Let neighbouring nations feel, with dread and reverence,
Th' aſcendant of your genius: while your ſon,
In ſuch a ſhining path, ſhall count it glory
With his laſt blood to ſeal a father's fame!

ALONZO.

Such talk may ſuit the foe of human kind,
A hero's mouth, whoſe buſineſs is deſtruction:
But I muſt act a nobler part—a King's!
The father and preſerver of his people!

We war for them alone, to make them safer
And happier by our triumphs. Other wars,
Of mad ambition or of blind revenge,
But shame the prince, and curse the land he rules.
And may the Nimrods of each blood-stain'd age,
Th' exterminating Demons of mankind,
Reap horror for their portion! Are we rais'd
Alone to conquer? Are mankind but made,
That we, as lust or fury drives our will,
Should traffic with their blood? We are the guardians
Of free-born men, not lords of slavish herds.
Upon their bliss is built our truest fame:
And when we deviate from that glorious end,
We are not kings, but robbers, but assassins.
  Keep these fair maxims ever in your eye;
And when my death shall make this sceptre yours,
Remember and fulfill them. Now, Don Pedro,
My subject now, submission is thy part.
Acquit my promise, make Almeyda thine;
For thus, and in one word, thy king commands it.

DON PEDRO.

O hear me, and recall the stern command——
Ah then—in one word too—for what I am
Permits no more—I cannot.

ALONZO.

Ha!

SCENE IV.

ALONZO, DON PEDRO, *the* QUEEN, ELVIRA.

ALONZO.

This rebel
Resists me to my face, and shews unveil'd

That

That unſubmitting pride, which my fond love
Durſt not foreſee. By this determin'd inſult
To your Caſtile, he covers me and you,
And your Almeyda, with one common ſhame:
And doubt I ſtill to puniſh him?—But, tell me,
Say, is there not ſome partner of his guilt,
Some dark accomplice, whoſe pernicious counſel
Thus hardens him in guilt?

QUEEN.

You ſee her there,
Th' accomplice you would find!

ALONZO.

Elvira!

ELVIRA.

Me!

QUEEN.

Drawn from his duty by her feeble charms,
Aided, no doubt, with all th' enſnaring ſkill
Of female arts, to this degenerate paſſion
He poorly offers up Almeyda's worth,
And feeds a ſubject's vanity by boaſting,
How rich a victim bleeds before her ſhrine!

ALONZO.

Amazement! Can it be?

QUEEN.

It is not now
I firſt diſcover whence his coldneſs grows.
Day after day have I beheld his eye
Of love and ſoftneſs ever hung on hers:
Nay, when alone, when I the dreadful truth
Try'd to explore, the ſtarting tear, that ſtole
Down her fluſh'd cheek, diſcover'd all I fear'd.
Even now—I ſcarce had reach'd my own apartment—

The

They met in ſecret; and in ſecret long
Converſing, parted, each with ſtreaming eyes.
And ſee, my Lord, read on their guilty cheeks
Diſorder and alarm!

ELVIRA.

I am accus'd——
But 'tis in vain—Suſpicions are not proofs——
Th' imputed crime——

DON PEDRO.

Elvira, we are born
Above diſſimulation. Yes—I love;
And dare, without a bluſh, avow my paſſion;
The object makes it glory—But, on me,
On my devoted head fall your full vengeance:
Elvira, Sir, is guiltleſs. She——

ALONZO.

Be dumb!
Ungrateful! cruel!

ELVIRA.

Hear Elvira ſpeak.
Make her, untry'd, unjudg'd, the ſacrifice!
If ſo fair peace betwixt you and the prince
Might be reſtor'd, a death ſo juſtly due
Would be my deareſt wiſh!

ALONZO.

What? what remains?
Let her own chamber henceforth be her priſon,
Till ſhe her conduct juſtifies at full.
Madam, with you I truſt her: be it yours
To keep her perſon ſafe.

DON PEDRO.

Good angels guard it!
With whom, my gracious Lord—Ah! in what hands
Do you entruſt her tender frame?

ALON-

ALONZO.

Peace! peace!
Nor farther urge my fury—I ſuſpend
Thy fate ſome moments: this laſt day is given thee
Yet to reflect; yet to efface thy crime
By prompt obedience. Should it paſs in vain——
Thou art no more my ſon! Away.

DON PEDRO, *aſide.*

Too ſoon
I may return—more guilty than I go!

SCENE V.

ALONZO, *the* QUEEN, ELVIRA.

ALONZO.

Thou ſeeſt, O heaven! the horrors of my lot;
That I may ſoon, in this offending ſon,
Be forc'd to puniſh whom I hold moſt dear.
Oppoſe not now the Monarch to the Father!
My heart would be the firſt: imperious duty,
Alas! may drive me to aſſert the King.
Then teach ſubmiſſion to his ſtubborn will,
That he may yet repent, and I be bleſt!

SCENE VI.

The QUEEN, ELVIRA.

QUEEN.

You ſee, your eyes enjoy the cruel triumph
Of our deſpair. But you are now my priſoner,
[*Guards enter.*
And, with your head, ſhall anſwer what befalls!
For could your arts diſarm Alonzo's wrath,

You

You never ſhall entreat a Mother's heart,
By jealous honor made inexorable.
Nay more; ſhould I reſign the looſen'd rein
To my full rage, one victim were too few!
The cruel Prince, who dares to ſtain our name
With this diſgrace, may then—The blood forſakes
Your cheek at his imagin'd danger—Know,
And let it ſhake your inmoſt ſoul! the fear
You ſhew for him—but wings the fate of both!

SCENE VII.

ELVIRA.

I riſe above all horrors for myſelf
Of torments or of death. Don Pedro's fate,
Inhuman queen! his fate alone can wound
Elvira's breaſt: her own ſhe ſcorns to feel.
Ills, that but touch ourſelves, all diſappear;
For what we love, we only know to fear!

End of the ſecond ACT.

ACT III. SCENE I.

ALONZO, *the* QUEEN.

ALONZO.

YES, let her come. The juſtice of a King,
That law ſupreme which ever ought to guide
His public will, requires ſhe ſhould be heard.
Her virtues too, and the fair ſervices
To former monarchs and to me perform'd
By her forefathers, make it juſter ſtill.

QUEEN.

What would you more? Is not her guilt confeſs'd
In that unworthy paſſion ſhe inſpires?
Nor is the pride of her ambition bounded
Barely to ſuffer it: I know, my Lord,
That drawing glory from her conqueſt won,
She ſpares no grace, no favor, to maintain it.

ALONZO.

Such oft is woman ſeen: to Vanity,
To that mere idol---yet their greater god;
For Love himſelf holds but the ſecond place——
Devoting even that honor they oppoſe
To Nature's law!

QUEEN.

And will you leave her then
To boaſt this triumph o'er a monarch's oath?
Leave her at large to ſtretch her boundleſs ſway,
Up from your meaneſt ſubject to the throne;
Where ſhe will reign imperious in a heart
By love enſlav'd: perpaps decide the fate,

The being of an infant, yet unborn,
Who is to heir your throne!

ALONZO.

I hear, and weigh
What you ſo juſtly urge: and my firſt thought
Was, with her death, to have atton'd her crime.
But no: that were on the wild ſea of paſſion
To drive at random, as th' unguided bark
Is borne before the blaſt---She ſhall be heard——
Yourſelf ſhall hear her; ſound her ſecret aims,
And ſearch thro all the woman in her ſoul.
You know my thoughts, and what I purpoſe for her:
Set thoſe in open light before her eyes,
With firmneſs---but with temper.

SCENE II.

QUEEN.

Wiſe men tell us
That deep diſſembling is th' imperial art
By which kings reign; and that its myſtic veil
Muſt ſtill be drawn betwixt them and the eyes
Of their preſuming ſubjects. Muſt I ſtoop
To this felt baſeneſs? Is a ſovereign's will
By thoſe to be controll'd whom heaven ordains
The vaſſals of his nod; to crouch and kiſs
The foot that ſpurns them? Well; this art for once,
Deſcending from myſelf, I will eſſay——
Guard, call your priſoner hither---and aſſume,
If yet I can---for juſt diſdain forbids it——
This gentleneſs of look that is preſcrib'd me.

SCENE

SCENE III.

The QUEEN, ELVIRA.

QUEEN.

Draw near---Elvira.

ELVIRA.

Now aſſiſt me, heaven!

QUEEN.

Your fears, perhaps, have form'd ſome direful image
Of the King's wrath; ſome ſanguinary purpoſe,
By which your doom already is pronounc'd.
Thoſe fears repreſs, and with the calmeſt ear
Attentive mark me. You, beneath this roof,
Have wide-diffus'd the flames of hateful diſcord,
It may be, undeſigning; and the crime
Your eyes have caus'd, your heart may diſavow.

ELVIRA.

You judge me fairly, Madam!

QUEEN.

Yet, attend.
I dare not think you ſhare Don Pedro's fault,
Encouraging the rebel in his breaſt
By favor or connivance. You too well
Muſt know the diſtance, not to be ſurpaſs'd,
Betwixt you and the throne. It is a height
A ſubject's eye muſt from afar behold,
With reverent awe, but never hope to reach!
I know you fair and virtuous: theſe endowments,
That now adorn you, if beſtow'd aright,
May make you happy too.

ELVIRA.

What mean you, Madam?

QUEEN.

QUEEN.

Hear what Alonzo ſpeaks by me. He owns
The ſtate a debtor to your great forefathers,
For conqueſts won, for blood profuſely ſpilt,
Not here alone in this our weſtern world,
But in remoteſt regions, where the ſun
Looks down direct at noon. He bids me dwell,
With chief regard, on what he owes Alphonſo,
Your Grandſire, that good man who form'd his youth
To love of virtue; whoſe paternal care
Taught him, with no unequal hand, to wield
This kingdom's ſceptre.

ELVIRA, *aſide.*

Whither tends her purpoſe?

QUEEN.

And when a king recounts a ſubject's worth,
What he has prais'd his glory bids him pay
With ample retribution. You ſhall find
He now reſolves no leſs---Rodrigo loves you;
Rodrigo, near of kindred to the throne.
I know he loves you.

ELVIRA, *aſide.*

I am loſt for ever!

QUEEN.

He oft has urg'd Alonzo to reward
His ardent flame: and by a gift ſo noble,
Your ſovereign deems not his imperial houſe
Diminiſh'd in its luſtre. No: the world,
By this great inſtance, ſhall be taught to know,
He holds that man, who train'd a king to honor,
As ſecond only to the Prince he form'd

ELVIRA.

I hear with wonder this exalted ſtrain
Of royal gratitude. Yet, Madam, think,

The

The blood, they ſhed for him, of right was his;
And to have loſt it, at fair honor's voice,
Its own bright recompence! He who is call'd
To ſerve his country, if he has deſerv'd
That glorious truſt, is paid by ſerving well!
But if, too generous, great Alonzo's bounty
Deigns to reward their ſervices in me,
Tho duty has no right—

QUEEN.

You heſitate.
Speak boldly: let your ampleſt claim be ſhewn.

ELVIRA.

Then know, the ſole return Elvira aſks—
Is to be miſtreſs of her humble fate;
That far from courts, and to Rodrigo loſt,
She may with gentle peace live out her days!

QUEEN.

Your pride diſdains him then?

ELVIRA.

Pride dwells not here:
To ſuch a gueſt this boſom is a ſtranger.

QUEEN.

Yet can refuſe, thro mere humility,
A prince from great Alonzo's blood deriv'd?
And dare to tell it me?

ELVIRA.

I dare to think,
That all the brighteſt honors Hymen ſpreads,
When he would join our hands, are airy toys,
Or glittering load; if love attends not too,
To plight conſenting hearts.

QUEEN.

I ſee thro yours!
I fathom its laſt depth!

D ELVIRA.

ELVIRA.

Then you may find,
What equal Nature has to all indulg'd,
Even to its poorest creatures, truth and worth,
The inmates of this heart!

QUEEN.

To boast thy virtues
Before thy queen is insult.

ELVIRA.

Madam, no—
O my full soul!*—but justice done myself [*Aside.
To you is highest reverence. Truth should ever
Be found a subject's language to the throne:
And I but meant to say, our weaker sex,
Even I, may think up to that height of honor,
Which in all ages has enobled Man!
The same blest power—

QUEEN.

'Tis well! thy soul is trac'd
Thro all its doubling mazes. Those suspicions
I sought to banish, now are truths confirm'd!
Ambitious! yes; I mark the daring height,
The wild excess, to which your pride of heart
Elates imagination! you reserve
That beauty for Don Pedro! you revolt
A prince, a son, against his king and father!

ELVIRA.

You wrong me, madam. By the faith sincere
I owe my king, this bosom never lodg'd
A thought against his dignity or peace.
And if the Prince—*I shall betray my heart— [*Aside.
If I had power upon Don Pedro's will,
Eternal Concord with her sheltering wing,
Should ever guard the throne.

QUEEN.

QUEEN.

And what is ſhe,
Whoſe great ambition buſys thus itſelf
In matters of ſuch weight? unſummon'd too
To this high taſk?—Am I awake? Elvira!
What art thou?

ELVIRA.

Mock me not—A ſubject, madam;
A ſubject and your ſervant—yet the child
Of Reaſon, born to think and act with choice!
Sprung too from ſuch a race, ſo great and good,
Their daughter dares not deviate into baſeneſs,
By wedding where ſhe loves not!

QUEEN.

I have found it!
A ſlave to this rebellious paſſion's force,
Don Pedro burns to mount a vacant throne,
That you may there be worſhip'd as his queen—
Ha! yet—who knows—it may, it may be true,
That, ſpurning all the ties of ſacred law,
He is already yours! Perhaps, his fate
A ſecret marriage has already fix'd!
Should it be ſo, ſhould he have ſunk the throne
To that diſgrace—the bolt is lanc'd already,
That ſtrikes you into duſt! Your grand-ſire, yes,
The very man, whoſe loyalty I boaſted,
Preſcrib'd this law. Think of it well—Ah heaven! *
What mingled uproar this way ſwells its ſtorm?

[* *A great ſhout is heard, and the ſound of trumpets at a diſtance.*

SCENE. IV.

The QUEEN, ELVIRA, MENDOZA.

QUEEN.

Mendoza! speak.

MENDOZA.

Madam, the city swarms,
In every street, with multitudes enrag'd,
Who to the palace urge their furious course.
I came to know—

SCENE V.

The QUEEN, ELVIRA, MENDOZA.

RODRIGO.

Not here! Where is the king?

QUEEN.

Rodrigo—what!

RODRIGO.

The sum of all misfortunes!
Arms in his hands and fury in his eyes,
Don Pedro, with a host of gather'd rebels,
Already fills the square, and threatens loudly
Destruction on our heads—I must return:
The king may want our swords.

SCENE VI.

The QUEEN, ELVIRA.

QUEEN.

Perfidious! see,
Behold the curs'd effects—

ELVIRA.

ELVIRA.

O Madam, ſpare
This fruitleſs inſult. Can Elvira dread
Your impotence of anger, while her fears
Embrace alike Alonzo and his ſon?
My boſom bleeds for both! But Oh the prince!
Whate'er his fate may be, the ſame deſpair
Abides this tortur'd heart—ſince I muſt weep
His life, or virtue, loſt!

QUEEN.

And dares thy pride
Affect this glorious ſorrow, when 'tis you,
You only who have plung'd him into guilt?
But yet—and let it as the knell of death
Sound in thine ear—alone he ſhall not fall!
The thunder o'er thy head—think of it—think
Thou art my priſoner ſtill!

ELVIRA.

I think withall,
The death you threaten is but my enlargement
From life's low dungeon, from its galling chains,
To boundleſs freedom and to bliſs ſupreme,
Reſerv'd by gracious heaven for every wretch
Who ſuffers here unjuſtly!

Trumpets ſound again.

SCENE VII.

The QUEEN, ELVIRA, *an Officer.*

QUEEN.

Ha! what means
Thy look of wild diſtraction?

OFFICER.

Mighty Queen,
Don Pedro—

QUEEN.

What of him?

OFFICER.

Has broken down
The palace-gates; and now is rushing forward
To where you stand—

QUEEN.

Confusion! he is here—

SCENE VIII.

DON PEDRO, ELVIRA.

DON PEDRO, *to those behind.*

Keep clear the secret passage; plant your friends
Thro all its downward windings to the garden:
I follow on the instant.
Have I found thee,
My heart's sole wealth, the jewel of my bosom!
Let me secure it, let me lodge it safe
Beyond the reach of robbers.

ELVIRA.

Ah Don Pedro!
What have you done? O you have lost for ever
A brighter gem, of dearer worth and price,
Your Faith and Innocence! And now, your deed
Opens my eyes on mine, and sets it full
In all its horrors, all its guilt before me!

DON PEDRO.

Cruel! what mean thy words?

ELVIRA.

Ah me! what means

This

This blood upon thy ſword? Forbid it, heaven!
That what my fears ſuggeſt—

DON PEDRO.

Thy fears are vain.
With care I ſhun'd where ſtern Alonzo ſtood,
And ſtem'd the tide, majeſtic tho alone,
Oppoſing a king's firmneſs to it's fury.
I turn'd another way: and what you ſee,
Theſe ſanguine ſtains are from a vulgar breaſt,
That would have barr'd my paſſage on to you.
Then, let us fly, my love.

ELVIRA.

Ah, hope it not.
I dare to dye—but tremble at a crime!
I dare be deaf to love itſelf, and you!
Return, defend a parent and a king.
Yes, throw that rebel-ſword beneath his feet:
I leſs ſhall ſuffer from the hand of fate,
To loſe you, innocent, than ſave you, guilty!

DON PEDRO.

What I have done, the meaneſt of mankind,
The peaſant, would have dar'd; have boldly met,
With face erect, earth's univerſal Lord,
Who from his cottage had preſum'd to tear
The partner of his boſom.

ELVIRA.

By the hold,
I have upon your heart! More dear than life;
Than fame itſelf more ſacred! yet reſume
Your better thoughts. Let me behold your ſorrow,
Your filial penitence—

DON PEDRO.

Ah, let me then,
Let me lodge Thee, where my diſtracted fondneſs

No more may tremble for thy life. I then
Return to beg an injur'd sovereign's mercy;
To ask it at his knees: but, while I fear
For thy dear safety, duty pleads in vain!

ELVIRA.

Then, know, Don Pedro—should this guilty passion,
Deaf to the voice of reason, take no counsel
But from its headlong fury— here I stay!
I here remain, your hostage and your victim!

DON PEDRO.

Thou Angel-Cruelty! does then a wife
Reject her husband's aid—

SCENE IX.

ALMEYDA, ELVIRA, DON PEDRO.

ALMEYDA.

Don Pedro, fly!
Your life is on the cast: this minute's chance
Decides your future fate. Alonzo comes:
Those clamouring multitudes, at sight of him.
Shrunk into tame submission. Not their boldest
Could bear the mingled dignity and wrath
That threaten'd from his brow. Be gone, my Lord,
Let not a father's vengeance find you here.

ELVIRA.

O unexampled goodness!

DON PEDRO.

Can it be?
Do you take part, Almeyda, for his life,
The life of One, who merits all your hate?

ALMEYDA.

Ah no! The jealousy of slighted love
I stifle here. My soul is rais'd beyond

The

The baſeneſs of revenge. I pardon all,
So you are ſafe. Fly then, this inſtant fly,
Even were it with my rival—

ELVIRA.

See! Don Pedro,
The King appears—

SCENE X.

ALONZO, DON PEDRO, ALMEYDA, ELVIRA.

ALONZO.

Yes, thou of many crimes!
Thou complicated traitor! thou art loſt,
Where mercy cannot find thee—But behold,
Lo where he ſtands! Say, is thine arm ſtill rais'd,
Still eager for the ſin of parricide?
This inſtant yield thy ſword; or plunge it here
Full in a father's breaſt.

DON PEDRO.

That word, my Lord,
That dreadful ſound has wrench'd it from my hand.
One moment's madneſs has not ſo effac'd
Great Nature's law, that I ſhould ballance here.
And now, diſarm'd, I know my ruin ſure!
My doom already paſt! But O, my Lord,
O let impartial Juſtice draw her line,
And ſeparate ſtrictly innocence from guilt!

ALONZO.

Ha! innocence?

DON PEDRO.

Elvira's ſafety, Sir,
Unſheath'd my ſword. I thought her life in danger:
And to ſecure my bliſs in guarding that,

Tempeſtuous

Tempeſtuous paſſion bore me into guilt.
But her firm virtue, firm above all fear,
Deny'd to be th' accomplice of my crime.
She choſe to ſtay, and anſwer with her life
For my returning reaſon. Save ſuch goodneſs:
Protect it, Sir, from one revengeful arm.
I aſk no more.

ALONZO.

Far other cares ſhould now
Employ thy thoughts. To ſerve her better, know
Thou ſhouldſt defend her leſs. 'Tis thine to tremble
For her and for thyſelf!

DON PEDRO.

If I muſt dye,
Let Puniſhment at once lift up her axe,
And ſtrike this rebel: for, while life is mine,
That life, in her defence, will be employ'd.
You think this recent tumult quench'd and dead;
An inſtant blows it into ſevenfold flame.
Your ſubjects then, let looſe from all regards,
May force my priſon-doors, may ſet me free:
And I, amidſt the horrors of my rage,
May to its deep foundations ſhake this realm!
Do things that reaſon ſhudders but to think!
In that wild ſtorm, diſcerning, ſparing none,
Noble or baſe, but you and this fair princeſs!

ELVIRA.

His paſſion blinds him! All the guilt is mine,
Who thus have arm'd a ſon againſt his ſovereign.
Then let my head attone it; let my death
Reſtore that peace—

ALONZO.

Who waits?—Confine the Prince
[*Guards enter*.
To his apartment,—

ALMEYDA,

ALMEYDA.

Dear unhappy youth!

ALONZO.

And guard him at the peril of your Heads.

[*Two conduct* Don Pedro *to his Apartment.*

Secure Elvira too.

[*She is attended to hers by two others.*

Stern Juſtice—no,
I have no ſon! I am no more a father!
Follow me not *—I would avoid myſelf, [* *To Almeyda.*
Fly from mankind, forſake this hated light,
And hide my woes in death's eternal night!

End of the third ACT.

ACT

ACT IV. SCENE I.

RODRIGO, ALVAREZ.

ALVAREZ.

YOU ſeem much mov'd.

RODRIGO.

The horrid viſion ſtill
Purſues my wounded fancy!

ALVAREZ.

Speak, my Lord,
What have you ſeen?

RODRIGO.

I am not prone to ſhape
Unreal forms, with Superſtition's eye:
But thus it was. There, in that reverend pile
Where reſt the bones of our departed kings,
And where in animated marble riſe
Their ſceptred forms around; as on my knees
I pour'd to heaven my heart in ſecret prayer,
At once a more than midnight-darkneſs ſpred
O'er all the ſolemn ſcene: at once was heard
A peal of groans, reſounding from below!
While ſudden lightnings, darted thro' the gloom,
Shew'd every ſanguine ſtatue red with blood!
Chief that of old Alphonſo—you have ſeen him,
Elvira's grandſire.

ALVAREZ.

Yes: to crown whoſe virtues,
The reigning Monarch plac'd his honor'd form
Next thoſe of our dead kings.

Of winds and ſeas in his ungovern'd paſſions!
Your ſubjects too, the rebels of to-day,
Who now will think him formidably theirs,
Are from this moment his. A nod from him
Will be their law; and each licentious hour
Wear its red mark of civil broils and murders:
The crown, the ſceptre may remain with you,
The power, that ſhould ſuſtain them, will be his!

ALONZO.

Heroic proof of loyalty and truth!
I can diſcern the painful throes of ſoul
This firmneſs coſts thee: but its felt aſcendant,
The ſovereign influence of ſuch virtue, chides
Fond nature from my boſom. Now, who elſe
Among you, Lords, ſtands forth to give his ſuffrage?—
What! no one riſe?—Alas! the tears that ſtream
From each dejected eye, this mournful ſilence,
Big with all horror, but too clearly ſpeak,
What you have judg'd—My ſon is then condemn'd
For you, for all my people, for mankind,
I here devote him—Were I but a father,
He ſtill might live—A monarch muſt be juſt:
Who has betray'd the law would be a tyrant!
He ſhall not reign: No, from that threaten'd danger
I now deliver *you*, your wives, and children.
Let all retire: and you, Mendoza, go,
Inform him of his fate—

SCENE V.

ALONZO.

What will be mine?
O tyrant-Duty! art thou ſatisfy'd,
While I with Roman names of cruel greatneſs,
With Brutus, Manlius, ſhare the fame abhorr'd
Of being more, or leſs, than man was meant?

But

RODRIGO.

The very ſame.
Down his ſtain'd armor ran the crimſon drops,
And his ſhook image trembled on its baſe!
Now, if I live, I ſaw it.

ALVAREZ.

That good angel,
Who watches o'er our ſtate, avert the dangers
Such omens may foreſhew—The King! he gnaws
His angry lip, and ſtorm is on his brow.

SCENE II.

ALONZO, RODRIGO, ALVAREZ.

ALONZO.

Then—it is fix'd—The Lords that you have ſummon'd,
Say, are they come?

ALVAREZ.

They wait your pleaſure, Sir,
In the near council-chamber——

ALONZO. *Aſide.*

Could they ſee
Their ſovereign's breaſt unveil'd! but no: the curtain
Muſt be cloſe-drawn, that each man may adviſe
As unimpaſſion'd reaſon guides him—Leave me.

SCENE III.

ALONZO.

Adviſe!—Thou general Parent of mankind!
Who bidſt thy ſun ariſe, thy rain deſcend
On all the various creatures thou haſt made,
Juſt and unjuſt alike! is one ſad father
Reſerved, in his grey years, himſelf to puniſh
A lov'd, an only ſon? And muſt he ſit
In judgment on him? hear the doom of death—

My

My soul revolts, all nature in my bosom
Shrinks and starts back from this detested duty;
But 'tis a King's——and thou, Alonzo, thou
Art he, that king! O did the beggar know
What splendid misery is lodg'd within
The circle of a crown, he would not stoop
His palsy'd hand to take it from the dust,
And be its wearer——What, or how determine?
Was it for this I weary'd heaven with vows
To give my throne an heir? Was it in wrath,
Heaven granted my request? and have I form'd
His youth to glory, seen his steps outrun
The swiftest in her race, that he, this son,
With her fresh laurel wreath'd, should bleed at last
Beneath the murderous axe?

Guards—bring my son;
Conduct Don Pedro hither.

Once, once more
I mean to hear him—could I pardon too,
I yet were blest! for my torn bosom feels
The pangs of guilt, in following Virtue's call.
Then summon all the monarch to thine aid!
For think, the present, think, each future age
Will fix their eyes of censure or applause
On this one act of thine. Altho a father,
That private name must bend before the large,
The universal duties of a sovereign.
Quit we the sceptre, or its rights assert;
Chastise offence, while weeping o'er th' offender
That humankind may tremble to transgress,
Who see inexorable Justice stretch,
O'er all alike, her rod of punishment;
Not even a prince, a throne's immediate heir,
Exempted from her arm!

SCENE

SCENE IV.

ALONZO, DON PEDRO.

ALONZO.

The council, Prince,
Is now aſſembling. Your own breaſt muſt tell you
Th' inevitable ſentence it will paſs:
And when your fury plung'd you into guilt,
You on yourſelf pronounc'd it. Yet there is,
There ſtill remains one door of mercy open:
Take warning then in time. Your prompt obedience,
To me a ſon, to you reſtores a father.
Fulfill the treaty, wed that virtuous Princeſs:
You live on theſe conditions. Theſe refus'd—
I may be wretched—but your doom is paſt!

DON PEDRO.

Then—know your Son, with all his failings on him.
My Soul, like yours, thus guilty as I am,
Beholds, unmov'd, the neareſt face of danger:
And you would bluſh, would deeply bluſh for both,
If fear or force debas'd me to ſubmiſſion.
What love and reverence, to a parent due,
Could not perſuade, no tortures can obtain.

ALONZO.

Thou Cruel! why, deſerving all my hate,
Preſerve this greatneſs, that but more embitters
The grief I feel already? Shew me rather
A mortal enemy, a Son ingrate
Prepar'd to ſtrike his parricidal knife
Deep thro my heart. Reduc'd to wiſh thy death,
Let me behold it too—without deſpair!

DON PEDRO.

I have deſerv'd to die.

ALONZO.

My pity ſtill
Would bid thee live.

DON PEDRO.

What muſt I do?

ALONZO.

ALONZO.

Obey!

DON PEDRO.

Then all is o'er. It cannot be.

ALONZO.

Retire—

A tear would follow—but I blot it out.

SCENE V.

The back scene opens and discovers the Lords of the council met, RODRIGO, ALVAREZ, *and others.*

The King walks slowly up to his chair of State.

ALONZO.

Be seated, Lords—Alas! I look around,
And read on every face the secret pangs
Your bosoms share with mine. The ready drop
Stands trembling in each eye, as if yourselves
Had each a son to judge and to condemn!
But let us rise above all private feelings;
Remorse should have no place, where Justice reigns:
And those, whom heaven appoints to counsel kings,
Must shed no tear, but for offended laws.
All other grief is weakness, or is guilt.
The Prince, a rebel to the law and us,
Has set at nought the binding faith of oaths;
The solemn ties of treaties ratify'd,
Whatever links one nation to another,
And king to king. Nor is this all. You saw,
With horror and astonishment you saw him,
In arms and at the head of traitors arm'd,
Assault this palace! force its gates against me!
And, if he shun'd himself the guilt supreme
Of parricide, he left his king expos'd,
His father at the mercy of those rebels
Whom he had made so!—These are his offences.

'Tis

'Tis yours to judge them; and pronounce his doom.
Rodrigo, ſpeak.

RODRIGO.

Alas! I ſhould be ſilent.
You know, and have approv'd the tender love
I bear Elvira: To my happineſs
Don Pedro is the ſole, the fatal bar:
And you command me, Sir, to judge a rival!
But far be from me each imagin'd hope,
However dear, that but reſpects myſelf!
Is it a queſtion, can it bear debate,
If he, tho deem'd a criminal, ſhould live?
Search your own breaſt: the powerful pleadings there
Will beſt inform you what I ſhould adviſe.
Forgive, my Lord, this tranſport.

ALONZO.

Let calm reaſon
Guide all you ſay. Proceed.

RODRIGO.

I aſk again,
Is it in queſtion, whether your renown
Should live by him, or be for ever loſt?
He—and there is none other—can ſupport
The ſceptre's weight; he only, after you,
Preſerve this kingdom flouriſhing and happy.
Weigh then, with candor weigh, againſt his crime,
Th' acknowledg'd prize of benefits like theſe.

ALONZO.

But treaties ſeal'd, and ſanctify'd by oaths,
He dares to violate.

RODRIGO.

Are treaties then,
But leagues of regal cruelty and force?
Muſt you, to pleaſe a neighbouring monarch's pride,

In your own ſon exterminate your race?
Extinguiſh every future hope? and would not
The cheek of Ferdinand burn red with ſhame,
Should his lov'd ſiſter owe a huſband's hand
To cold obedience; while, in other realms,
New thrones, new hearts, attend the fair one's choice?
He forc'd the palace gates. The crime is own'd:
But no deſign againſt your crown or perſon
Urg'd that blind violence: Alas! his aim
Was but to ſcreen th' endanger'd life of one,
His fondneſs trembled for. You ſee him thus—
A rebel? no: a lover in deſpair!
And can a moment's raſhneſs merit death?
No: let him live—and tho my boſom bleeds
At what I utter—yes, indulge his love!
His life is all: a life like mine is nothing!

ALONZO.

You prove the blood you ſpring from: and this effort,
This generous violence you do your heart,
While it miſleads, both honors and exalts you.
But 'tis the hero, not the judge has ſpoken.
What ſays Alvarez?

ALVAREZ.

Could your eye, my Lord,
Pierce inward to my heart, the conflict there,
The war that gratitude and duty wage,
Would leave it doubtful which you moſt ſhould pity,
Don Pedro or his judge. He ſav'd my life.
Beneath an African's uplifted ſabre,
Faint, bleeding thro my former wounds, I lay.
He ſaw, he flew, and on his ſhield receiv'd
Th' impending ſword! Was it, good heaven, for this,
That I, who but for his protecting arm
Had now been duſt, ſhould ſit to judge his fate?
Ah no, my Lord: I would be dumb for ever!

ALONZO.

ALONZO.

Fair honor and the duty of this place
Exact it of you ; call on you to speak
By truth's unbiass'd dictates. This great cause
Imports ourself, our realm, and all mankind.

ALVAREZ.

Alas, my Lord, to what alternate horror,
As subject and as man, am I expos'd ?
But hence all private ties, the first and dearest !
My life is his ; my duty, Sir, is yours :
And from the fear, so busy here within,
Of being deem'd ungrateful to a friend,
I dare not be a traitor to my king.
The law *has* spoke. His sentence *is* pronounc'd,
Is past already ; in despight of tears,
Of all the pain'd reluctance pity strives with :
For when the sovereign majesty of kings
Is once invaded, but one way remains
To expiate that offence. Th' insulted rights,
You sit to judge of, are not yours. They grow
Inherent to the throne : And you, my Lord,
Are to all present, all succeeding princes
Accountable for what you now decree.
I go too far.

ALONZO.

Proceed.

ALVAREZ.

It cannot be :
Tears choak my voice.

ALONZO.

Keep nothing from my view :
Thy virtue here demands it.

ALVAREZ.

I obey.
Should pity now prevail in his behalf,
You are no more a king ! You reign at mercy

Of winds and ſeas in his ungovern'd paſſions!
Your ſubjects too, the rebels of to-day,
Who now will think him formidably theirs,
Are from this moment his. A nod from him
Will be their law; and each licentious hour
Wear its red mark of civil broils and murders:
The crown, the ſceptre may remain with you,
The power, that ſhould ſuſtain them, will be his!

ALONZO.

Heroic proof of loyalty and truth!
I can diſcern the painful throes of ſoul
This firmneſs coſts thee: but its felt aſcendant,
The ſovereign influence of ſuch virtue, chides
Fond nature from my boſom. Now, who elſe
Among you, Lords, ſtands forth to give his ſuffrage?—
What! no one riſe?—Alas! the tears that ſtream
From each dejected eye, this mournful ſilence,
Big with all horror, but too clearly ſpeak,
What you have judg'd—My ſon is then condemn'd
For you, for all my people, for mankind,
I here devote him—Were I but a father,
He ſtill might live—A monarch muſt be juſt:
Who has betray'd the law would be a tyrant!
He ſhall not reign: No, from that threaten'd danger
I now deliver *you*, your wives, and children.
Let all retire: and you, Mendoza, go,
Inform him of his fate—

SCENE V.

ALONZO.

What will be mine?
O tyrant-Duty! art thou ſatisfy'd,
While I with Roman names of cruel greatneſs,
With Brutus, Manlius, ſhare the fame abhorr'd
Of being more, or leſs, than man was meant?

But

But how ? or when ?—The blackeſt hour of night
Muſt cover this dire deed—Ha ! there, behold
Th' uplifted axe ! Ha heaven ! it falls—and lo
A headleſs trunk ! a ſcaffold red with blood !
O thou, All-Juſt, who doom'd me to a throne !
Why, with its duties, leave this writhing boſom
Acceſſible to pangs, that but a Child
Can pierce the ſoul with—and a Parent know ?

SCENE VI.

ALONZO, *the* QUEEN, ALMEYDA.

ALMEYDA.

What have I heard ? This moſt inhuman ſentence
Is it then paſt ? Each face bedew'd with tears,
And every eye caſt in deſpair on heaven,
I ſaw the Council part : and on your brow
I read my fate in characters of horror !
You have condemn'd your ſon !

ALONZO.

I have done juſtice.

ALMEYDA.

O heaven ! can you avow, and can I hear it ?

QUEEN.

This wound, my Lord, muſt in a father's heart
Be deeply felt. Why, by his guilty raſhneſs,
Why has Don Pedro puſh'd you to the brink
Of dire neceſſity—

ALONZO.

Madam, no more.
If in obedience to relentleſs duty,
If deaf to all that bleeding Love can plead
In this ſad boſom, I condemn a ſon ;
'Tis yours to think, that mercy was his due.
Unhappy boy ! alas it is too plain,
He has no mother.

SCENE VII.

The QUEEN, ALMEYDA.

ALMEYDA.

If my life is dear
To her who gave it, ſeize, O ſeize, this moment—
You ſee Alonzo ſoftening into nature—
Kneel, preſs, adjure him—and you ſave the prince!

QUEEN.

I go. Your pains and pleaſures all are mine:
Be moſt aſſur'd they are—And, tho' the ſkies
Look frowning round us, yet methinks a beam
Of day-light breaks upon the doubtful horror!
It lights me—yes, it points the ſecret path,
I ſhould purſue! Almeyda—truſt to me.

SCENE VIII.

ALMEYDA.

Sir, bring your priſoner: by the Queen's command
I have to talk with her,

[*Guard goes out.*

It muſt be ſo—
Yes, to preſerve him, I will ſtoop to beg
A rival's aid. Even ſhould he live for her;
Is any price too high, at which we ſave
The life of him we love? She comes—

SCENE IX.

ALMEYDA, ELVIRA.

ALMEYDA.

Alas!
Don Pedro is found guilty!

ELVIRA.

O deſpair!
O death to all my hopes!

ALMEYDA

ALMEYDA.

Elvira, now,
On this important, this deciding moment
Our mutual fate depends. You long have mark'd
My paſſion for the prince; that, in deſpite
Of ſcorn in him, of jealouſy in me,
Beyond whatever nature elſe can boaſt
I hold him dear—

ELVIRA.

I have with heart-felt grief,
And flowing eyes beheld it—and even now
They ſtream afreſh!

ALMEYDA.

The Queen is gone to try
Her tendereſt influence on a huſband's heart.
I too will claſp his knees, and beg for mercy:
But will theſe arts, theſe little aids prevail
Againſt his dread ſeverity of nature?
If you have thought, or if inventive Love
Can prompt your breaſt with more ſucceſsful means,
Adviſe, Elvira; for your counſels here
Shall be my law. Whatever you ſuggeſt,
At peril of my life I will perform.

ELVIRA.

Ah! how reply? What equal anſwer find
To ſuch exalted worth? All that my thought
Is big with, your true virtue, my diſtreſs,
All preſs me with confuſion. In your ſight
The Prince muſt ſeem ungrateful and unjuſt;
And I a worthleſs rival, caſt beneath
Your leaſt regard.

ALMEYDA.

Let virtue make us equal.
The Prince to both is dear: let both unite,
Without a farther thought, to ſave his life.

ELVIRA.

O amiable goodneſs! Wonder fills
And joy again attempts to chear my boſom!
There riſes to my eye one glimpſe of light,
One ray of hope: but you, and only you
Can make it real. Cloſely here confin'd,
Alas! I have no means—Go then—and heaven
Suceed your purpoſe! from the King intreat,
Obtain a moment's audience for Elvira—
I yet may calm his anger; yet prolong
Don Pedro's threaten'd days—perhaps for you!

ALMEYDA.

It would be cruel, as 'tis moſt unjuſt,
To think ſuch hopes could animate my zeal.
Elvira, no: the fire that warms this breaſt
Is of a purer beam. I go to find
Th' unhappy King; with prayers and tears to try
If he is yet a parent, or a man!

ELVIRA.

O may the fair attempt ſucceſsful prove!
May ſtern Alonzo hear the voice of love!
O may we both preſerve, what both adore!
So he but lives—I aſk of heaven no more!

The guards conduct her back.

End of the fourth ACT.

ACT

ACT V. SCENE I.

MENDOZA, RAMIREZ.

RAMIREZ.
Condemn'd to die, you ſay?

MENDOZA.
This very moment
The fatal preparations are begun;
The gloomy pomp that ſhews us death more dreadful!
Surrounding guards, whoſe ſilence terrifies
Beyond the din of their conflicting arms;
The bloody theatre, with cypreſs hung—
Alas! the color that ten thouſand mourners
Muſt ſhortly wear—And then the victim comes!
'Tis horrible to thought!

RAMIREZ.
Who has in charge
To ſee this murder done?

MENDOZA.
On me, my friend,
On me the cruel duty is impos'd
By our relentleſs Maſter.

RAMIREZ.
Is the hour
Appointed, and the place?

MENDOZA.
Both, both are fix'd:
And when the midnight-bell with mournful call
Tolls up the cloiſter'd Fathers of Saint Francis,
Who have been nam'd on his departing ſoul

To

To beg heaven's mercy—when that fatal warning
Has ſtruck my ear, Don Pedro is brought forth.

RAMIREZ.

And whither then?

MENDOZA.

To that ſequeſter'd ſpot,
Wall'd high around, where oft the nobleſt blood
Of Portugal has flow'd. 'Tis there the Prince
Muſt loſe his head.

RAMIREZ.

Mine ſhall be riſk'd, by heaven!
Nor mine alone: a thouſand more ſhall fall,
Ere that inhuman ſentence takes effect.
A deed like this will ſtain our hated annals
Thro all deſcending time. Let us prevent it.
The people, ſtill tumultuous, like their ſea,
May ſoon be blown into a ſecond ſtorm,
It ſhall be try'd.

MENDOZA.

You caſt yourſelf away,
And ſerve not him your friendſhip aims to ſave.
The palace-gates are ſtrongly barr'd; at each
A triple guard is planted: and the King
Commands, on pain of death, that none approach him.

RAMIREZ.

But ſure theſe orders are not for the Queen;
And ſhe, a woman, by thoſe tender feelings,
That are her ſex's glory, muſt be ſway'd—
She moves this way, and with her, fair Almeyda.

SCENE II.

The QUEEN, ALMEYDA, MENDOZA,

RAMIREZ.

O Queen! and you, lov'd Princeſs! hear me ſpeak—

QUEEN.

QUEEN.

Withdraw at once.

RAMIREZ.

Don Pedro, gracious Miſtreſs—

QUEEN.

Ha!—leave us—go.

RAMIREZ.

Heaven! in her lateſt hour,
When ſhe would plead to thee, remember this!

SCENE III.

The QUEEN, ALMEYDA.

QUEEN.

Elvira ſee the King! What haſt thou done?
Diſhonor'd as we are, you ſeem to dread
The vengeance due to your diſgrace and mine.
Far from reſenting theſe repeated inſults,
You, by your tears, ſolicite new and greater;
For they may live, the hated pair may live
To ſee our mutual ſhame, and triumph o'er it!

ALMEYDA.

Let not the pious meltings of compaſſion
Offend you, Madam. Let her virtue ſtill
Be your Almeyda's happineſs and pride.

QUEEN.

What is your aim? what viſionary purpoſe
Deceives you into wiſhing they may meet?
'Tis madneſs all.

ALMEYDA.

When Liſbon firſt beheld
It bleſt your daughter's ſteps. As Peace and Eaſe
Came, her companions, ſhouting thouſands rais'd
Her name to heaven, and hail'd their guardian-genius.
But what a peace, good Angels? writ in blood,

And

And ſeal'd with murder ! Was I then but meant
The Meſſenger of heaven's ſevereſt vengeance ?
To tear aſunder nature's cloſeſt ties ;
And by the Sire aſſaſſinate the Son ?
'Tis more than horror ! May Elvira's tears
Prevent theſe threaten'd miſchiefs—

QUEEN.

May the rage,
This boſom ſwells with, rather be aſſwag'd
By ſeeing both expire ! Rejected ! heaven !
The daughter of a king ! in whoſe high veins
Flows undebas'd from a long line of heroes
The nobleſt blood ! Shall Europe hear it told,
She has been ſet at nought ? Ha !—and for whom ?
Degenerate boy ! I, with my own, could purchaſe
His death, this moment !

ALMEYDA.

Do you then wiſh mine ?

QUEEN.

Ah, can'ſt thou love him ſtill ?

ALMEYDA.

I ſtill adore him,
Ungrateful, cruel as he is !

QUEEN.

O ſhame !
O fall ignoble from the high rais'd ſenſe
Of that reſentment, wrongs like ours demand,
Nay ſanctify, and make our vengeance, virtue !
Can ſhe, a child of mine, whoſe every pulſe
Should beat with driving fury and diſdain,
Whoſe boſom ſhould expand to take in all
That brave revenge avows, thus melt away
In tears and ſighs ? like ſome fond village-maid

 Beneath

Beneath her willow, by the brook obſcure
That ſoothes her amorous folly?

ALMEYDA.

O yet think,
There is revenge more noble, more divine,
That ſpreads no bluſh upon the injur'd cheek,
By rendering good for ill.

QUEEN.

My Ferdinand!
Son of thy mother's ſoul, when thou ſhalt know
Thy ſiſter's abject ſpirit, thus reſign'd
To injuries and ſcorn, thy breaſt will flame
With anger uncontroul'd! On thee alone
My hopes, my life depend—Who waits?—'Tis glory
To fall reveng'd.

GUARD.

Your pleaſure, Madam?

QUEEN.

Go,
Call in th' Ambaſſador of Spain.

ALMEYDA.

Ah me,
Whence this new ſtorm of paſſion?

Enter AMBASSADOR.

QUEEN.

You have had
Your audience. Then be gone; this moment go;
On all the wings of haſte to Spain return:
And there, this letter, as you prize your head,
Deliver on the inſtant to my ſon.
Yet, ſtay—You may be uſeful, and inforce
With your beſt reaſon what my letter urges;

That

That he ſhould arm inceſſantly, and lead
His troops the neareſt road towards hated Liſbon.
Extremeſt need, mine and Almeyda's ſafety,
Requires he ſhould. That writing will explain
What elſe remains.

Exit Ambaſſador.

My brain turns round—Aſcend
From night eternal and profoundeſt hell,
Ye Powers of vengeance! Puniſh home with me
This object of my hate! thro all her frame
Spread fires unquench'd! then, with his funeral torch,
Let Death attend, to light her bridal bed!
And thus compleat my great revenge, as fits
A mother and a Queen!

SCENE IV.

ALMEDYA.

My blood ſtops ſhort
And freezes in its courſe to hear her threats.
But love and rage diſtract her.

SCENE V.

ALONZO, ALMEYDA.

ALONZO.

Princeſs, yes,
Your tears have vanquiſh'd. I will hear Elvira:
But be moſt ſure her hopes are empty air.
Leave me: ſhe comes.

SCENE

SCENE VI.

ALONZO, ELVIRA.

ELVIRA.

This moment, Sir,
This awful moment is, perhaps, the laſt
That e'er Elvira's voice ſhall reach your ear,
Or ſight offend your eye— But let me now
Intreat this guard may go—He is already
Poſſeſs'd of what I purpoſe.

ALONZO.

Be it ſo.
Do what you have in charge.

ELVIRA.

Speed wing thy ſteps!
You have, againſt the voice of earth and heaven,
To day condemn'd your firſt, your only hope!
A Son who loves you, who reveres the voice
That dooms him to the block! an early Hero,
By you belov'd—O heaven!—and tho I ſee
Remorſe ſit ſad and ſilent on your brow,
You yet devote this victim; that mankind
With dread amazement may revere the Juſtice,
They tremble to behold—You turn away—
May I proceed?

ALONZO.

Go on.

ELVIRA.

Thus far is well:
But then—'tis ſtill the firſt, the law ſupreme,
On kings moſt binding, to be juſt in all.
Guilt may appear, where yet no crime is found;

A rebel,

A rebel, an ingrate, deserves to die.
And yet these names may not belong to him,
To your unhappy Son.

ALONZO.

Thy words are wild:
Despair and love thy reason have unsettled.

ELVIRA.

Ah no—If he, against the faith of treaties,
Refus'd Almeyda's hand, it was not, Sir—
Believe these tears—'twas not the crime suppos'd
Of disobedience—

ALONZO.

How!

ELVIRA.

And if he forc'd
These palace-gates, his noble soul abhorr'd
All criminal attempt against his king.
A word, a breath his innocence had prov'd:
But he, a hero in his cruel silence,
To save Elvira, greatly chose to die!
'Tis therefore mine, the sole remaining purpose
Of my last hour, to clear his injur'd name;
And lead you into truth. Don Pedro's faults
Were those of duty, Sir—He is my husband!

ALONZO.

Ha! husband! he! my son!—And dares thy fondness
Think, by discovery of this daring crime,
To move compassion? When no hope remains
Of grace to his offence, dost thou presume
On mercy for thy own acknowledg'd guilt?

ELVIRA.

I ask for none! my parting thoughts are fix'd
On something nobler, dearer far than life.

The

The rigid law, by you declar'd inviolable,
I only have transgress'd—

ALONZO.

True: and thy life
The penalty shall pay.

ELVIRA.

It is most just.
I bring no plea, I urge no vain defence,
That love for him—such love as would in heaven
Be held no crime—

ALONZO.

Away—that very love
Makes thee but still more guilty!

ELVIRA.

Sir, recall
The dreadful moment, when your court beheld
This Son, this blooming promise of a hero,
His eye extinguish'd and his fading cheek
Of its fresh rose forsaken, to the grave
Untimely sinking! and a father's tears
In hopeless silence streaming o'er his face!
I urge it not, that, to preserve his youth,
And save your only hope, I gave my hand
Where I had vow'd my heart—I urge not this:
But now at last devote myself for both!
In death exulting to have sav'd him twice!

ALONZO.

Thro all the horrors guilt has thrown around thee,
Thy virtue yet looks lovely—but in vain:
Thy crime and his stand manifest to view,
And what the laws exact shall be fulfill'd.

ELVIRA.

Juſt heaven! ſhouldſt thou, when kings addreſs thy throne
For mercy on their own offences, then
Be deaf to them, as he is now to me—
But on, my Lord; purſue theſe ſavage-maxims;
Without remorſe conſummate your revenge!
Yet, other victims, other heads attend,
To ſatiate its full fury—See, O King!
Lo! where they ſtand—

[*Her two children are brought in by their Governeſs.*

Acknowledge them for yours,
By dooming both to bleed!

ALONZO.

Ye holy Powers!
What do I ſee?

ELVIRA.

Yes, by one common fate,
Wife, children, huſband—let us periſh all!

ALONZO.

What ſay'ſt thou!—Juſtice! Mercy! how ye rend
My heart!

ELVIRA.

Forgive the language of deſpair.
My children, kneel with me. Your infant-tears
May wake at laſt the parent in his breaſt.
Sir, they are yours—behold them not as mine.
The law demands a victim: here, on me
Exhauſt its utmoſt rage—but O, to theſe
A father ſave, and to yourſelf a ſon!
Yet ſome few moments from his ear conceal
Elvira's death—for ſhould it reach him now,
His own too ſure would follow—

ALONZO.

ALONZO.

Call my ſon!
Fly, let him know—Elvira is his own!
My daughter—

ELVIRA.

O unutterable Joy!
Here at your feet, to heaven and you I pour
My grateful boſom—

ALONZO.

Nature! thou haſt conquer'd.
I am a man, a father!—Riſe, Elvira;
Live, and be happy long—O my dear children!
Take, take me all—

SCENE VII.

ALONZO, ELVIRA, DON PEDRO.

ALONZO.

My ſon!

DON PEDRO.

My King and father!
Elvira—from the grave to me reſtor'd!
To theſe deſpairing arms!—and you my little ones!

ELVIRA.

O I am bleſt—beyond all utterance bleſt!
And my tranſported heart—Ah me—

ALONZO.

Elvira!
Thy cheek is pale!

ELVIRA.

Oh I have death within me!

DON

DON PEDRO.

This flood of Joy, my ſoul's beſt happineſs.
O'erpowers thy tender frame.

ELVIRA.

Ah no, I burn :
A kindled furnace rages in my boſom—
Convulſions ſhake me—ſweats of death bedew
My trembling limbs !

DON PEDRO.

O Source of life ! look down
With pity on her—

ELVIRA.

Ha ! a ſudden night
Spreads dark around—You ſwim before my eyes—
Their light is loſt !—but I will hold you faſt—
Again I burn !

ALONZO.

O moſt inhuman Queen !
This Stygian draught, too ſure, was by thy hand,
Thy fatal hand prepar'd.

DON PEDRO.

Did heaven look on
And ſuffer this ?—Yet, by my ſoul's ſtrong anguiſh !
Not ſhe alone, her Spain ſhall weep in blood
This deed accurſt !

ELVIRA.

'Tis paſt—Don Pedro, love
My memory—Alonzo, cheriſh theſe—
O my poor babes !—and bleſs their dying mother !
But that fair princeſs—yes, reward for me
Her nobleneſs of virtue – My lov'd Lord !
Theſe arms would fold thee ſtill—but Oh—

ALONZO.

ALONZO.

She dies—
In that laſt ſigh the gentle ſpirit fled!

DON PEDRO.

Mine ſhall rejoin it, ere it finds that heaven
Prepar'd for ſouls like hers—I will not live?
This ſword reſtor'd—

ALONZO, *ſeizing his hand.*

Away—Shall fury ſtill
Sway all thy actions? No: reward her truth
A nobler way. Theſe Infants claim thy care:
And thou muſt ſuffer life, to guide their ſteps
Safe from the ſnares that courtly Fraud and Falſehood
Spread daily in a youthful Prince's walk;
Spread for his ruin. And now, warn'd thyſelf,
Let all mankind, by one example, know,
From paſſions unreſtrain'd what miſchiefs grow!

THE END.

POSTSCRIPT.

HAVING found by frequent experience, how much the mind is apt to flag under the ſame kind of employment, too long and too uniformly continued; I had an inclination to try whether a different ſort of labor might not be, at the ſame time, a ſort of relief. To this experiment only, the reader is indebted for the pleaſure, or diſtaſte of the preceding poem. The melancholy event, on which it is built, has a foundation of truth in hiſtory; and was celebrated long ago by the famous Portugueſe poet, CAMOËNS, in his *Luſiad.* There he has deſcribed at large, and with all the graces of his poetry, the beauty, the virtue, and the tragical fate of that lady, to whom I have here given the name of Elvira. Don Pedro, to whom ſhe had been privately married while ſhe lived in a pleaſing ſolitude on the banks of the Mondego, was long happy in her truth and tenderneſs. After her death, when he became king of Portugal, he had her ſkeleton taken out of the coffin, placed on a magnificent throne, ſolemnly crowned and acknowledged for his queen. It is reported, that he obliged the principal perſons of his court to kiſs the bones of thoſe hands which had once been the object of his love and fondneſs. But it is true, that he ordered ſuch of her enemies, as fell into his power, to be puniſhed with circumſtances of great ſeverity. They were burnt alive.

A writer of diſtinguiſhed reputation, who found the ſubject extremely fit for a tragedy, brought it on the French theatre, with great and univerſal applauſe. The reader, who cares to give himſelf that trouble, will eaſily diſcover how much, and how generally I have followed my original: and he only has a right to determine, whether I have done it well or ill. If he is acquainted likewiſe with the hiſtory of our ſtage, he muſt have remarked, that it was no unfrequent practice among our poets, eſpecially during the laſt part of the former century; firſt to borrow very freely from our neighbours on the continent; and then, in their prefaces, to boaſt how much they had excelled their benefactors. But ſurely the practice is too unfair to be juſtified, and too illiberal to be copied. Let the reputation therefore of Monſieur de la Motte remain entire and inviolate.

EPI-

EPILOGUE.

By Mr. GARRICK.

Spoken by Mrs. CIBBER.

LADIES and Gentlemen——'Tis ſo ill bred——
We have no Epilogue, becauſe I'm dead;
For he, our Bard, with frenzy-rolling eye,
Swears you ſhan't laugh, when he has made you cry.
At which I gave his ſleeve a gentle pull,
Suppoſe they ſhould not cry, and ſhould be dull:
In ſuch a caſe, 'twould ſurely do no harm,
A little lively nonſenſe taken warm:
On critick ſtomacks delicate and queaſy,
'Twill ev'n make a heavy meal ſit eaſy.
The town hates Epilogues—*it is not true,*
I anſwer'd that for you—*and* you—*and* you—
(To pit, boxes, and 1ſt gallery.)
They *call for Epilogues, and Hornpipes too*—
(To the upper gallery.)
Madam, the Criticks ſay—*To you they're civil,*
Here *if they have'em not, they'll play the devil;*
Out of this houſe, Sir, and to you alone,
They'll ſmile, cry Bravo! Charming!—Here *they groan:*
A ſingle critick will not frown, look big,
Harmleſs and pliant as a ſingle twig,
But crouded here *they change, and 'tis not odd,*
For twigs, when bundled up, become a rod.
Criticks to bards, like beauties to each other,
When tête à tête their enmity they ſmother;
Kiſs me, my dear—how do you?—Charming creature!
What ſhape! what bloom! what ſpirit in each feature!
You flatter me,—'pon honor, No.——You do—
My friend—my dear—ſincerely yours—adieu!

But

1

EPILOGUE.

But when at Routs, the dear friends change their tone—
I ſpeak of foreign *ladies, not our own.*
Will you permit, good Sirs, theſe gloomy folk,
To give all tragedy, without one joke?
They gravely tell us—tragedy's deſign'd,
To purge the paſſions, purify the mind;
To which I ſay, to ſtrike thoſe blockheads dumb,
With phyſick, always give a ſugar plumb;
I love theſe ſugar plumbs in proſe or rhimes;
No one is merrier than myſelf ſome times;
Yet I, poor I, with tears and conſtant moan,
Am melted down almoſt to ſkin and bone:
This night, in ſighs and ſobs I drew my breath;
Love, marriage, treaſon, priſon, poiſon, death,
Were ſcarce ſufficient to compleat my fate;
Two children were thrown in to make up weight.
With all theſe ſuff'rings, is it not provoking,
To be deny'd at laſt a little joking?
If they will make new laws, for mirth's ſake—break 'em,
Roar out for Epilogues, and let me ſpeak 'em.

THE LIST OF TITLES

1. **Restoration Adaptations.** Edited with an introduction by Edward A. Langhans.

2. **The State and the Licensing Act, 1729–1739.** Edited with an introduction by Vincent J. Liesenfeld.

3. **The Performers and Their Plays.** Edited with an introduction by Shirley Strum Kenny.

4. **The Plays of Isaac Bickerstaff.** Edited with an introduction by Peter A. Tasch. *Three volumes.*

5. **The Plays of James Boaden.** Edited with an introduction by Steven Cohan.

6. **The Plays of Henry Carey.** Edited with an introduction by Samuel L. Macey.

7. **The Plays of Susanna Centlivre.** Edited with an introduction by Richard C. Frushell. *Three volumes.*

8. **The Plays of Colley Cibber.** Edited with an introduction by Rodney L. Hayley.

9. **The Plays of Theophilus and Susanna Cibber.** Edited with an introduction by David Mann.

10. **The Plays of George Colman, The Elder.** Edited with an introduction by Kalman Burnim. *Two volumes.*

11. **The Plays of George Colman, The Younger.** Edited with an introduction by Peter A. Tasch. *Two volumes.*

12. **The Plays of Hannah Cowley.** Edited with an introduction by Frederick M. Link. *Two volumes.*

13. **The Plays of Richard Cumberland.** Edited with an introduction by Roberta F.S. Borkat. *Three volumes.*

14. **The Plays of John Dennis.** Edited with an introduction by J.W. Johnson.
15. **The Plays of Samuel Foote.** Edited with an introduction by Paula R. Backscheider. *Two volumes*.
16. **The Plays of David Garrick.** Edited with an introduction by Gerald Berkowitz. *Four volumes*.
17. **The Plays of Charles Gildon.** Edited with an introduction by Paula R. Backscheider.
18. **The Plays of Eliza Haywood.** Edited with an introduction by Valerie C. Rudolph.
19. **The Plays of Aaron Hill.** Edited with an introduction by Calhoun Winton.
20. **The Plays of Thomas Holcroft.** Edited with an introduction by Joseph Rosenblum. *Two volumes.*
21. **The Plays of John Hoole.** Edited with an introduction by Donald T. Siebert, Jr.
22. **The Plays of John Home.** Edited with an introduction by James S. Malek.
23. **The Plays of Elizabeth Inchbald.** Edited with an introduction by Paula R. Backscheider. *Two volumes*.
24. **The Plays of Robert Jephson.** Edited with an introduction by Temple Maynard.
25. **The Plays of Samuel Johnson of Cheshire.** Edited with an introduction by Valerie C. Rudolph.
26. **The Plays of Hugh Kelly.** Edited with an introduction by Larry Carver and with textual notes by Mary Jean Gross.
27. **The Plays of George Lillo.** Edited with an introduction by Trudy Drucker.
28. **The Plays of David Mallet.** Edited with an introduction by Felicity Nussbaum.
29. **The Plays of Edward Moore.** Edited with an introduction by J. Paul Hunter.
30. **The Plays of Arthur Murphy.** Edited with an introduction by Richard B. Schwartz. *Four volumes*.

31. **The Plays of John O'Keeffe.** Edited with an introduction by Frederick M. Link. *Four volumes.*
32. **The Plays of Mary Pix and Catherine Trotter.** Edited with an introduction by Edna L. Steeves. *Two volumes.*
33. **The Plays of Frederick Reynolds.** Edited with an introduction by Stanley W. Lindberg. *Two volumes.*
34. **The Plays of Edward Thompson.** Edited with an introduction by Catherine Neal Parke.
35. **The Plays of James Thomson.** Edited with an introduction by Percy G. Adams.